HISTORY

The Hum

THE HUMP

The 1st Battalion,
503rd Airborne Infantry,
in the First Major Battle of
the Vietnam War

Al Conetto

McFarland & Company, Inc., Publishers
Jefferson, North Carolina

LIBRARY OF CONGRESS CATALOGUING-IN-PUBLICATION DATA [new form]

Names: Conetto, Al, 1941– author.
Title: The Hump : the 1st Battalion, 503rd Airborne Infantry, in the
    first major battle of the Vietnam War / Al Conetto.
Other titles: 1st Battalion, 503rd Airborne Infantry, in the first major
    battle of the Vietnam War
Description: Jefferson, North Carolina : McFarland & Company, Inc.,
    Publishers, 2015 | Includes bibliographical references and index.
Identifiers: LCCN 2015035125| ISBN 9780786499250 (softcover : acid
    free paper) | ISBN 9781476622057 (ebook)
Subjects: LCSH: Conetto, Al, 1941– | United States. Army. Infantry,
    503rd. Battalion, 1st—Biography. | Vietnam War, 1961–1975—
    Campaigns—Vietnam—Biên Hòa. | United States. Army—Officers—
    Biography. | Post-traumatic stress disorder—Patients—Biography. |
    Vietnam War, 1961–1975—Regimental histories—United States. |
    Vietnam War, 1961–1975—Personal narratives, American.
Classification: LCC DS559.5 .C64 2015 | DDC 959.704/342—dc23
LC record available at http://lccn.loc.gov/2015035125

BRITISH LIBRARY CATALOGUING DATA ARE AVAILABLE

Front cover images © 2015 iStock/Thinkstock

Printed in the United States of America

McFarland & Company, Inc., Publishers
    Box 611, Jefferson, North Carolina 28640
    www.mcfarlandpub.com

To the 49
young paratroopers
who fought and died on Hill 65;
to the hundreds of young paratroopers
who fought and survived Hill 65;
and to Ramrod 6, Rawhide 6 and
especially Diesel Stamp 6:
"Airborne, All the Way!"

Those of us who survived must have been spared for a purpose. I choose to believe that we were chosen so as to serve as spokesmen for those who can no longer speak for themselves. All of us—the living and the dead—ask for nothing special in return for what we did. We merely ask that we be remembered by our countrymen as good and honorable men who did our country's bidding as had been done by our forefathers down through the ages.

Col. John E. Tyler
U.S. Army (Ret.)
November 24, 1991

TABLE OF CONTENTS

TABLE OF CONTENTS

ACKNOWLEDGMENTS

I began this project more than 20 years ago, but the journey actually began November 5, 1965, the first day of Operation HUMP. Either way, it has been a long process. In that time I have encountered many people who have helped in their own way: some with advice, some who kicked me in the butt for motivation, some for their stories, and some by just being there. I wish to acknowledge them all, but time has removed many names and faces from my mind. So let me begin with those I do remember.

First, COL Walter B. Daniel, my former company commander. Walt was an enthusiastic supporter of this project as he also felt the story had to be told to the general public. He sent me his recollections of the battle and contacted COL John Tyler, our former battalion commander, and notified him of the project. He also sent pictures and drawings of our unit's movements. He contacted MG Ellis W. Williamson, former brigade commander, and also let him know. And he helped me get their accounts of what happened between November 5 and 9, 1965. He encouraged me to find LTC Lowell Bittrich, B Company, and LTC Henry "Sonny" Tucker, C Company, to get their stories. And he helped me in that search. To me Walt Daniel was the epitome of an airborne soldier. He was tough, knowledgeable, a leader and a motivator. He led his company with enthusiasm and courage. And he passed those traits down to his platoon leaders. In my mind he was the best airborne infantry company commander in the Army and I deeply respected him. Unfortunately, Walt did not live to see this project come to fruition. On a turkey hunt with friends in March 1997 he had a massive heart attack and passed away. I deeply miss him—he was my hero.

Next, I cannot give enough credit to my friend and mentor, Larry Engelmann. Larry was my professor for the Vietnam Wars class I took when returning to college for my master's degree. He was also my thesis advisor. His inspiration and encouragement gave me the impetus to think about converting my thesis into a book. I called on him many times for guidance, to ask a question, or to get a little kick in the butt to get me started again. He was the one who encouraged me to return to Vietnam in 1992. He was always there for me, but unfortunately he passed away April 1, 2015.

Obviously, I want to thank the members of the 1/503. They were there and many are not with us anymore. Some contributed their stories and their words and their actions speak for themselves. I have given them credit for the stories they have shared. Some were there, but don't want to revisit that time again. I respect their position. But I thank all of you guys for your service and especially those who were willing to tell their stories. There is no story without you; actually you are the story. You demonstrated the best of what a paratrooper represents.

Thank you to one special member of 1/503, Dutch Holland. Dutch has been as enthusiastic about this project as anyone. He has ensured that I kept going and kept telling me that the book had to get out as soon as possible as we were losing more members every year. Thanks, Dutch. You are my brother.

To those of you I have missed, I apologize but at my age the mind does not function as well as it used to. Please understand I have not forgotten your assistance, I just cannot remember your names.

Finally my wife, Melody. This journey has taken more than 20 years and she has stood by me. She was there for the beginning and has always been there. There were times when I wasn't so sure I could reach the end, but she encouraged me and challenged me to keep going. There were times when she had enough of hearing me talk about what I was going to do rather than doing it. In those times she took me to task and got me back on the right track. Thank you, Melody, you are the love of my life and you deserve the best of everything.

PREFACE

We were the children of the 1950s and we went where we were
sent because we loved our country.
—LTG Hal Moore (Ret.) and Joseph Galloway,
We Were Soldiers Once ... and Young

This is my story. This is what I saw. This is what I heard. This is
what I experienced, what I read and what I believe. This is my truth,
but it is also our story: the men of the 1st Battalion, 503rd Infantry, 173d
Airborne Brigade.

This is the story of how I challenged myself to face my personal
hell: battling my lack of confidence, my weaknesses and my fears while
in combat. It also is the result of my search for what happened 50 years
ago. In the late '70s and early '80s I began to have flashbacks. The first
one was of a battle I participated in, but I didn't know where, against
whom, the name of the operation, and what the outcome was. But the
flashback continued until I began my search to find out the truth. Only
then did it recede and another one follow.

But within my story is also the story of the first major battle of the
Vietnam War between the United States Army and the Viet Cong
(VC)/People's Army of Vietnam (PAVN). It was the first battle that would
change the nature of the war. It would elevate the intensity of the conflict
from a hit-and-run guerrilla war to a contest between large-scale American and enemy main force units (battalions, regiments, and divisions).
For the first time the enemy decided that instead of breaking contact
and melting back in the jungle, he would stand and fight an American
unit on his own terms. Many lessons would be learned by both sides in
the jungles of War Zone D and in the second major battle, the 1st Cavalry
Division's later engagements in the Ia Drang Valley.

"During 1965 and 1966, the Communists fought the Americans toe

1

to toe, making little effort to act like guerrillas. Those years saw the largest percentage of attacks by battalion-size enemy units or larger—even greater than in the years of the two biggest enemy offensives of the war, 1968 and 1972."[1]

So for the first time we found that we were engaging main force troops and not just VC guerrillas, thus destroying the contention that this was a civil war between South Vietnamese factions. After all, in July 1959, North Vietnam's Communist leadership ratified a resolution affirming that the Vietnamese revolution was led by the Party.[2] For the first time we also found that the North Vietnamese were using Chinese advisors, who would be reported later in other battles by other units.

Captain Al Conetto, Fort Lewis, Washington. Early 1967, prior to returning to Vietnam (author's collection).

Also, for the first time the enemy was willing to engage the American Army to test our strengths and weaknesses and how best to counter them or take advantage of them, especially our helicopters and air mobility.

And maybe worst of all, for the first time we, the foot soldiers, saw (but probably didn't recognize) that we would not be allowed to win. We would not pursue the enemy into Cambodia to destroy his units and supplies. We had established a safe haven for him, an imaginary line in the sand, and he would take advantage of it over the next seven years.

In addition, this battle and the ones at Landing Zone (LZ) X-Ray and Landing Zone Albany in the Ia Drang Valley would escalate the commitment of the United States to Vietnam. Indirectly this battle would result in the increase of American troops to nearly 200,000 by year end with another 100,000 in the pipeline for 1966.

Operation HUMP started on November 5 and ended on November 9, 1965. The battle at LZ X-Ray in the Ia Drang Valley started November 14 and the battle at LZ Albany started on November 17.

I did not write this book to take anything away from the 1st Battalion, 7th Cavalry or 2nd Battalion, 7th Cavalry, 1st Cavalry Division. Although they were greatly outnumbered, their fights in the Ia Drang were bloody, vicious, heroic, and courageous and brought great glory to already highly decorated units. Their stories are well told in LTG Hal Moore's and Joe Galloway's book, *We Were Soldiers Once ... and Young*.

Instead, my purpose is to pay tribute to the hundreds of young paratroopers who for two days in War Zone D, Republic of Vietnam, fought against a reinforced VC/PAVN regiment and destroyed it. And I want to recognize the 49 young men who gave their lives in the hot, steamy jungles of South Vietnam 10,000 miles from home.

Unlike most Army units, the 173d consisted of volunteers. Each man had signed up for jump school at Fort Benning, Georgia. Each had completed the tough 3-week course. Each had earned the right to wear bloused boots, the glider patch and silver jump wings, the symbols of the Airborne. We became part of that proud tradition, and we loved it. Plus, we now earned monthly jump pay ($110 for officers, $55 for enlisted men) to supplement our meager base pay. The 173d was the Army's main reaction force for the Pacific Theater. The officers were from West Point, the Reserve Officers Training Corps, and Officer Candidate School. The noncommissioned officers were mostly professional soldiers, many with Combat Infantryman Badges (CIBs) from Korea, and even World War II. The enlisted men came from all walks of life and every part of the nation. Some were draftees but most were volunteers who had joined the Army for excitement and the challenges it entailed. We were all this, but most of all we were America's hope for the future, America's finest.

We were the first Army ground combat unit ordered to Vietnam and we arrived on May 5, 1965. We were sent by a president who had inherited the war from his predecessor and chose to expand it. His micromanagement of the war and its horrible results would force him not to seek re-election. We were brought home by another president

3

who said he had the solution to the conflict: "Peace with honor."[3] At least that was what he indicated in the presidential election of 1968. More than 58,000 young Americans would die to fulfill the political dreams and ambitions of these two American presidents.

And so, we went into War Zone D and we met the enemy. And for the first time the enemy decided to stay and fight rather than run. So we fought and we killed and we endured. Did we win? I think so. But the enemy may have thought he won, too. Who really will decide?

Either way, this battle was only a prelude to seven more years of bitter fighting and sacrifice on both sides that would end with the withdrawal of American troops in 1973 and the fall of Saigon on April 30, 1975.

PROLOGUE

I knew wherever I was that you thought of me, and if I got in a tight place you would come—if alive.

—William Tecumseh Sherman,
in a letter to Ulysses S. Grant

My breath came in short gasps. I tried to burrow into the ground and crawl inside my helmet at the same time. The other men were spread out in groups of two or three. We waited for the enemy to attack as we were heavily outnumbered and outgunned. It was only a matter of time.

It was 1745 hours, 9 November 1965. Dusk. The rest of the battalion had been airlifted to Bien Hoa. The remnants of a battered Viet Cong/PAVN regiment were scattered throughout the jungle that surrounded us. My commanding officer, Captain Walter B. Daniel, and his radio telephone operators were only a few yards away. 1st Sergeant William Workman was there, too. It was eerily quiet except for occasional sniper fire. I looked around and assessed our situation. We were in War Zone D, approximately 20 kilometers north of Camp Ray, our base camp. There were 14 of us securing a small landing zone, it was getting dark and there were no helicopters in sight. I didn't like our chances.

I was a 23-year-old first lieutenant, a rifle platoon leader with Alpha Company, 1st Battalion (Airborne), 503rd Infantry, 173d Airborne Brigade. My 24th birthday was only four days away, and I had less than three months left in my tour. I was anxious and scared, and I could hear my heart pounding in my chest. My thoughts drifted to home and my wife, Kathy, and our 1-year-old daughter, Krissy. I had not seen either of them since August when I left Fort Benning, Georgia, to travel by ship to this island paradise. The odds were not very good that I would ever see them again.

Christ, I did not want to die here in this stinking jungle, 10,000 miles from home! But the choice was not mine. I was a soldier, an infantry officer, and a volunteer. I was trained to fight, and die if necessary, for my country. I had welcomed and accepted that challenge years before. I had an obligation to do my duty, to stand with my comrades, to pay the price.

So with my M-16 rifle, .45 caliber pistol and a few hundred rounds of ammunition, I was ready to take as many of them as possible with me into death.

Charlie controlled our fate now. And so we waited.

1

THE ROAD TO WAR

Older men declare war. But it is youth that must fight and die.
And it is youth who must inherit the tribulation, the sorrow,
and the triumphs that are the aftermath of war.
—Herbert Clark Hoover

"Good morning, sir," the sergeant said, throwing me a salute.

I had just been commissioned in the office of Lieutenant Colonel Edwin Rios, professor of military science. It was my first salute as an officer, and I returned it with, "Good morning, sergeant." I then handed Sergeant First Class Raymond Leong, a staff noncommissioned officer for the Reserve Officers Training Corps detachment, a silver dollar. We officer candidates had been told it was a military tradition, and we better have a silver dollar on our person for the first NCO to offer a salute. Sure enough, Leong was waiting outside the door. (See Appendix 6, Glossary, for military abbreviations.)

I graduated from San Jose State University on January 24, 1964, with a degree in business-industrial management. In addition to receiving my degree, I was made a second lieutenant in the United States Army. I was the first in my family to graduate from college and the first to be commissioned an officer.

As a youngster, I became fascinated by the military and warfare. I read popular war novels like *Battle Cry*, *The Barren Beaches of Hell*, *The Angry Hills*, and *On the Beach*. My favorite movies were also about war, especially the ones starring John Wayne. They included *The Sands of Iwo Jima*, *The Flying Leathernecks*, *The Fighting Seabees*, and *Operation Pacific*. Other favorites were *Battle Cry*, *To Hell and Back*, *Battleground*, and *Retreat Hell!* I was entranced with the concepts of honor, sacrifice, daring, courage, glory, patriotism and military tradition that were extolled in these movies and books.

Yet war and the military did not rule my early life. Baseball did. My favorite team then was the New York Yankees—the "Bronx Bombers." I grew up with Joe DiMaggio, Casey Stengel, Mickey Mantle, Yogi Berra, Billy Martin, Whitey Ford, and Phil Rizzuto—they dominated the game in those days. And DiMaggio was a young Italian kid from San Francisco. Since I had been born in San Jose, he was almost a hometown boy.

I was born just before the attack on Pearl Harbor and have no recollections of World War II and very few of Korea. The one incident that I did recall, however, was General (GEN) Douglas MacArthur's return to the United States after President Harry S. Truman fired him as commander of Allied forces in Korea on April 11, 1951.[1] I remembered the tumultuous welcome he received from the American people, the parades and the adulation. He was an American hero returning in triumph to his homeland. It left a lasting impression on me.

Also, at that time, in another Far East country named Indochina, the French were fighting a ragtag peasant army called the Viet Minh. The French were determined to bring the country back under their rule, while the Viet Minh wanted reunification and independence. Reunification was an interesting idea in that the North and South, prior to 1954, had been united for just 58 years, from 1802 to 1859. This in an area with more than 2,700 years of history.[2]

And in Saigon, in October 1951, a young congressman from Massachusetts, John F. Kennedy, age 34, arrived by plane at the city's Tan Son Nhut Airport with his brother Robert and sister Patricia. He was on a seven-week, 25,000-mile tour of Asia and the Middle East to burnish his foreign-policy credentials before his Senate run the next year. The Kennedys were told they could not venture outside Saigon by car as the insurgents ruled the roads after twilight. So they would spend their first evening on the fourth-floor rooftop bar of the waterfront Majestic Hotel, observing gun flashes from French artillery firing across the Saigon River, hoping to hit Viet Minh mortar sites.[3]

Kennedy would later write in his trip diary: "'We are more and more becoming colonialists in the minds of the people because everyone believes that we control the UN [and] because our wealth is supposedly inexhaustible, we will be damned if we don't do what they [the emerging nations] want.' The United States should avoid the path trod by the declining British and French empires and instead show that the enemy is not merely Communism but 'poverty and want', 'sickness and disease', and 'injustice and inequality', all of which are the daily lot of millions of Asians."[4]

Anyway, I was nine years old at the time, and the most important thing to me was not Korea or Indochina, but the National League play-offs. In the third game, Bobby Thomson of the New York Giants hit the "home run heard around the world" off Ralph Branca and the Giants defeated the Brooklyn Dodgers for the pennant. In the World Series, my Yankees whipped the Giants in six games. Gil McDougald drove in seven runs and DiMaggio drove in five.

In 1952, after his defeat by GEN Jean de Lattre de Tassigny at the French fortified city of Vinh Yen, North Vietnamese Defense Minister GEN Vo Nguyen Giap moved back to harassing the French at every opportunity using guerrilla tactics.[5] Giap had lost 6,000 dead and 8,000 wounded in that battle. French airpower using napalm had proved decisive.[6]

I began the sixth grade in September, and in October the Yankees and Dodgers battled in the World Series with the Yankees finally winning, four games to three. Johnny Mize batted around .400 and hit three home runs to spark the Yankees. Vic Raschi and Allie Reynolds won two games each and struck out 36 batters between them.

Also in November 1952 GEN Dwight D. Eisenhower was elected president of the United States in a landslide. A new administration took power. His "first policy priority was to make good on his campaign promise to end the Korean War as quickly as possible. But his very willingness to discuss peace terms with the North Koreans and the Chinese made him all the more determined to show firmness toward Communism elsewhere in Asia."[7]

"In early February, in his first State of the Union, he characterized the Indochina struggle as part of a worldwide fight against Communist aggression."[8]

In January 1953, GEN de Lattre died in Paris. And in May, GEN Henri Navarre replaced him as the new French commander in Vietnam. His lack of experience in Indochina was an asset, according to Paris, as he could approach the issue with an "absence of prejudice." An old cavalryman, he declared, "We shall give back to our troops the mobility and aggressiveness they have sometimes lacked."[9]

The Korean Armistice, signed on July 27, had a devastating effect on French morale, including a lowering of the will to continue the fight in Indochina. The French "saw the United States securing a truce in Korea and Britain trading with China and could not understand why their allies should expect them to continue a war in Indochina in which there was no longer a direct French interest."[10] France was the now the only Western nation shedding blood on a major scale to fight Communism.

Meanwhile, Navarre and his staff came up with the idea of establishing a mooring point, or base camp, from which the French and their native troops could penetrate the Viet Minh's rear areas. The site he chose was a remote valley, 11 miles long and five miles wide, in the northwestern section of North Vietnam. The ethnic minority T'ai who lived there called the place Muong Thanh. To the Vietnamese, and to the French, it was known as Dien Bien Phu.[11]

It was certainly a strategic position. The basin was one of the few hollows in the vast and largely impassable highland region. The Laotian border was ten miles to the west, just over the mountains. The village was also at the junction of three routes. One went north to China, another went to the northeast to Tuan Giao, and the third ran southwest to Laos. Legend taught that whoever controlled the basin, controlled the region and the entry to Laos and the upper Mekong. The native T'ai referred to it as the Arena of the Gods.

At 0815, on November 20, 1953, French Foreign Legion and South Vietnamese paratroopers were dropped into the valley at Dien Bien Phu (Operation Castor) from 60 Dakota aircraft (C-47s). These aircraft bringing in the paratroopers formed a column seven miles long. The cream of the French Expeditionary Corps dropped into the valley north and south of the village. The operation was commanded by gruff, one-eyed BG Jean Gilles (he carried his glass eye in his jacket pocket when he jumped). The Viet Minh in the village contested the jump, resulting in 15 French dead and 53 wounded. The Viet Minh lost 90 men.

The news of the French occupation of Dien Bien Phu caught the Viet Minh commanders by surprise. Vo Nguyen Giap was preparing to present the 1953–1954 offensive campaign to his division commanders in the Dinh Hoa district of Thai Nguyen province, approximately 300 miles east of Dien Bien Phu.

GEN Giap responded by moving 33 infantry battalions, six artillery regiments, and an engineer regiment to meet the French.[12] His marching orders from Ho Chi Minh were: "You are the general commanding the troops on the outer frontier.... I give you complete authority to make all decisions. If victory is certain, then you are to attack. If victory is not certain, then you must resolutely refrain from attacking."[13]

But now, GEN Navarre's chief subordinate, Major General (MG) René Cogny, changed his mind. Instead of a "mooring point," he saw Dien Bien Phu more as a "meat grinder" of French troops. GEN Navarre discarded his subordinate's misgivings.[14] Author Fredrik Logevall disputes this claim by Cogny. "For Cogny no less than Navarre, the concept had the virtues of being versatile and of having both a defensive and offensive purpose: It was a 'hedgehog' that would thwart a major attack, and it was an 'anchor point' that would support mobile operations in the enemy's rear."[15]

Both sides had the opportunity to win a decisive victory at Dien Bien Phu. The French faced dwindling support for the war at home, but militarily they held pretty good cards, especially in view of their strong positions in the Red River Delta and in Cochin China. In addition, Navarre calculated that Giap's logistical problems so far from home would be too severe to overcome: "He would not be able to maintain a large body of troops in the area due to the harshness of the terrain and the presence of the French Air Force." Although the Viet Minh had trucks and cannons, how could it transport them as far as Dien Bien Phu? It couldn't. Its inferiority in transport meant that Giap would not be able to match the weight of French weaponry and would be crushed when battle came. A colossal miscalculation in hindsight, it was less so at the time.[16]

The Viet Minh did have greater problems. A senior Hungarian diplomat heard Giap lecture that the battle of Dien Bien Phu was the last desperate exertion of the Viet Minh army. Its forces were on the verge of complete exhaustion. The rice supply was running out. Apathy had spread among the populace. Morale in the fighting units was plunging.[17] Plus, how was Giap to bring his troops to the battlefield? They would have to cover 300 miles on foot, and supply lines from China would be up to 500 miles. The road system, rudimentary at best, would have to carry every piece of equipment, every bullet, for thousands of soldiers. And the vulnerable supply lines would have to be kept open, in forbidding terrain, over a period of weeks or months.

But Giap had a battle plan. Its fundamental premise was that the fortified French camp would be a formidable defensive complex, but that it suffered a grave weakness: its isolation. It would have to be supplied largely by air, completely so if Giap's army could surround it. That would be the aim: to encircle the encampment with a ring of steel and then close in.[18]

I graduated from grammar school in June and started junior high school in September. In the Fall Classic in New York, the Yankees continued their dominance over the Dodgers winning the Series four games to two. Billy Martin batted .500 with 12 hits and eight RBIs and Mickey Mantle hit a grand slam in game five.

With the signing of the Korean armistice, there was optimism in the world that the Indochina conflict could also be settled. Soviet leaders were seeking to relax tensions, the French were sick of war, and the Chinese favored a negotiated settlement. These trends troubled the anti–Communist Vietnamese, who feared that the French would sell them out. American leaders were also alarmed. Secretary of State John Foster Dulles saw the U.S. policy of the containment of Communism crumbling.[19]

Meanwhile, BG Gilles was leaving Dien Bien Phu, and the new commander for the French was Colonel Christian Marie Ferdinand de la Croix de Castries, a 51-year-old, tall, debonair, aristocratic cavalryman. Descended from a long line of high military officers, one of whom served with Lafayette during the American Revolution, de Castries was dashing and courageous, and a notorious womanizer. He would meet the Viet Minh threat.

When he was introduced to the officers, it was quickly pointed out to him that commando operations outside the valley were already encountering severe problems. "The enemy was in close, they told him; they were hemmed in."[20]

And so, de Castries got to work supervising the construction of strongpoints in the valley. There would be nine of them, all given female names which were reputedly those of former de Castries mistresses.

By Christmas Eve, the number of French troops in the valley totaled 10,910, the steady stream of C-47s was bringing in large amounts of weaponry and ammunition, the American-supplied Bearcat fighter planes were in place, and the first platoon of three U.S. made M-24 tanks were being readied for action.

"There was a strange atmosphere in the camp," recalled USIA correspondent Howard Simpson, who had been there two days earlier. "The officers remained cocky and determined, but the men, particularly the North Africans, T'ai, and Vietnamese, seemed to have been affected by the boredom, the lack of movement, and the threat of what was 'out there.'"[21]

By the middle of January 1954, GEN Giap was ready to attack. His Chinese advisors urged a "human wave" assault, such as they had used against the Americans in Korea. Giap at first agreed and then doubts plagued him. He knew the French entrenched positions were encircled by barbed wire and minefields, and the French possessed tanks—a deadly weapon against frontal assaults. He realized a setback here could be fatal to the Viet Minh cause. Giap concluded he could not risk defeat. "It was the most difficult decision of my life," he recalled. "Suddenly, in the morning, I postponed the operation. My staff was confused, but no matter. I was the military commander, and I demanded absolute obedience—*sans discussion, sans explication!*" Instead, Giap adopted a more cautious strategy: he hauled his cannon higher in the hills, and he ordered tunnels dug to surround the French garrison.[22] If the attack failed, Giap feared it would inflict huge damage on the People's Army and hand the French a major military and political victory. "He had not forgotten Ho Chi Minh's admonition: Unless you are certain of victory, don't proceed."[23]

By March 13, 1954, Viet Minh combat forces were estimated at 49,500 with another 31,500 in support and 23,000 dispersed along its supply lines. The French, meanwhile, numbered 13,200, of whom about 7,000 were front-line troops.[24] Finally, Giap gave the order to advance, and the Viet Minh attacked the base camp. Within 48 hours the French lost four battalions and two strongholds: artillery bases Gabrielle and Beatrice.[25] Colonel (COL) Charles Piroth, the officer in charge of the French artillery, had pledged to Navarre two months earlier, "[N]o Vietminh cannon will be able to fire three rounds before being destroyed by my artillery." At dawn, March 15, Piroth pulled the safety pin out of a grenade and blew himself to bits. The night before he had said he was completely dishonored.[26]

The French Chief of Staff, GEN Paul Ely, flew to Washington on March 20 to request U.S. support. He proposed American air strikes against the Viet Minh perimeter at Dien Bien Phu. Admiral (ADM) Arthur Radford, chairman of the Joint Chiefs of Staff, and GEN Nathan Twining, Air Force Chief of Staff, endorsed the idea. But GEN Matthew Ridgway, Army Chief of Staff, was dead set against it. He had a clear idea of the limitations of air action and felt in all likelihood it would be followed by a commitment of large American combat troops to another inconclusive and costly war on the mainland similar to Korea. LTG James Gavin, chief of research and development, fully backed Ridgway, as did Secretary of Defense Charles Wilson. President Eisenhower stood his ground against Dulles and the other service chiefs.[27]

President Dwight Eisenhower further discouraged the French by insisting that he would authorize the strike only if Congress and our allies approved. On April 3, eight congressional leaders were called to a meeting, including Senator Lyndon B. Johnson. After their briefing all eight agreed that the United States should not support France alone. With time running out, Secretary Dulles resorted to shuttle diplomacy, but France decided to negotiate a settlement at the upcoming Geneva Conference, and England feared an air strike would sabotage the Geneva talks. Dulles returned home empty-handed.[28]

On May 7, 1954, Dien Bien Phu was overrun and fell. The French did not surrender. One source listed French casualties as 2,242 killed; 6,463 wounded; 2,711 missing; and 10,754 taken prisoner.[29] Bernard Fall would also report 2,242 killed and 6,463 wounded, but would list 3,711 missing and 13,050 taken prisoner.[30] The exact number of casualties will probably never be known.[31] "For the first time in the annals of colonial warfare, Asian troops had defeated a European army in fixed battle."[32]

The next day, the Geneva Conference began discussions of the Indochina problem. Distrust and tension pervaded the conference. The Viet Minh avoided Emperor Bao Dai's representatives from the south and boycotted the French. The Russians made degrading remarks about the Chinese. The French resented American attempts to use them as intermediaries. The Americans, under orders to shun the Chinese and the Viet Minh, criticized the French for secret maneuvering and were impatient with the British lack of toughness. The Viet Minh, having prevailed at Dien Bien Phu and controlling more than two-thirds of the country, came on strong. Led by Pham Van Dong, they insisted on a political settlement giving them all of Vietnam.

The new French Prime Minister Pierre Mendes-France was appointed in mid–June and promised to resign if he did not secure a cease-fire within one month. China's Chou En-lai, seeking to keep the United States out of Asia, preferred a divided Vietnam with a French presence in the south, as well as independent governments in Laos and Cambodia. A partitioned Vietnam better suited the Chinese policy to fragment Southeast Asia in order to influence its states. With Chou's assistance, Mendes-France met his deadline.

On July 20, the Geneva Agreement called for a cease-fire. France and the Democratic Republic of Vietnam agreed to a temporary division of the country at the 17th parallel with nationwide elections within two years. The French forces would withdraw from the north and the Viet Minh from the south. The United States did not sign these accords, but reluctantly pledged to abide by the agreements. Bao Dai's representatives refused to sign. All along they had opposed ceding the entire northern half of Vietnam to the Viet Minh because its population exceeded that of the south and it contained large pockets of staunchly anti–Communist Catholics.[33] "In the words of Canadian diplomat John Holmes, the Geneva Agreements constituted a 'nasty bargain accepted by all parties as the only way to avoid a dangerous confrontation.' The major issues over which the war was fought were not settled."[34]

For the Chinese and the Viet Minh, only one thing mattered most of all: keeping the United States out of Southeast Asia:

> The only real answer, Eisenhower and Dulles determined, was to accept the likelihood that part of Vietnam would be lost at Geneva and to plan for the defense of the rest of Indochina and Southeast Asia. They had been contemplating this solution for several weeks … but only now did they take concrete steps to realize it.
>
> It was a monumental decision, as important as any made by an American administration on Indochina, from Franklin Roosevelt's to Gerald Ford's…. The United States would thenceforth take responsibility for defending most of Indochina … and without "the taint of French colonialism."[35]

After the Geneva conference, the Eisenhower administration moved forward to implement its vision of creating and sustaining an anti–Communist government in Vietnam. One of its first moves would be to secure a defense grouping similar to NATO. Including the United States, Britain, France, Australia, and New Zealand, together with the Philippines, Thailand, and Pakistan, SEATO (Southeast Asia Treaty Organization) would be that grouping. Although they were not members, Dulles secured inclusion of a separate protocol that designated Laos, Cambodia, and southern Vietnam as areas that, if threatened, could "endanger" the "peace and security" of the SEATO signatories.

With SEATO providing the foundation for establishing a U.S.–protected state in southern Vietnam, the administration set about making that state a viable entity. This new venture retained the name of the state of Vietnam, and Bao Dai stayed on as chief of state.

But not all of the Eisenhower administration was convinced that we should back South Vietnam. In August 1954, a National Intelligence Estimate cautioned that even with robust backing by the U.S., the chances of establishing a strong government with broad popular support were "poor." The Joint Chiefs of Staff said it would be "hopeless" to build an army without a "reasonably strong, stable civil government in control." And Secretary of Defense Charles Wilson "recommended that the United States get out of Indochina 'as completely and as soon as possible.' With the French experience firmly in mind, Wilson warned that he could 'see nothing but grief in store for us if we remained in that area.'"[36]

In mid–June, prior to the signing of the accords, however, Emperor Bao Dai had appointed Ngo Dinh Diem, a little-known nationalist, to the office of prime minister of South Vietnam.[37] In keeping with the dignity of his position, Diem assumed a formal and reserved air in public. Although honest, courageous, and dedicated, he delegated authority with a miser's hand. He worried that subordinates might use official authority against him. In addition, he used this approach because South Vietnam had relatively few men with strong executive abilities.[38]

But I was in the eighth grade and was only concerned about how many games it would take the Cleveland Indians to annihilate the New York Giants in the Series. After all, Cleveland's top three pitchers had won 65 games between them during the season. But Willie Mays made a tremendous back-to-the-plate catch of a 440-foot fly ball in the first game and Dusty Rhodes had four hits in six at bats, seven RBIs, and two home runs. The Giants swept the Indians in four.

By October 1955, Diem had deposed Bao Dai in a referendum in which he received 98.2 percent of the vote.[39] He even received more than 605,000 votes from the 450,000 registered voters in Saigon.[40] His official title became president and chief of state of the Republic of Vietnam. In the north, President Ho Chi Minh sought and accepted aid from the Soviet Union and China.[41]

Meanwhile, I began my final year of junior high school and suffered as my beloved Yankees lost to the Dodgers for the first time in the World Series. Johnny Podres won two games for the Dodgers with a 1.00 ERA, and Duke Snider had eight hits and four home runs to lead the offense.

The year 1955 was also when Graham Greene published *The Quiet American*, a superb story that included a warning to Americans about Vietnam: "They killed him because he was too innocent to live. He was young and ignorant and silly and he got involved. He had no more of a notion than any of you what the whole affair's about, and you gave him money and ... books on the East and said, 'Go ahead. Win the East for democracy.' He never saw anything he hadn't heard in a lecture-hall, and his writers and his lecturers made a fool of him. When he saw a dead body he couldn't even see the wounds. A Red menace, a soldier of democracy."[42] A haunting metaphor of what lay ahead for the United States.

In 1956 the world focused on the Hungarian revolt against Soviet rule and the Suez Canal crisis and paid little attention to Vietnam. Neither did I. I was entering high school, and my hero was the Yankees' Don Larsen, who pitched a perfect game in the World Series as the New Yorkers took Brooklyn four games to three. Yogi Berra had nine hits, three home runs, and 10 RBIs to spark the Bombers.

With the departure of the last French troops and advisors from Vietnam in April 1956, the United States began to funnel aid directly to the Saigon government. The American commitment in Vietnam began to harden, and Diem made it known that he did not expect to participate in the forthcoming countrywide elections called for in the French–Democratic Republic of Vietnam agreement.[43]

President Eisenhower welcomed Diem to the United States in May 1957, hailing him as the "miracle man" of Asia—he had virtually annihilated the Communists in the south. One of the most significant achievements in Diem's early presidency was land reform. The previous October he had issued a presidential ordinance that restricted individual land holdings to 100 hectares of rice land. Ultimately, this land reform did succeed in breaking up vast estates and changed the landless in the South from the large majority to a minority.[44]

In early October, Hanoi issued instructions to the remaining Communists in the south to organize 37 armed companies.[45]

I was now a junior in high school and thinking about the military as a career. But even then, the most important thing to me was baseball. The Milwaukee Braves won their first World Series ever by beating the Yankees four games to three. Lew Burdette won three games and had an ERA of 0.67. Hank Aaron batted .393 and had 11 hits. Incidental to the Series was the announcement that the Brooklyn Dodgers and New York Giants were moving to Los Angeles and San Francisco, respectively, for the following season.

The year 1958 was a quiet one in Vietnam. But this would turn out to be only a short dormant interlude before the storm. In the United States, the junior senator from Massachusetts, John F. Kennedy, began talking to his friends about a run at the presidency.[46] This was also the beginning of my senior year in high school, and thoughts for my future gathered importance. I began thinking more seriously of a professional military career and how I could become an officer. As my senior year began, I decided to attend San Jose State College and join the Army ROTC, with a military career firmly in mind. Of course, baseball was still number one. The Yankees repaid the Braves by winning the Series four games to three. Hank Bauer led the Yanks with 10 hits, four home runs and eight RBIs.

As 1959 dawned, Kennedy prepared to run in the Democratic Party's primaries.[47] He knew a tough fight lay ahead to get to the nominating convention a year and a half off. Vice-President Richard Nixon was the Republican front-runner. In the South Vietnamese countryside, assassinations of village officials rose sharply. Vigorous campaigns were mounted against schoolteachers, forcing thousands of schools to close. Terrorism, sabotage, and subversion became continual, concentrated, and ominous.[48]

> During the second session of the Fifteenth Plenum of the Central Committee, held in July 1959, North Vietnam's Communist leadership ratified a resolution "affirming" … that "the Vietnamese revolution was led by the Party and that it had two strategic missions to be carried out in parallel: the social-

ist revolution in North Vietnam and the people's national democratic revolution in South Vietnam. Although these two missions were different in nature, they were intimately connected with one another, because they affected, influenced, and supported one another." The plenum also pronounced that "the fundamental path for the advancement of the Vietnamese revolution in South Vietnam is an insurrection to place the reins of the government into the hands of the people.... Based on the specific situation and the current requirements of the revolution, that path is to use the power of the masses, relying primarily on mass political forces supported by armed forces, to overthrow imperialist and feudalist rule in order to establish a popular revolutionary government."[49]

"The North's political establishment, not apolitical rice farmers rebelling against governmental oppression, had ultimately chosen the path of political agitation and armed revolt in South Vietnam."[50] The Central Committee declared: "'Our Party must make active preparations in all fields' for 'staging an insurrection to overthrow the U.S.–Diem regime' and 'to unify the nation.'"[51] "The die had been cast and it had been cast in North Vietnam."[52]

Also in 1959, the Military Commission of the Central Committee created Group 559, which had the mission to create the first foot-travel route (the Ho Chi Minh trails) connecting the North and the South and organizing the sending of people, weapons, and supplies to the South.[53]

The year 1959 also marked my graduation from high school and entrance into college and ROTC. I was on course, and baseball was still important. The Los Angeles Dodgers, playing in Memorial Coliseum, won their first World Series over the Chicago White Sox four games to two. Unheralded Charlie Neal had 10 hits and a .370 average to lead the Dodgers.

The American presidential election was in November 1960. John F. Kennedy was the Democratic nominee and Richard M. Nixon was the Republican. For the first time, two presidential candidates debated each other on national television. In the closest race ever at the time, Kennedy defeated Nixon to become the 35th president of the United States.

"On December 20, 1960, officials from the 'southern branch' of the Communist Party headquartered in Hanoi convened in Cambodia and established the National Liberation Front (NLF) which publicly espoused the goal of overthrowing the 'dictatorial Ngo Dinh Diem administration.' Ostensibly a sovereign South Vietnamese political invention, the NLF was little more than a North Vietnamese contrivance designed to deflect suspicions and put an 'independent,' ideologically neutral southern face on the movement to unseat Diem's anti–Communist government."[54]

Baseball became less important, and school and ROTC took on a more serious note. But I was still annoyed when Pittsburgh Pirate Bill Mazeroski hit a home run in the bottom of the ninth inning of the seventh game of the World Series to defeat the Yankees.

John Fitzgerald Kennedy was inaugurated on January 20, 1961. His moving speech stirred a generation: "Let every nation know, whether it wishes us well or ill, that we shall pay any price, bear any burden, meet any hardship, support any friend, oppose any foe to assure the survival and the success of liberty."[55]

In April, Kennedy agreed to send an additional 100 American military advisors to Vietnam, bringing the total to nearly 800. At the same time, he sent Frederick Nolting to Saigon as our new ambassador. Diem at this point resisted the effort to bring American combat troops to his country.

By October, however, when large Viet Cong forces attacked South Vietnamese army posts in Phuoc Thanh and Darlac provinces, inflicting heavy casualties, Diem reversed himself. He told Nolting he would welcome American troops as a "symbolic" presence.[56] In the same month, Kennedy sent his military advisor, GEN Maxwell Taylor, to Vietnam on a fact-finding mission with Walt Rostow. Upon his return, Taylor proposed an initial commitment of 8,000 American troops. Secretary of Defense Robert McNamara rejected Taylor's proposal as inadequate and urged the deployment of six American divisions, some 200,000 men, to show the Viet Cong "we meant business."[57]

Initially, Kennedy continued the pattern the United States had followed through the years regarding Vietnam: he rejected withdrawal and balked at rushing into total war.[58]

I was beginning my third year at San Jose State, and baseball began to lose its importance to me. But what a year! Yankee teammates Mickey Mantle and Roger Maris competed all year in a battle of home run hitters. After 162 games, Maris broke Babe Ruth's record with 61 and Mantle had hit 54. The Yanks as a team had 240 for the season and they beat Cincinnati in the Series four games to one.

1. The Road to War

During the summer of 1962, between my junior and senior years, I attended the six-week Army ROTC Summer Camp at Fort Lewis, Washington. One of the most fascinating events happened to me while training there. During bayonet training in the middle of a large open field, the instructor yelled, "What is the spirit of the bayonet?" And the class responded, "To kill!" He yelled louder, and we replied even louder. As we were screaming "To kill" at the top of our lungs, a strange transformation took place. At that time I realized I could kill someone.

In October, the San Francisco Giants played in their first World Series against the Yankees. In the seventh game, with two on and two out in the ninth inning, Willie McCovey hit a line shot at second baseman Bobby Richardson. Richardson made the catch and the Giants' hopes died.

Turmoil marked the New Year. On January 2, 1963, a South Vietnamese division was mauled at Ap Bac by a smaller Viet Cong force. On this day, the Viet Cong decided to stand and fight, although they were outnumbered ten to one.[59] In the end, South Vietnamese casualties were 80 dead and more than 100 wounded. Three American advisors were killed, eight wounded, and five helicopters were shot down. Eighteen Viet Cong were killed.[60] The senior American military advisor there, Lieutenant Colonel John Paul Vann, accused the South Vietnamese commanding general of being afraid to fight and choosing to reinforce defeat.[61] It was later found that the failures Vann mentioned could also be blamed on him and his faulty decisions during the battle.[62]

As the war intensified, disillusionment with Diem increased. Even within the United States government, the presidential advisors were split between supporting Diem or pushing for a coup to overthrow him. Nobody could come up with suggestions for relaxing the tensions in Saigon. On McNamara's advice, President Kennedy did what is usually done in times of indecision: he sent out a fact-finding mission.

"This one, composed of Marine Corps GEN Victor Krulak and Joseph Mendenhall, a State Department official who had served in Vietnam, flew a total of 24,000 miles for a four-day survey to confirm their prejudices. An optimist, Krulak concluded from speaking almost exclusively with American and South Vietnamese army officers that 'the shooting war is still going ahead at an impressive pace.' A pessimist,

Mendenhall concluded from talks primarily with urban bureaucrats and politicians that the Diem government was near collapse. After they presented their divergent reports to him on September 10, Kennedy quipped: 'You two did visit the same country, didn't you?'"[63]

Finally, South Vietnamese generals conspired to overthrow Diem with CIA support. On November 1, the generals moved against Diem and his brother, Ngo Dinh Nhu. The Presidential Palace was surrounded, and Diem attempted to negotiate and gain time for loyal units to come to their rescue. But there were no loyal units except for the Palace guard. When the rebels took the Palace the brothers slipped away through a secret tunnel. They fled to the Chinese suburb of Cholon, where they accepted from the generals a guarantee for safe-conduct out of the country. Instead they were picked up and killed in the back of an armored personnel carrier.[64]

Three weeks later, President John F. Kennedy was assassinated in Dallas. Like the rest of the country, I spent endless hours in front of the television absorbing and trying to make sense of the unfolding events. I never did. Lyndon Baines Johnson was the new president.

My interest in baseball continued to fade even while the Dodgers swept the Yankees in four straight. The Dodger pitching staff held the Yanks to only four runs in four games for an amazing 1.00 ERA. Sandy Koufax, Don Drysdale, and Johnny Podres recorded the victories.

I graduated in January 1964, and still Vietnam was not a major concern of our government, our citizens or me. We had about 16,500 military advisors there, but no official troop commitment.[65] But events changed my outlook and interest. I completed the Infantry Officers Basic Course (IOBC) and now felt that I was ready for my new assignment. Like all new 2LTs, I wanted an infantry rifle platoon to lead and train. I did not get my wish. Instead, I was assigned to Headquarters and Headquarters Company, 2nd Brigade, 2nd Infantry Division at Ft. Benning as the communications platoon leader. This unit had a second designation: the 11th Air Assault Division (Test). The 11th was the unit designated by the Howze Board to test and prove that air mobility worked.

The American military had used helicopters in combat since the end of World War II, but the Korean War accelerated their use.[66] The United States Marine Corps conducted the first air mobile landings of troops. In the summer of 1951, HMR-161, the first helicopter transport squadron, airlifted troops into combat in Korea.[67] The Army, meanwhile, used helicopters to evacuate the wounded.[68]

After the Korean War, LTG James Gavin wondered what had happened to the cavalry made famous by the likes of Jeb Stuart, J.F.C. Fuller, and Erwin Rommel. Commenting on GEN Walton Walker's withdrawal to Pusan in June 1950, Gavin asked, "Where was the cavalry? And I don't mean horses, I mean helicopters and light aircraft."[69]

When Kennedy was inaugurated as President, Robert McNamara was named Secretary of Defense. McNamara was determined to reorganize the Department of the Army and its methods of warfare. He felt that the Army aircraft procurement plan was inadequate, that there was no unified aviation effort, and that officers with progressive air-mobile ideas were not being heard.[70]

On April 19, 1962, McNamara sent a blunt memorandum to Secretary of the Army Elvis Stahr ordering the Army to implement air mobility, telling him how to do it, and stating who should be involved. This memorandum became the birthright of the new air mobile division.

THE SECRETARY OF DEFENSE
Washington, D.C.
April 19, 1962

Memorandum for Mr. Stahr

I have not been satisfied with Army program submissions for tactical mobility. I do not believe that the Army has fully explored the opportunities offered by aeronautical technology for making a revolutionary break with traditional surface mobility means. Air vehicles operating close to, but above, the ground appear to me to offer the possibility of a quantum increase in effectiveness. I think that every possibility in this area should be explored.

We have found that air transportation is cheaper than rail or ship transportation even in peacetime. The urgency of wartime operation makes air transportation even more important. By exploiting aeronautical potential, we should be able to achieve a major increase in effectiveness while spending on air mobility systems no more than we have been spending on systems oriented for ground transportation.

I therefore believe that the Army's re-examination of its aviation requirements should be a bold "new look" at land warfare mobility. It should be conducted in an atmosphere divorced from traditional viewpoints and past policies. The only objective the actual task force should be given is that of acquiring the maximum attainable mobility within alternative funding levels and technology. This necessitates a readiness to substitute air mobility systems for traditional ground systems wherever analysis shows the substitution to improve our capabilities or effectiveness. It also requires that bold, new ideas which the task force may recommend be protected from veto or dilution by conservative staff review.

In order to insure the success of the re-examination I am requesting in my official memorandum, I urge you to give its implementation your close personal attention. More specifically, I suggest that you establish a managing group of selected individuals be considered as appropriate for service thereon: Lt. Gen. Hamilton H. Howze, Brig. Gen. Delk M. Oden, Brig. Gen. Walter B. Richardson, Col. Robert R. Williams, Col. John Norton, Col. A.J. Rankin, Mr. Frank A. Parker, Dr. Edwin W. Paxson, and Mr. Edward H. Heinemann.

Existing Army activities such as Fort Rucker, RAC, STAG (Strategic and Tactics Analysis Group, Washington, D.C.), CDEC (Combat Development Experimental Center, Ft. Ord), and CORG (Combat Operations Research Group, Ft. Monroe), combined with the troop units and military study headquarters of CONARC, and in cooperation with Air Force troop carrier elements, appear to provide the required capabilities to conduct the analyses, field tests and exercises, provided their efforts are properly directed.

The studies already made by the Army of air mobile divisions and their subordinate air mobile units, of air mobile reconnaissance regiments, and of aerial artillery indicate the type of doctrinal concepts which could be evolved, although there has been no action to carry these concepts into effect. Parallel studies are also needed to provide air vehicles of improved capabilities and to eliminate ground-surface equipment and forces whose duplicate but less effective capabilities can no longer be justified economically. Improved V/STOL (Vertical/Short Takeoff or Landing) air vehicles may also be required as optimized weapons platforms, command and communications vehicles, and as short-range prime movers of heavy loads up to 40 or 50 tons.

I shall be disappointed if the Army's re-examination merely produces logistics-oriented recommendations to procure more of the same, rather than a plan for implementing fresh and perhaps unorthodox concepts which will give us a significant increase in mobility.

(Signed) Robert S. McNamara

Thus began the formation of the U.S. Army Tactical Mobility Requirements Board, the Howze Board. McNamara ensured that the board was not impartial in its views of the air-mobile concept. All of the military personnel supported it, and the civilians were by and large positive about it.[71]

The Howze Board report was submitted in four months and recommended: formation of an air assault division; an air cavalry combat brigade; a corps aviation brigade to move reserves rapidly; an air transport brigade to provide logistical support to the air assault division; and a special warfare aviation brigade to support units in combat.[72]

When I arrived in the late spring of 1964, the 11th had been testing and training for 18 months. The experiments were conducted in three-day and four-day operations, and this continued until the fall.

Meanwhile, events in Vietnam heated up. In South Vietnam, American forces were still supposedly advisors with no combat role. On August 2, 1964, in the Gulf of Tonkin, however, the American escalation began. The United States Navy destroyer *Maddox* was patrolling off the North Vietnamese coast. These operations, code named DeSoto, were conducted with South Vietnamese commandos who would harass enemy radar transmitters, thereby activating them so that American electronic intelligence vessels cruising in the Gulf could learn their locations and measure their frequencies. In addition, they could chart and photograph the coastal region, and monitor its traffic.[73]

By 1100 that morning, the *Maddox* had come within ten miles of the Red River delta, the northernmost point of its mission. The day was clear and calm. Captain John J. Herrick commanded the mission aboard the *Maddox*. He now noticed three North Vietnamese patrol boats emerge from an estuary and then disappear behind an island. Confident he was in international waters, Herrick was not concerned. His technicians, however, intercepted an order to the patrol boats to attack after they had refueled.

As the *Maddox* turned towards the open sea, the North Vietnamese patrol boats followed in pursuit at twice its speed. Tracking the enemy on radar, the *Maddox* opened fire when they reached a range of 9,800 yards. The *Maddox* fired three or four shells as warning shots. In addition, Herrick radioed the aircraft carrier *Ticonderoga*, also patrolling in the Gulf, for air support.[74] At 1508 the destroyer began rapid fire at a range of 9,000 yards. The *Maddox* was 28 miles from shore at the time the shooting started. The speeding PT boats didn't hesitate or change course. With the boats spread 500 yards apart and approaching torpedo range, the *Maddox* fired with all six guns.[75]

Closing in at a range of 5,000 yards, two of the patrol boats launched torpedoes. Both missed. The third boat, with its weapons pumping fire, sped directly at the destroyer to discharge its torpedo. It turned out to be a dud. The gunners on the *Maddox* hit one of the enemy craft as three Crusader jets from the *Ticonderoga* arrived on station to strafe the other two patrol boats. The enemy boats turned away and the *Maddox* turned, still firing, and pursued them.[76] The skirmish, which barely lasted 20 minutes, ended in a clear American victory. Only one enemy bullet had struck the *Maddox* with no casualties. In contrast, the Americans had crippled one North Vietnamese boat and damaged the other two.[77] Reports from the incident reached Washington, D.C., that morning. (Washington is 12 hours behind Vietnam.)

President Johnson was in the middle of a presidential election campaign and knew the voters would not look favorably to a candidate moving towards war. Thus, since there were no American casualties, he felt no further action was necessary and specifically rejected reprisals against North Vietnam. At the same time, however, Johnson directed the *Maddox* and another destroyer, the *C. Turner Joy*, as well as protective aircraft, to return to the Gulf of Tonkin. Their orders were to "attack any force that attacks them." Johnson also sent a note to Hanoi warning that "grave consequences would inevitably result from any further unprovoked offensive military action" against American ships deployed in international waters off North Vietnam.

Meanwhile, the Joint Chiefs of Staff felt differently. They identified targets in North Vietnam, such as harbor installations and oil depots. Admiral Ulysses S. Grant Sharp, Jr., Commander-in-Chief-Pacific (CINCPAC), ordered the carrier *Constellation* to join the *Ticonderoga* in the South China Sea. He also outlined a new mission for the *Maddox* and the second destroyer, the *C. Turner Joy*. Their mission was to be superseded by more vigorous maneuvers made to "assert the right of freedom of the seas." The two destroyers were to stage direct daylight runs to within eight miles of the North Vietnamese coast and four miles off its islands.

Summer in the Gulf of Tonkin is volatile, and thunderstorms throughout the night battered the destroyers as their crews, blind in the darkness, sat glued to their instruments. The sonar aboard the *Maddox* was functioning erratically, and atmospheric conditions distorted the radar beams reaching both ships. In addition, there is a phenomenon in this area called "Tonkin Gulf Ghost" or "Tonkin Spook" that generates radar images much smaller and more clearly defined than normal.[78] Around 2000 the *Maddox* intercepted radio messages that gave Herrick the impression North Vietnamese patrol boats were preparing for an assault. He requested air support from the *Ticonderoga*. Soon eight jets were overhead, but their pilots saw nothing.

Approximately an hour later, both destroyers started firing in all directions and turning wildly to avoid what they believed to be enemy torpedoes racing towards them. Their sonar counted 22 torpedoes, none of which scored a hit. Their officers reported sinking two or maybe three patrol boats during the engagement, which went on for more than two hours. But hardly had the shooting stopped than Herrick developed doubts about the whole incident.[79] Herrick immediately communicated his concerns up the chain of command. He stated that the "entire action leaves many doubts," and he urged a thorough air reconnaissance in daylight. Herrick then ordered his officers to question the crews of both ships. Not a single sailor had seen or heard enemy gunfire. And the jet pilots had detected no enemy craft during their 40 minutes of flying over the area.

Herrick now reported that the *Maddox* had not made any "actual visual sightings" of North Vietnamese patrol boats. The radar blips showing such had been due to "freak weather effects," and an "overeager" sonar operator. Admiral Sharp relayed the message to Washington.

At 1800 Washington time, while Herrick was still attempting to furnish additional evidence, a Pentagon spokesman declared that "a second deliberate attack" had occurred. And just before midnight, nearly an hour after the carriers *Ticonderoga* and *Constellation* had sent their aircraft to bomb North Vietnamese territory, President Johnson appeared on television.

Somber and determined, Johnson announced: "The initial attack on the destroyer Maddox, on August 2, was repeated today by a number of hostile vessels attacking two U.S. destroyers with torpedoes.... Air action is now in execution against gunboats and certain supporting facilities in North Vietnam which have been used in these hostile operations."[80] Aircraft from the carriers *Ticonderoga* and *Constellation* flew 64 sorties against four North Vietnamese patrol boat bases and a major oil storage depot. Enemy antiaircraft guns shot down two of our jets, resulting in the death of one pilot and the capture of the other. LT Everett

Alvarez would spend the next eight and a half years in a North Vietnamese prison. Thus, *one of the first steps in the coming war with North Vietnam was based on a complete fabrication.*

After the incident in the Tonkin Gulf, President Lyndon Johnson asked for and received authorization from Congress to take all necessary measures to repel attacks against American forces and to prevent further aggression. On August 7, 1964, the Tonkin Gulf Resolution passed the Senate with only two dissenting votes and passed the House unanimously. Senators Wayne Morse (D-OR) and Ernest Gruening (D-AK) were the dissenting votes.[81]

American actions tapered down after the initial attack, as President Johnson was not yet committed to the idea of war. He was, however, a believer in the domino theory and desired to stabilize the South Vietnamese government and remedy its military position in the field. He feared if Saigon fell, so would Laos, Cambodia, and Thailand.

As we tried to stabilize the South Vietnamese government, it had a succession of coups and changes in leadership. From January 1964 to February 1965, nine different men ran South Vietnam. These constant changes proved to Johnson that he could not count on the South Vietnamese to have the will or capacity to prevent a Communist victory in the South. He felt he had no choice but to Americanize the war.[82] As he said two days after becoming President, "I am not going to lose Vietnam. I am not going to be the President who saw Southeast Asia go the way China went."[83]

Meanwhile, the 11th's six-week exercise "Air Assault II," conducted in North Carolina, South Carolina and northern Georgia, successfully concluded in November 1964. Shortly thereafter, I was reassigned. I was sent to Charlie Company, 2nd Battalion, 38th Infantry. Captain Ed Boyt became my new commanding officer. I was now a rifle platoon leader.

After a landslide victory in the 1964 presidential election, Johnson began to move relentlessly toward war. On February 7, 1965, the *Coral Sea* launched 49 aircraft to attack the North Vietnamese barracks at Dong Hoi.[84] On March 2, Operation Rolling Thunder began by hitting minor targets in the southernmost third of North Vietnam.[85]

And on March 8, 1965, two battalions of U.S. Marines splashed ashore at Da Nang to provide security for the huge air base there. They were the first American combat troops to set foot on the Asian mainland since the end of the Korean War.[86] On May 5, the Army's 173d Airborne Brigade landed at Bien Hoa and Vung Tau. And in mid–September the 1st Cavalry Division (Airmobile) landed at Qui Nhon after 30 days at sea.

By the end of the year there were 184,300 American troops in Vietnam.[87]

We were at war. I was at war.

2

173D AIRBORNE
BRIGADE

On Okinawa a lady remarked that I commanded the most conceited unit she had ever encountered. She was told, "Oh no! last
year we were conceited. This year we are perfect."
—MG Ellis Williamson (Ret.)

The 173d was activated on June 25, 1963, and assigned to the
Ryukyan Islands with an authorized strength of 3530 officers and men.[1]
Its organic units were the 1st and 2nd Battalions (Airborne), 503rd
Infantry Regiment; Company D, 16th Armor; 3rd Battalion, 319th
Artillery; 173d Engineer Company; 173d Support Battalion; and Troop
E, 17th Cavalry.[2] Brigadier General Ellis W. Williamson was Brigade
Commander.

Its mission was to be the Army's response force for the western
Pacific theater: to quickly drop onto an objective by parachute and hold
it until reinforced by a larger force. To meet that mission, the brigade
conducted extensive airborne, guerrilla, and jungle warfare training in
Okinawa, Taiwan, Korea, and Thailand. It had received the nickname
"Sky Soldiers," or "Tien Bing," from its many airborne exercises conducted in Taiwan. By the end of 1963, more than 10,719 parachute jumps
had been made and six field exercises conducted.[3]

As a result of BG Williamson's tireless efforts and those of his subordinates, the 173d quickly established itself as one of the finest units in
the United States Army. Morale was so high that the brigade often
achieved a 100 percent reenlistment rate, an unheard of achievement.

Officers selected to attend career-enhancing courses in the United
States sometimes turned them down in order to remain with the brigade.
This practice became so prevalent that Williamson had to promise those

officers that he would make room for them in the brigade when they completed their stateside courses.[4]

By 1964, the units within the brigade were trained, tested and operationally ready. For the remainder of the year, the brigade conducted varied and diversified training, most of it based on previously formulated contingency plans. The Sky Soldiers conducted 26,339 parachute jumps that year, proving they were "Airborne, All the Way." In addition to its airborne training, the brigade constantly and continuously worked on air-mobile tactics, developing and refining the new concept of vertical envelopment by helicopter.

Early on the morning of April 25, 1965, BG Williamson, his S-3 (Operations), S-4 (Logistics) officers, and his aide arrived at Ton Son Nhut airport outside of Saigon. GEN William C. Westmoreland, MACV commander, had summoned him. Williamson's trip to Saigon was in response to a top-secret message received at his headquarters the previous day. GEN Westmoreland had requested deployment of the 173d to Vietnam, and the Department of the Army had ordered the unit to prepare for movement.

At MACV, Westmoreland outlined his plan for the 173d. With the expansion of Operation Rolling Thunder, a program of measured and limited air action against North Vietnam, Westmoreland was concerned about the ability of the Army of the Republic of Vietnam (ARVN) to provide adequate security for the American Air Force bases supporting the raids. Also, the introduction of U.S. Army units in country to provide base security would free those ARVN units currently providing security to perform offensive operations against the enemy.

In addition, Westmoreland revealed to Williamson that several American divisions were scheduled to arrive in South Vietnam within a few months. Thus, the 173d would also have the mission to clear the enemy from the proposed base campsites. Westmoreland stated that the brigade's deployment to Vietnam would be temporary, no more than 60 days.[5] General Williamson spent the next three days visiting the air bases that the brigade would be guarding, meeting with a variety of American military advisors, as well as key ARVN commanders, and formulating plans for the brigade's deployment. Preparing for the unit's mission in Vietnam would involve a tremendous amount of work, but Williamson had a history of overcoming difficult obstacles.[6]

General Williamson was born and raised in Raleigh, North Carolina. He joined the North Carolina National Guard in 1935. He would spend ten years with the regiment, rising from private to lieutenant colonel—the regimental commander.[7]

Just before World War II, his unit was called to active duty as part of the massive American military buildup. They would enter France through Omaha Beach in Normandy on June 10, 1944—four days after D–Day.

Soon after the armistice, Williamson was promoted to lieutenant colonel and given command of the 120th Infantry Regiment. Convinced that the Army was his true calling, Williamson applied for and received a regular Army commission. He saw combat in Korea, making the famed Inchon landing in September 1950 as Assistant G-3 for GEN Douglas MacArthur's X Corps. His superior performance during the "forgotten war" led to his promotion to full colonel.[8]

A Pentagon tour followed Korea, and here Williamson was a key staff member during the planning stages for the new aforementioned air-mobile concept, which led to the activation of the 1st Cavalry Division (Airmobile). The Army made several alterations to the Howze board recommendations, recognizing the need for an airborne unit in the Pacific to fulfill the mission of a theater quick-reaction force. COL Williamson was unanimously selected to command the new airborne brigade.[9]

But the real heart and soul of the 173d, or at least the 1st Battalion, was LTC Richard H. Boland, call sign Rawhide 6. LTC Boland was a tall, lean, tough airborne officer who already had a Combat Infantryman's Badge with 2 stars signifying combat service in World War II, Korea and Vietnam.

He had been an enlisted man in World War II like Williamson, but had made combat jumps into Normandy during D–Day and into Holland during Operation Market Garden. He had participated in the battle at Bastogne, the Battle of the Bulge, with the 101st Airborne Division. Boland would later command a rifle company in Korea and earn a Silver Star for his actions during a night attack on Hill 472.

LTC Boland came to the 173d in late November 1963. He was originally assigned as the S-3, Brigade Operations Officer. But that didn't last long. "And when I got to Okinawa, Williamson and I never hit it off right from the beginning. And he had me in there initially as his Operations Officer, but then he threw me out of there and down to the 1st Battalion to get rid of me, I guess."[10]

As the battalion commander of the 1st Battalion 503rd Airborne, LTC Boland brought his unit up to combat readiness by embarking on a rigorous physical training schedule. And to build morale at the same time, he played the theme song from the television show *Rawhide*. He wanted to lift the troops' spirits so that "everything is not as shitty as it looked."[11]

The playing of the theme from *Rawhide* would result in the 173d getting the nickname of "The Herd." The story behind his selection of the song was typical Boland. He was walking down the street, and he heard somebody in a store playing the TV series theme record. He walked in, slapped the arm off the record, picked it up and asked how much they wanted for it. He then paid and walked out the door. One of his subordinates remembered, "At the next formation we were in Battalion formation, and Boland was spit and polish. The troops were in khakis and were looking sharp. As the companies marched by he was standing on the back of a truck and it's 'Rolling, rolling, rolling, Rawhide.'"

But it wasn't just *Rawhide* that would endear Boland to his troops; it was his leadership abilities and his caring for his men:

> My thinking always was that before you take troops out on something, when you go out on an exercise and operation, have briefings on it and everything. Most of the commanders come back and they don't explain it to the troops in such a way that the troops understand what they're doing and what is required of them. And they don't feel a part of the operation.
>
> So, in other words, they feel like they are just being pushed into something. And then they come back and no one gives them a basic critique on what was wrong, including what you did wrong and what was the results of what you did wrong and what you learned. Ask them what they thought of the operation that wasn't brought up by me in the critique. You know, let people get up and have the confidence that they can say, "Well, I think you screwed up in that one, I think we did the wrong thing here." Or, "I don't think we should have done that. I think we should have done this."
>
> Then you discuss it, and then the people begin to have an understanding of what in the hell is going on and feel that he, too, has a part to play in this thing. Drill into them that we stand or die. We either die alone or we die together.[12]

Private Richard White remembers arriving at Camp Kubasaki (Okinawa) in early 1965 with Pat Gaffney. They knocked on the door of the Quonset hut that was the Battalion headquarters orderly room. They removed their headgear and reported for duty. "Shortly, we were standing at attention in front of COL Richard Boland. The colonel welcomed us and invited us to 'stand at ease.' Without further ado, he proceeded to fill our heads with graphic accounts of his war record. At one point in his speech he said in effect, 'I have stepped over more dead soldiers in my career than you two have seen live ones in yours.' And, 'But there's one damn thing that I want you men to know. I have never left a man on the battlefield. If we ever go to war together, you can bet your ass I'll bring you back one way or the other.' I think it was at that particular time that I realized that the army must have invented the parade rest position to keep a slick sleeved private's knees from knockin' while the brass was busy scaring the shit out of him."[13]

"Boland was a magnificent leader in the Patton mold: Hard as nails and really knew his stuff. Bn [Battalion] was extremely well trained esp [especially] in live fire which was very rare in those days.... I personally saw him knock out the BN XO on one occasion in the Sukiran O [Officers'] Club at a Friday night Happy Hour, and deck an Army Doctor who talked back to him on a DZ on Oki [Okinawa]; unbelievable stuff. The troops were in awe of him and he was very hard on them; even more demanding on the Officers esp the CPTs. The NCOs cut a wide path away from him and he generally did not screw with them."[14] Many of his troops would later credit LTC Boland's tough training for saving them from being killed in combat.

On May 5, 1965, the 173d became the first American Army ground combat unit assigned to Vietnam.[15] The 1st Battalion, 503rd Infantry arrived at the port city of Vung Tau at 0500 and set up perimeter defense. At approximately the same time the 2nd Battalion arrived at Bien Hoa and set up its perimeter defense.[16]

Richard White recalls that the jungle around Vung Tau was filled with huge insects and strange creatures. "Jokingly, we would refer to the mosquitoes as being the size of B-52s and scorpions the size of backhoes were frequently seen. I was stung by one such scorpion while I slept and awoke with a knee the size of a football.... There were lizards in the dense forested areas the size of alligators and at night they kept you awake with their vulgar cries of 'fuckyou, fuckyou.' We just called them 'fuckyou' lizards. There was an equally aggravating message from a bird which beckoned us to re-enlist with its cries of 'reeup, reeup.' Of course we just called 'em reup birds."[17] PFC Harry Allen remembers the first patrol he went on in Vung Tau:

> We were moving through the jungle, and it was the very first patrol I had been on, and I was probably 6 or 8 guys back from the front when all of a sudden we heard a loud explosion, a grenade or booby trap, some type had gone off. And then there was some automatic weapons fire and everybody hit the dirt. The first time we had been under fire, really. And all of a sudden there was a call for "Medic." And the medic was about 2 or 3 guys behind me and CPT Daniel was about 2 guys behind him. I remember the call went out, you know, "Medic, medic!" And the medic lifted his head up and said, "Yeah, what do you want?" And about that time Daniel jumped and ran up there and kicked the guy right in the butt and said, "They want you, Goddammit! Get up there!"[18]

The Brigade's initial missions were to protect the Bien Hoa airfield and the Vung Tau seaport; to keep the enemy off balance until more American units arrived; to assist the ARVN; to protect the entry of American units in country and orient them; and to open up and pacify the countryside. By early June[19] the Brigade was back together in Bien Hoa and incorporated the crack 1st Battalion, Royal Australian Regiment (1/RAR) to bring it up to its Tables of Organization & Equipment (TO&E) strength. It would now train for offensive operations.[20]

But before the 1st Battalion would conduct offensive operations, it would lose its Battalion Commander. LTC Boland had hurt his back during a jump in Okinawa. Not realizing how bad the injury was, he made another jump over a rice paddy and that re-injured his back and forced his evacuation from Vietnam. LTC John Tyler, the Brigade S-3, replaced Boland.

I arrived in Bien Hoa on October 6, 1965, at 1700, and reported into Company A, 1st Battalion (Airborne) 503rd Infantry, by 1800. CPT Walter B. Daniel, radio call sign Diesel Stamp 6, was my new company commander. The airborne's history was riddled with famous names and glory. And now, I was part of it.

CPT Daniel was born in Kingsport, Tennessee, and had enlisted in the Army in 1955. An Airborne Ranger, he graduated from the Infantry Officers Candidate School in 1960. Although he was only four years older than me, he wore Master Jump Wings and already had 10 years Army experience. I looked at him and thought, "Uh-oh, he looks like one tough SOB. I better get my shit together and fast."

Wayne Downing, retired 4-star general and former member of the 173rd, told Walt Daniel "that he always measured the Ranger Battalions that he commanded by the standard set by A Co. on Okinawa and in Vietnam. He said that none had ever come up to the standard."[21]

I had been transferred to the 173d from the 1st Cav as part of a new policy called the Officer Infusion Program. Although I was proud to be a charter member of the Cav, now I was with the Army's most elite unit: the airborne. The airborne! Silver jump wings, glider patches, bloused Corcoran jump boots. Three weeks of intense training at Fort Benning. Bastogne, Normandy, Market Garden, Corregidor; the 82nd, the 101st, the 503rd, the 187th. James Gavin, Maxwell Taylor, William Westmoreland, Harry W.O. Kinnard, Anthony McAuliffe, Matthew Ridgway. We were part of the legacy of "Those Devils in Baggy Pants."

But, it wasn't just the uniform, jump school or famous names that made the airborne. It was more than that. It was volunteers. It was a mindset that allowed a normal human being to jump from a perfectly safe aircraft at 1500 feet or less into hostile territory. It was pride: in one's unit, in oneself. It was dedication: to succeed, to be the best. It was camaraderie. Paratroopers took care of each other; it was knowing that the wounded and killed in action would never be left on the battlefield. Like all elite units, the airborne accounted for all its men. It was an attitude: that airborne troopers were better. It was a drive for perfection.

It was all of these that led to the heroic defense at Bastogne, the jump behind enemy lines at Normandy, and the airborne assault to free the Philippines at Corregidor. It was all that that made my chest swell with pride. It was the airborne, all the way! Everyone else was a "leg."

After initially conducting movements around Bien Hoa and Vung Tau, the Brigade expanded its area of operations to War Zone D, Phuoc Tay, Pleiku-Kontum, Ben Cat (Iron Triangle), Phuoc Vinh, Di An, Phu Loc, and Phu Loi.[22] All were preludes to the first major unit engagement of the war between the American Army and the Viet Cong/PAVN. It would take place in War Zone D.

Brigadier General Williamson named the operation THE HUMP (OPORD 28–65) to signify the halfway point in the 12-month tour for members of the Brigade. The unit had deployed to Vietnam on May 5, and HUMP would begin on November 5.[23]

War Zone D was named by the French in 1950 and was located approximately 15 kilometers due north of the Bien Hoa Air Base. The zone, some 60 kilometers (37 miles) wide and some 35 kilometers (22 miles) deep, had belonged to the Viet Minh since the early days of the French Indochina War and subsequently was controlled by the Viet Cong. It was predominantly jungle terrain bounded by rice paddies and small villages near the banks of the Song (river) Dong Nai and Song Be. For the most part, the South Vietnamese government and military failed to challenge the Viet Cong for its control.

War Zone D [Chien Khu D]: A war zone in Eastern Cochin China during the Vietnamese people's wars against the French and against the Americans. It was formed in early 1946 and at that time was made up of five villages (Tan Hoa, My Loc, Tan Tich, Thuong Lang, and Lac An) in Tan Uyen District, Bien Hoa Province. Initially it was called the Dat Cuoc War Zone or the Lac An War Zone. Beginning in 1948 it began to expand and became the base area for many Party, government, mass organization, and armed forces headquarters of many districts of Bien Hoa and Thu Dau Mot provinces as well as of the headquarters of Region 7, the Eastern Sub-Inter-Zone, and of all of Cochin China. During the resistance war against the Americans, the center of the war zone gradually shifted to the northeast... It was a node in the strategic transportation corridor from the Center [North Vietnam] to Cochin China. It was the base area for Party, government, NLF, and armed forces units and headquarters of Eastern Cochin China, from the district level up through province and Military Region, right up to the Central Office of South Vietnam [COSVN]. It was a location where Liberation Army and Eastern Cochin China main forces units were formed and that they used as a springboard for their attacks and as their direct rear area. It was a local logistics base for Cochin China and for Region 6.[24]

In 1965, War Zone D was home to the 9th Viet Cong Division and its three main force regiments: 271st VC Infantry, aka Q761; 272nd VC Infantry, aka Q762; and 273rd VC Infantry, aka Q763. This division was the first Communist main force unit fielded entirely in the South under the Central Office for South Vietnam in September 1965. Its origins could be traced back to two battalions organized from "regroupees" in 1961. Each of the 9th's regiments was structured with three main force battalions, and each of its battalions consisted of three main force companies. Elements of the 9th faced the 173d in War Zone D in late

June (OPORD 16–65) and early July (OPORD 17–65). For the most part the Viet Cong refused to fight and avoided contact whenever possible.[25]

The mission for the 1st Battalion, 503rd Infantry and 1st Battalion, Royal Australian Regiment was to air assault into War Zone D and search for the Viet Cong's Q762 Regiment and D.800 Battalion (an independent VC main force battalion) rumored to be operating in the area. The Brigade S-2 estimated that the enemy could mass up to 8500 men within 48 hours. Their armaments reportedly included 81mm and 82mm mortars, 57mm and 75mm recoilless rifles, and .50 caliber and .30 caliber machine guns.[26] (A note on the size and organization of the Viet Cong military: The "principal VC and NVA combat organization was based on a triangular system. Three men made up a cell, three cells a squad, three squads a platoon, three platoons a company, three companies a battalion, and three battalions a regiment. This 'system of three' continued through division, corps and army. The triangular system was not totally rigid. It was not unusual for the 'system of three' to vary from a 'system of two to five.'")[27]

The 1/503 would search north of the Song Dong Nai and west of the Song Be while the 1/RAR would search south and east of the two rivers. The rumor was that the Viet Cong were massing for an attack on the Bien Hoa Air Base. The 2/503 would remain in reserve in Bien Hoa to defend the air base.

3

5–7 NOVEMBER 1965

Battle is the most magnificent competition in which a human being can indulge. It brings out all that is best; it removes all that is base.

—Gen. George S. Patton

The Brigade Staff Journal recorded the following:

0530 E/17 Cav departed base area.
0540 E/17 Cav CP 1 at 0538.
0547 E/17 Cav CP 2.
0554 E/17 Cav CP 3 at 0550.
0600 3/319 reports 1st march unit SP.
0618 3/319 CP 1.
0619 All elements 3/319 crossed SP.
0630 Air relay on station.
0635 3/319 Arty CP 2.
0650 3/319 Arty (D/16) at RP.
0709 3/319 Arty closed RP.[1]

Early in the morning of November 5, the 3rd Battalion (Airborne), 319th Artillery, protected by Troop E, 17th Cavalry and Company D, 16th Armor moved by convoy to Position Ace, a few kilometers southwest of the operational area. The artillery registered its batteries in preparation for the helicopter assaults to begin later that morning.

0720 CG announces 30 min. delay.
0745 XO informs of 1½ hour delay for weather.[2]

The 1/RAR's scheduled air assault at 0800 on LZ Queen was delayed by heavy ground fog.

0810 FSCC reports one battery has registered from Psn Ace as of 0700.

0825 FSCC informs DO that alt LZ will be used.

0830 XO reports opn. a go on new schedule.

0845 XO reports TAC Air Prep on Jack commencing.

0915 Arty prep commenced.

0917 1st lift off at Snakepit [name of our pickup area for helicopter combat assaults].

0927 Arty prep completed.

0930 1st element 1st lift on LZ.

0936 1st lift completed.

0955 1st element 2nd lift down.

1001 2nd lift completed.

1014 1st element 3rd lift on LZ.

1015 1/RAR reports neg contacts all elements on LZ Jack. Phase II in progress.

1021 1/RAR lift complete.[3]

The Australians completed the assault on alternate LZ Jack with no opposition.

1130 1/503 elements moving to Snakepit.

1200 Air strike on King in progress.

1230 Arty prep commencing.

1237 1st element 1st lift off from Snakepit.

1240 Arty prep complete.

1245 1st element 1st lift down.

1250 1st lift 1/503 on LZ.

1307 1st element 2nd lift on LZ.

1313 2nd lift 1/503 on LZ.

1330 1st element 3rd lift on LZ.

1335 1/503 reports choppers receiving heavy SA fire west of LZ YT122245 during landing.

1335 1/503 landing complete.[4]

By 1335, the battalion was on the ground at LZ King with no ground opposition and began sweeping north-northwest with the Song Be to our east and the Song Dong Nai to the south.

The terrain initially consisted of low paddies, but as the 1/503 moved, small hill masses came into view. These hills seldom exceeded

70 feet. The vegetation on the LZ was tall grass and reeds that stood six to ten feet high. As the unit progressed, the terrain became semi-jungle with thick undergrowth near the stream beds. The first layer of canopy was thick, reaching a height of 40 to 50 feet; the second was 250 feet high.[5]

The paratroopers were overpacked: 100 rounds of 7.62mm ammunition for the machine guns, one mortar round, more than 800 rounds of 5.56mm M-16 ammo, 4 grenades, 1 bar of C-4, 3 C-ration meals and 1 poncho. All told there was more than 70 pounds of equipment on the young soldiers' backs.[6]

We spent the rest of the first day sweeping the immediate area around the LZ, encountering only light sniper fire. Walt Disney nature photographer and noted outdoorsman Chuck Keen was on the operation with the 1/503rd. He remarked, "[U]ntil now he would have called anyone a dam [sic] liar that told him it would take most of the day to cover 800 meters in any kind of terrain. But there we were just 800 meters from where we landed and preparing to secure the perimeter for the night."[7]

The Aussies swept south and east. Both units encountered jungle with "wait-a-minute" vines. These vines grow vertically as well as horizontally and invariably caught on pieces of equipment as we bent to go underneath them. They hooked onto almost anything; and as you moved forward, they restrained you then jerked you back. In other words, two steps forward, one step back. The point man in each unit used a machete to cut a path through the jungle, but he could not get all the vines. So for the rest of us it was two steps forward, one step back; two steps forward, one step back. Men cursed as the vines dragged them back, and it echoed up and down the column. Progress was very slow. The heat and humidity were oppressive. Sunlight seldom appeared through the canopy, so the moisture never evaporated; the ground remained wet and soggy and the humidity high. Fighting in 90 to 100-degree heat was one thing, but 90 to 100 percent humidity was another. Sweat quickly soaked through our uniforms, burned our eyes, and dehydrated us. Water became a precious commodity. The jungle has never been a pleasant place for American soldiers with 50 to 70 pounds of equipment on their backs and steel pots on their heads. And it never will be.

Chaplain James Hutchens from Indianapolis, Indiana, recalled:

The jungle canopy overhead gave some relief from the burning sun, but still we marched through steaming humidity in clothes that were drenched with sweat almost as soon as we began. Burning thirst gave our mouths a coating like chalky glue. Each man carried at least two quarts of water and some had three or four. It was imperative that fresh water be supplied every day. The cool mud of swamps and marshes was a welcome sensation to our tired, burning feet.

Added perils were the legions of leeches which found their way to any open flesh, and every low hanging branch had its own army of biting, stinging red ants which invariably found their way down the backs of our necks if we even brushed against a tree.[8]

The first day ended with no contact.

1720 1/503 reports loc sta A,B,C on obj #1 YT134288.
2400 All units neg sit rep.[9]

On D+1, November 6, we continued our north-northwest movement with platoon-sized patrols operating out of company patrol bases. We made only light contact.[10]

0650 1/503 observed 9 people across the river, 5 female, 4 male, do not appear to have weapons.
0910 1/503 sit rep: B Co found VC water point at 135295. Loc sta: A Co-138294, B Co-129291, C Co-126288, Bn CP-144290.
1030 1/503 operating in sectors A1, B1, C1.
1105 Rept to Danger: 10–12 foxholes, 2 huts, 2 gas masks at YT133305.

Observation tower at YT123293. Searching area.

1115 B Co 1/503 used cry baby on VC tunnels at YT135307. No enemy personnel.
1710 1/503 reports will move to obj 2 tomorrow.[11]

PFC John "Dutch" Holland, of Nicoma Park, Oklahoma, was with Bravo Company: "We patrolled for a couple of days with no enemy contact at all. At nights we'd sit into defensive perimeters with half on full alert while the other half slept. This kind of routine will quickly wear down the best of soldiers because we stayed on edge expecting to fight the enemy instead of the difficult elements presented by this unforgiving terrain."[12]

Battalion Commander LTC John E. Tyler from Winona, Mississippi, had just turned 40 years old on 4 November. He was short, wiry and tough, but he was taller than most when he stood on his heart and courage. He reported that the "operation proceeded smoothly with little or no enemy contact. We frequently employed small arms fire and artillery fires to 'feel out' suspicious areas in a reconnaissance by fire role. This was standard 173d procedure, which prescribed that we use fire power rather than fatigue jackets to rout the enemy from his hiding places. The nights of November 5 & 6 passed with no contact other than minor brushes with enemy forces of no significance."[13]

This was only my second operation in country and already I was bored with the constant searching for the enemy with no contact. My mind became numb and I became unfocused. I found myself drifting to other times and other places. This was dangerous. I was not prepared for contact, to act decisively, to do my job. I had to kick myself in the ass. I needed to remember where I was and what I was doing, and that lives hung in the balance with my decisions or lack thereof.

0735 1/503 rpts all elements moving.

0900 1/503 rpts loc: A Co-135300, B Co-129305, C Co-126298.

0955 1/503 found tunnels at YT140301. Destroying them now.

1100 1/503 rpt loc: A Co-117309, B Co-116305, C Co-112307.

1240 1/503 reports all elements closed obj 2. [Dept of Army Combat After Action Report placed 1/503 at YT112306.][14]

1515 A/C received ground fire NE of obj 2.[15]

After the order for Operation HUMP was issued, but shortly before the air assault began, the Brigade's Radio Research Unit (RRU) held a special briefing with the battalion commander, the three company commanders, and the Battalion S-2 and S-3. "Most of the RRU that operated with the brigade were senior sergeants. All were fluent in Vietnamese, and seldom were they allowed to accompany any formation below battalion level."[16]

They were told that if they received the code words "Sour Apple" followed by map grid coordinates, that area was to be reconnoitered and findings reported. American forces were using radio direction finding equipment to locate enemy command and control sites in War Zone D. "Sour Apple" meant that such a site had been found and Brigade wanted to know what was there. This information was not disseminated below the company commander level.[17]

We neared the base of Hill 65 (Dat Cuoc) in the late afternoon of the 7th (D+2). We had been drained by the humidity, slowed by the terrain, and frustrated by the vines. We set up base camp about 1,000 meters east of the hill in a dense jungle with a wide former logging trail, equivalent to the size of an American two-lane road, running generally north-south through the eastern portion of the perimeter. This road, part of the Ho Chi Minh trail, would play a significant role later.

Bravo and Charlie Companies secured defensive positions northwest and southwest of the road, and Alpha Company deployed east of it. We hooked up with Bravo to the north and Charlie to the south.

As we set up our defensive perimeter, Brigade encrypted and transmitted "Sour Apple" to Battalion. With little daylight remaining, LTC Tyler initiated recon patrols from B and C.

One of the men from Company C remembered "that it was light when we left but in that thick jungle it gets dark early." He was in 2nd platoon and recalled going out that afternoon to the creek at the bottom of Hill 65. The creek formed south-southwest of the hill. He noted that there were many rodent fences and bamboo fish baskets, and when "you see those rodent fences it means that there are a lot of people eating in that area because they were down to rodents. And every wide spot and deep spot had one of those little bamboo fish baskets." They found nothing. However, C Company Commander, Captain Henry Tucker did report his units heard chickens cackling to his north. Not much attention was paid to CPT Tucker's report. After all, who ever heard of chickens in the jungle?[18]

1815 1/503 repts patrol cleared area of Sour Apple and returning to base operation. Sour Apple will be taken under fire tonight. A patrol will check area at first light.[19]

Platoon patrols from each company would be dispatched the next morning to follow up on the alert and to find and fix the VC/PAVN position.[20]

PFC Juan Jamie recalled that night: "During the night of the Seventh, we saw some lights, maybe flashlights or torches, and we passed the word, there was to be no smoking or any lights on and complete silence. The night passed quietly."[21]

With little contact during the operation's first three days, GEN

Westmoreland requested that BG Williamson fly to Saigon to help brief some VIPs from the States: two governors and several U.S. senators and congressmen. On November 8, only 30 minutes from Saigon, BG Williamson turned command over to his deputy and flew there. He would be gone about four hours and would be unaware for some time of the developments to soon take place.

4

8 NOVEMBER 1965
0800–1200

Look into an infantryman's eyes and you can tell how much war
he has seen.

—Bill Mauldin

At 0530 on 8th November, we received orders to attack a large force of Americans… Our fiery lads were hungrily searching for the few enemy reaction
force battalions left. HQ said this time we would clash head on with U.S.
combat troops, an entire airborne brigade of the Johnson-McNamara gang.

On learning we were to hit the Americans, we were enthusiastic, as for a
long time we had wanted to match our strength with the Americans, to see
what "spirit" they possessed. What made for our stomach's strength [trans-
lator note: courage] and belief in individual strength was the entire unit's
resolution to hold the battlefield to the last moment.

The political officers exhorted us to remember the compatriots and comrades slaughtered in North and South Vietnam by the Americans. Our wish
to come to grips with the Americans rose higher.[1]

At first light, D+3, patrols from each company moved out to search
for the enemy. Alpha Company was facing almost due east so we went
towards the Song Be.

Bravo, led by CPT Lowell Bittrich, sent patrols to the north and
northwest. Before they moved out, however, an interesting thing happened. Tom Marrinan was a medic assigned to Bravo Company. Early
in the morning, he checked his pack and medical kit and reported to
CPT Bittrich. Bittrich said, "Hey Doc, we won't need you here today.
We're just going up a hundred." Marrinan was shocked, as Bittrich normally was on his case to keep busy, but in the end he would stay in base
camp.[2]

Charlie Company sent two platoons with engineers and artillery
spotters to the west and southwest. As the platoons advanced, they again

radioed back that they had found fish traps in a small creek and numerous freshly cut trails. Robert Blango recalled hearing chickens and seeing a lot of portable latrines made with crossed bamboo.[3] As they started up Hill 65, they ran into unoccupied, but newly constructed, bunkers.

Charlie Company made contact first. At 0800, 2LT Sam Russ and his 1st platoon found a primitive Viet Cong village. He split his unit in half, with one searching to the left, one to the right. They had advanced, unknowingly, to within 50 meters of concealed Viet Cong positions. His point man, PFC Julius House, began checking a clothesline. An NCO hollered to him to watch out for booby traps, and then 2LT Russ ordered the unit to join up again. SSG Andrew Matosky, a squad leader, then saw 10 to 15 enemy soldiers coming down a trail towards his position. They were talking and carrying weapons, but didn't see him. He yelled for his men to get down, and then he fired and got most of them on the first burst. PFC House was then hit in the arm by enemy fire.[4]

Matosky noted that the VC were clad in Chinese style helmets and were in regular North Vietnamese uniforms, and knew immediately they were not up against an ordinary guerrilla force. These were regulars.[5]

Matosky fired the first shot of the battle; House received the first wound. The whole front then opened up with small arms, machine gun fire and grenades.

SP5 Lawrence Joel, a medic, was the last man in the center squad. "As soon as Matosky had opened up on the enemy, the whole jungle ... suddenly twinkled with the muzzle blasts of AK-47s and heavy machine gun fire. Fate was with Joel as the bullets whined around him, he was luckily behind a rock hill (they're six feet high in the jungle) and he and three other troopers came out of the initial burst untouched, though most of the rest of the entire platoon went down. The cry of "medic" was heard from all sides of him.[6]

PFC Bill Henry, a machine gunner with 1st platoon, with complete disregard for his own safety, remained in an exposed position and delivered devastating fire on the enemy. When it became apparent that the platoon could no longer hold against overwhelming odds, the order was given to break contact and withdraw to a secondary position. Again PFC Henry remained in his exposed position and covered the withdrawal.[7]

The first man Joel treated was SP4 James Belton, who had taken a bullet through an artery, blood spouting like a fountain. Joel quickly applied a tourniquet. Belton was conscious and was worried about his pals more than he was about himself. The medic did all he could for him, but in two hours Belton died.

Another man yelled for help and Joel took off from behind the rock to help him. He got about halfway across a small clearing when the VC opened up on him and he caught a round through his leg. Joel hopped back behind the rock, then went out to treat a man with chest, arm, and shoulder wounds and another with leg and belly wounds. From that time on it became a series of responses with Joel doing his best to treat his own wounds while running under fire from one wounded man to the next, doing what he could to help them. Since his platoon took almost 100 percent casualties, he was a busy man.[8]

About the same time, approximately 100 yards beyond the point reached by the patrol the previous night, 1LT Ben Waller and his 2nd platoon came across a similar camp set up. Waller ordered an immediate search of the area and found it was deserted, "but only recently for there was warm rice on the tables and hot coals from a fire someone had tried to smother."[9]

The platoon had a Vietnamese soldier with a scout dog assigned to it. The dog began acting up, jumping around. The platoon halted until the dog settled down and then began moving up the side of a hill. As they reached the top of the hill 1st platoon got hit. Waller put his squads abreast to move forward. They could hear .50 and .30 caliber machine-guns and knew that 2nd platoon was getting torn up.

0800 1/503 repts receiving .30 & .50 cal fire vic village at YT106309.[10]

1LT Waller moved his unit "forty more yards into the jungle when the whole earth seemed to erupt furiously" in front of them. "Claymore mines exploded all around the platoon, and interlocking machine gun fire rained down with deadly accuracy. Young men, who only seconds before had been strong and daring, now lay lifeless, their bodies torn apart, forever lost to this world."[11]

They moved another 15 meters or so and one of the troops saw Niles Harris go down. Then SGT Troy Williams was also hit and went down. All of a sudden other paratroopers were either hit or hitting the ground to fire back.

The Viet Cong "seized the opportunity ... when elements of Company C moved west in the direction of Hill 65, seeking enemy forces thought to be in the area, the jungle erupted in gunfire and exploding mines. Unseen and well entrenched, Viet Cong machine gunners pumped .30- and .50-caliber fire at the dazed paratroopers. Small-arms fire from other hidden VC soldiers amplified the din of battle. Pinned down and isolated, C Company had only to be flanked and destroyed for the [VC] to record a resounding victory over the Americans."[12]

Niles Harris recalled that he "was nailed instantly. I can't remember if I was 2nd, 3rd or 4th man in the line. Everybody got nailed. Everybody was killed or wounded. My friend Bell was up front and they were chopping people with machetes, our wounded. And there was no wounded or ... you know, when they came across those folks up front were killed, they were murdered."[13] 1LT Waller's platoon was on Hill 65. Waller and Russ were effectively pinned down, with Waller's unit surrounded.

Chaplain Hutchens was with Waller's platoon. He recalled that the contact happened with nerve-shattering speed. There was no time for thinking or philosophizing. The 2nd platoon's existence was now a matter of reaction by instinct. Indecision or hesitation meant death.[14] Every man still standing made a dive for cover and began to return fire.

Hutchens, recovering from the initial shock of the contact, began to see what had happened. The point man was killed instantly. Next in line, the Vietnamese dog handler and his dog were unscathed. 1LT Waller had been hit in the right shoulder and left wrist. Right behind him, his RTO's right thigh had been shattered by a .50 caliber round. Hutchens was next and not hit. But behind him, an engineer had both legs broken by machine gun rounds. The 12 men in the left file had been hit hardest, as they were closer to the enemy. The right file, although not hit as hard, had 50 per cent casualties.[15]

As one of the M79 grenadiers moved, he noticed that one of the first rounds fired was from a machine gun out of a bunker to his front. The point man went down and as he did the grenadier went with him. As he did, he was shot in the ammo pouch where he kept his M79 grenades. And as he went down, the left side of his face was looking right at the barrel of the machine gun. As the men behind him began firing, their red tracers were going over his head one way while the enemy's green tracers were coming from the opposite way.

Robert Blango recalled, "We were still firing. I mean it was so loud. I tell you I had to personally drop my weapon because I thought blood was coming out of my ears. I mean it was so high, and I dropped my weapon because I thought my head was bleeding. Of course it wasn't, and then I was able to hear again. Someone had gotten killed, my weapon jammed, the bolt didn't go forward all the way and I didn't have a cleaning rod. I remember trying to take a stick and … push it, but there was so much carbon in there."[16]

The Viet Cong newspaper quoted one of its soldiers as saying:

> We calmly let them come to within 20 metres before opening fire, to be sure of a hit. This group of "rice flower dandies" decided that they were not brave enough to close with the Liberation Forces' positions. We had not encountered an entirely American unit before, though we had put scores of American advisers to flight. 7 Section commander looked at me and said, "They are as big and as slow moving as buffalo. They crawl along with their behinds stuck up in the air, taking routes that make them good targets, and always move on old tracks." Each time they came in groups of 7 or 8 against we three. They were crying and yelling wildly, and at first this was strange to our ears… After we listened carefully and heard them crawling around, yelling and bellowing like cattle, we all couldn't help smiling. You can see their feeble spirit—how can this red-faced scoundrel Johnson stand against us?[17]

PSG Rick Salas, 2nd platoon, saw bullets flying all over the place; he didn't know where they were coming from. Salas had made it to the top of Hill 65 with a machine gunner and his assistant. The artillery recon sergeant had gone back down the hill and left his radio. When friendly artillery was fired on the hill, the machine gunner and assistant were killed. Salas was able to call off the artillery, but spent hours on that hill separated from the rest of the company. He finally was able to roll down it when friendlies began firing uphill at him.[18] As the battle continued, PSG Sylvester Bryant grabbed Niles Harris and dragged him with the platoon's radio.

1LT Waller had by now commanded his platoon to pull back and set up a defensive perimeter. He also ordered his artillery forward observer to request fire support ASAP. Chaplain Hutchens, with the medics, pulled the wounded engineer back into the small perimeter.

"Mindful of the potential for American air and artillery strikes, the Viet Cong hugged C Company to ensure that the subsequent engagement would force the paratroopers to fight for a time without close artillery support and in close quarters. Tucker's men returned fire and hung tough." The Viet Cong commander "then moved quickly to flank Tucker [Tucker's men] on the right (north) and encircle his company. The ongoing morning firefight had fixed the paratroopers, and a successful envelopment would finish them."[19]

At the Battalion Patrol Base, LTC Tyler recalled: "[n]ormally when enemy contact was first made, there was a gradual increase in the sound and intensity of the engagement that progressed from the sound of individual gunfire to an ever increasing crescendo of sound as soldiers on both sides joined the firefight. Such was not the case that morning, though, for there was an immediate thunder of sound that echoed through the jungle of both friendly and enemy fire.... Both sides responded with heavy gunfire, and heavy casualties were sustained on both sides from the first few minutes of the encounter."[20]

The platoon leader's voice crackled excitedly over the radio: "We found 'em ... lots of 'em ... they've got fifties ... we're taking casualties!" Tucker listened a moment longer. Machine gun staccato drowned out the platoon leader's voice. He depressed his hand mike and spoke loud and clear: "Okay, 2nd platoon is on your left. They'll move over and help you."

Time stopped. The radio crackled again. The 2nd platoon had been hit too, unable to move. CPT Tucker spoke as the rest of C Company moved. "Okay, I'm on the way. Pull your boys back to the left. Join us as we move up to 2nd platoon." Tucker and the rest of C Company were already moving forward on the double as he spoke.[21]

CPT Tucker and 1SG Board moved up with the reserve platoon and in a short time a burst of heavy .50 fire drove them behind a fallen log. As soon as he was able, Board, a stocky Korean War veteran, edged around the log and commenced making contact with what was left of the two platoons who took the brunt of the first gunfire. He took a slug through the shoulder from a 7.62 machine gun while hauling wounded men out of a fire lane cut by the enemy.[22]

PFC Juan Jaime was with 3rd platoon at C Company's command post as the reserve. He was making hot chocolate in his canteen using C-4 for fuel when he "heard a few rounds pop, followed by a few more and then all hell broke loose. Mortar rounds, machine gun fire and what seemed to be whistles blowing for a drill."[23] The word came down to Jaime and the rest of 3rd platoon to get ready, leave all the heavy stuff, bring only water and ammo; they were going to help out the rest of the company.

He saw tracer rounds going up the side of Hill 65 and recalled saying, "I hope these guys don't kill them all and leave some for us to shoot at." Jaime could make out M79 rounds being fired and also the slow "tat, tat, tat" of the powerful AK-47. The intensity of the firepower told him that there were more of them than us.[24]

Jaime's platoon, led by PSG George Hino, a Japanese-Hawaiian, was hurrying down a small opening when he saw a wounded RTO telling CPT Tucker that if he was planning on going up that hill, he was crazy; there had to be at least an enemy battalion up there. The medic was called to patch him up, and the platoon moved on.

With his entire company committed, Tucker attempted to join up his platoons. He would be unsuccessful, and his unit would end up split into four elements, unable to link up with each other.

Jaime was frightened and hot. "I could smell the gunpowder of all the rounds fired and a strong smell of torn leaves, broken branches and morning dew. Our first sergeant was screaming at us to hurry up and get up the hill; he was already wounded. Then I was really scared!"

Midway up Hill 65 Jaime saw the company interpreter, Ahn, lying lifeless with his head split open like a watermelon. He also saw a number of small bushes running around. He began firing. Scared, he crawled behind a tree and began to dig his body into the dirt as best he could. PSG Hino was walking around, coolly drawing enemy fire. It looked like a walk in the park to him. Hino's bravery calmed Jaime, and he began to take the enemy under fire. Receiving sniper fire from above, he engaged what looked like a big nest in the treetops, but nothing came down.[25]

"The fire fight became more and more fierce; men were screaming with pain. Our boys were getting hit from all over," he recalls. Jaime took an enemy machine gun under fire, but a grenade exploded nearby and all at once he was dazed—he couldn't see or hear. SP5 Lawrence Joel, C Company's medic, came over, talked to Jaime and calmed him down. Jaime then began blasting away at anything and everything that moved.

Although the fight had been going on for some time, it was still early in the morning. As it seemed to ease up, Jaime noticed that he was alone. Then artillery began landing on the hill above him. Was it enemy or friendly? He didn't have time to decide—he was still firing at the small trees running everywhere around the hill.[26]

SGT Blango remembered, "They hit us pretty much from all sides. And then, I didn't know until I got behind that termite mound and kind of looked back, was able to look back behind me that there were all these dead guys laying there. I don't know exactly who was killed or what, but I just seen bodies laying there. And some of the guys, a couple of the guys that were wounded credited SGT Troy Williams with saving their lives because they hid behind his body. I mean, his body was taking ... he was dead. But his body was taking round after round after round from that machine gun."[27]

At the sound of gunfire, shortly after 0815, CPT Bittrich of B Company took three actions: first, he ordered all platoons to halt and hold their positions; second, he told them to prepare to move out in direction of the fire; and third, he notified battalion that he had stopped his search and awaited orders.[28]

At 0830, LTC Tyler ordered Bravo Company to secure Charlie's right flank and Alpha to return to the Battalion patrol base. Alpha turned around and began to almost double-time back through the jungle.

0845 1/503 rpts 15 walking wounded. No LZ available. Will call for "Dust off" later.[29]

Meanwhile, CPT Bittrich decided to reorganize his company on the move rather than have them close on his position. He ordered 3rd platoon to move towards Hill 65, while his command element and 1st platoon caught up and 2nd platoon secured the rear. While on the move, CPT Bittrich attempted to establish radio contact with C Company, but was unsuccessful and became concerned that he might have problems with friendly fires. LTC Tyler informed CPT Bittrich that the situation on Hill 65 was unclear and that while speed was of the essence, he was not to take unnecessary risks. CPT Bittrich's final instructions to his platoon leaders were to move in the general direction of Hill 65 and to hold up short of the creek bed just east of the hill. Here he planned to move the 1st and 3rd platoons on line, with 1st platoon on the left and

3rd platoon on the right; 2nd platoon would follow 3rd for the assault up the hill.[30]

At approximately 0925, 3rd platoon leader 2LT Clair Thurston reported enemy movement on the far side of the creek, short of Hill 65. Thurston did not believe the enemy was aware of his unit's presence, but he was beginning to receive fire from C Company. Bittrich was able to raise C Company on the radio and alert them to his unit's presence. He also learned that CPT Tucker did not have contact with his forward elements, but that he would make every attempt to cease its fires. Tucker and Bittrich agreed that C Company only needed to halt its fires on the east side of Hill 65 as that was the direction in which B Company would attack.

Bittrich then deployed his company as previously planned and began to move west to the creek, totally surprising the enemy force to his front. His 1st and 3rd platoons opened up with everything they had and began to climb the hill, stacking enemy bodies as they went.

0930 1/503 rpts 2 Co. still in contact at YT106309. 1VCC w/wpn, 2 VC KIA (more to follow on body count), 1 MG captured.[31]

Sam Scrimanger, an M-79 grenadier, and 3rd platoon were crossing a stream when a mortar round detonated and knocked him down. Uninjured, he continued up the hill until a platoon sergeant from C Company stepped out and said, "Don't shoot. We are friendlies, Charlie Company." At that time 3rd platoon began receiving fire from its right flank. The platoon went to ground to return fire.

But before they could do so, 3rd platoon received a hail of incoming fire. A good portion of it was from an RPD light machine gun. Scrimanger would learn that distinct sound from three tours with the 173d. He not only served with the 1st Battalion at HUMP, but with the 2nd at Junction City and the 4th at Dak To.

Scrimanger returned fire and then realized there were only two of them together. Charlie Company was approximately 20 meters to their left, and the rest of 3rd platoon was 20 or 30 meters to the right. The two paratroopers continued to engage the enemy and then the firing settled down. At this point, low on ammunition, Scrimanger crawled approximately 40 meters to the rear, where Charlie Company's dead and wounded were grouped. He also grabbed an M-16, 15 magazines of ammo, and 3 grenades, and then crawled back to his previous position.

"We stayed there, I suppose, for an hour and a half to two hours," Scrimanger remembers. "And then the aircraft came. I don't know what type of aircraft it was or what it was, but there was a whistling sound that you knew were bombs dropping. They say in the movies that bombs do not whistle when they come down, but these did."[32]

Mike DeFrancesco was platoon leader with 1st platoon. He led a charge up the hill, which was covered with dense underbrush and tall trees. As he moved with his platoon, he looked down and could see tracers crisscrossing in a path low to the ground. There was a lot of noise and confusion for a long time as B Company tried to gain the top of the hill. 1LT DeFrancesco remembers passing VC machine gun emplacements and realizing they had moved across a major enemy area. At some point the VC had either had enough and retreated or had taken too many casualties.

When DeFrancesco attained the top, 1st platoon formed a defensive perimeter and started to care for its wounded. Although expecting an enemy counterattack at any time, DeFrancesco sent out small patrols to try to retrieve any casualties.[33]

Bill Acebes was with 2nd platoon, Bravo Company, and he remembered all of a sudden it sounded like an entire machine gun range opened fire at once with explosions every few seconds. The word came back: "Charlie Company's in contact, we're moving up." They didn't get very far when all hell broke loose, NCOs started yelling orders and the wounded yelled for medics.

At first, Acebes did not fire his weapon because he not only was scared, but also was afraid he might shoot a friendly to his front. He could not see anything until he hit the ground. Then it was clear not only where the VC were, but that they were dug in and camouflaged, and had well-prepared firing lanes cut knee high. Acebes listened for orders and when none came, he saw a VC firing straight at him. He rolled behind a tree that just wasn't big enough and returned fire. At this point he recalled someone passing the word to "fix bayonets." Someone else, in a halfhearted attempt at humor, replied that a bayonet would not fit on a .45 caliber pistol.[34]

SP4 Joe Diaz, from San Antonio, Texas, was a 26-year-old experienced medic who normally moved with the Battalion Aid Station during operations. For HUMP, however, he was asked to cover 2nd platoon, B

Company, as the regular medic had accidentally shot himself in the foot while cleaning his .45 pistol.

Diaz remembers booby traps being set off as the lead elements of B Company moved through the thick jungle toward the hill. He rushed to the front as the words "Medic, medic" rang in his ears. "With fear in my heart and a lump in my throat, I answered the call and went to work."[35]

He first came upon another medic, Joe Keys, administering first aid to the platoon leader's RTO, who had accidentally set off a booby trap underneath his legs and blown his testicles apart. "Doc" Keys assured him the situation was under control, so Diaz moved further forward and came across PFC Brown, who had a bullet hole clean through his hand. Diaz dressed it and continued forward.

Near the slope of the hill, Diaz came across a trooper with several bullet holes in his stomach but with no external bleeding. Diaz administered albumen intravenously.[36] He recalls:

> As I crawled forward in search of the wounded through the intense firefight, I could hear the sound of jets and helicopter gunships flying overhead and [could] feel the concussion of loud bomb explosions occurring within a few hundred yards from our position. The reluctant enemy pressed on his attacks, at times sounding separate bugle calls from both of our flanks ordering more assaults on our position. And every time the bugles sounded, it produced chills and an eerie sensation on the back of my neck. But just as quickly as the call was sounded, our troops dispensed a high volume of rifle, grenade, and small arms fire in the direction of the sound—neutralizing it completely.
>
> Along with air support, close artillery support was also heavily employed during this operation. The proximity of the enemy during battle forced the unit to call in friendly artillery fire, at times closer than 100 meters from our position. It also forced the enemy to fight in close quarters where many of his losses occurred.
>
> Equipped with only a .45 caliber pistol and unable to effectively fend for myself as I treated the wounded at the base of the slope of Hill 65, I asked one of the combat engineers armed with an M-16 to stay close to me and provide me with fire support. He did.[37]

All three of Bittrich's platoons were now under enemy fire from heavily fortified positions. 1LT DeFrancesco's 1st platoon reported incoming incendiary grenades just before his RTO was hit by automatic fire and killed. The VC then blew bugles and charged, and 1st platoon cut them down.

Three men in 1LT Bob Frakes's 2nd platoon were wounded by mortar fire, so he split his unit in half, leading one group forward and leaving one to guard the wounded. His two elements were then hit by another bugle charge. Frakes reported that every one of his men had been shot at least once.[38]

Acebes remembered the bugle charge as a "sound I can never forget. Everything seemed to go in slow motion. The VC rose and began running right at us—then past us. I couldn't understand. Then the bugle again and someone yelling at me to 'get ready, they are coming back.' And again humor, as someone yelled, 'Give the motherfucker some bugle lessons.' I was too up to my ass in fear to laugh until later."[39]

0952 1/503 rpts 5 additional VC by body count.[40]

PFC John "Dutch" Holland was part of the 18-man contingent from 2nd platoon left behind by 1LT Frakes to care for the wounded while the remainder of the platoon advanced to support Charlie Company. This seemed, at the time, to be the safest place on the battlefield. Holland remembers that they had positioned themselves into a small clearing about 20x30 meters. It was elevated to the right and surrounded by dense foliage. Security was placed facing the trail they had just moved from and forward where the rest of the platoon had gone. PFC Holland was to the right of the trail, hidden by the dense undergrowth, when he saw what looked like American soldiers coming up the trail. They were wearing jungle fatigues, steel helmets, boots and backpacks, and moving in formation. Holland whispered to his squad leader, SSG Theodore Shamblin, that it looked like friendlies coming up on their rear. Shamblin hollered, "B Company, 2nd platoon."

It was a deadly error. The Americans did not have a prayer. The enemy opened up—they had the paratroopers vastly outnumbered.[41] The VC immediately set up an RPD machine gun on the top of the slope. A young paratrooper not more than a couple of meters from the gun was the first to die. Although he was dead, the enemy continued to fire into his body, literally tearing it apart. Holland estimated the VC put more than 100 rounds into the young paratrooper's body, "just blowing the shit out of him."

PVT Everett Goias and Holland lay not three meters from the dead paratrooper behind a small log. It wasn't big enough to hide both of them and, besides, they were in the enemy machine gun's direct field of fire. Holland heard Goias grunt as the first round tore through his lung and saw smoke from a white phosphorus round come out Goias's right shoulder. Yet Goias continued to fire. Holland knew that the log they were behind would not stand up to much more of the intense small arms fire they were receiving. Too close to throw a fragmentation grenade, he decided instead to toss a tear gas canister. Unfortunately, it hit a branch close to their position, and the tear gas floated towards them. Holland grabbed Goias and began helping him down the hill. The VC also felt the effects of the tear gas and stopped firing the RPD. As Holland and Goias moved away from the VC, an enemy grenade hit the right side of Holland's helmet. He turned his head and waited for the grenade to detonate. It looked like the old German potato masher, and fortunately it was a dud. As Holland and Goias moved further down the hill, another grenade was thrown at them. Again, Holland waited. And again, it failed to detonate.[42] Holland and Goias reached the remaining half of 2nd platoon only to find most of them dead. It was apparent that some of the fighting had been hand-to-hand. Those still living poured a heavy volume of fire into the enemy positions. They used the bodies of their dead comrades to shelter them.

Just as Holland and Goias reached the remaining members of the unit, the enemy blew "that damn one note bugle" and "charged into the clearing, camouflaged with small tree branches and screaming their fucking heads off," said Holland. The Americans fired everything they had to stop this mad suicide assault.[43] The intense American small arms fire did stop the enemy, who retreated back into the jungle and continued to fire on the paratroopers. At this time, Holland noted that small arms fire was coming in from behind the American position. The sharp crack meant they were M-16s—they were Americans. Then a lull as both sides ceased fire. Holland yelled, "B Company, over here!"

Another mistake. Automatic weapons fire poured into Holland's position. Between volleys fired by the friendly patrol, Holland told Goias that he was on his way home with a million dollar wound. But Goias never made it. "When the second burst was fired in on us I was holding this brave man's head and looking into his eyes and, unlike action movies, there was no cry of pain, distortion of features, or animated facial expressions. Instead, his eyes just lost their glow of life, and I knew he was dead from friendly fire."[44]

Holland now thought he was the only one left alive. He knew the VC were going to kill him. They were going to come into the perimeter because they wanted the Americans' equipment, and they were going to kill anybody and everybody. Holland refused to play dead. He knew he was going to die, but he was going to kill as many of the bastards as he could. He rounded up as many M16 magazines as he could find. He hoped that if he put out a heavy enough amount of fire, the enemy would respond and kill him quickly. At that moment, a sudden peace engulfed the young PFC. It was a total calm; fear left him. There was no noise; everything was quiet, serene. It was total, total bliss. Holland would remember that feeling would last until an American patrol succeeded in reaching his position and saving what remained of the 2nd platoon.

At this point, however, he began to slowly crawl back down toward the dry ravine when SP4 Jerry Langston came inching up from that direction. Holland thought for sure that Langston had lost his mind; he was crawling towards the area that had been the main field of fire just moments before. But Langston was going for the field radio, which was still operational. He secured the radio, made contact, and led a patrol from Bravo Company in by firing a .45 caliber pistol for them to guide on.

Holland feared that the .45 firing would bring all kinds of fire down on them again, but it did not. The patrol arrived and found 15 dead paratroopers, two severely wounded, and SP4 Langston unconscious with a large hole in his helmet. There were dead Charlies everywhere. Holland later thought it was a small tribute to the gallant men who gave their all in that short, but very intense, battle for survival.

Langston recalled that the enemy tied bushes and branches "to their backs and they started blowing bugles and charged us from three sides. They came down off the hill behind us, from the flank, and across the creek to our front. The fighting was close in, real close. We were really cut off and there didn't look to be much chance left."[45]

The patrol worked to take the two seriously wounded first. Holland had a small piece of his scalp shot away, the flesh over the end of his right shoulder blade had a piece of frag, and his right buttocks was mostly gone from an RPD round. Rather than wait for a stretcher, he placed an arm around the shoulders of a brother paratrooper and attempted to walk out. Only a very short distance from the battle site, Holland was dropped to the ground as a sniper fired on them. When that danger passed, PSG Bernoski then assisted him back to Bravo Company's perimeter.[46]

Meanwhile, enemy bodies stacked up as the rest of B Company moved against the enemy flank and rear. It seemed to CPT Bittrich that C Company had pushed the VC off the hill and to the north. B Company had closed on the enemy's left flank and with the element of surprise moved virtually unopposed up the hill.[47] As Bittrich climbed the hill with his command element, he spotted a series of well-dug-in and covered enemy positions. None were occupied and a number of enemy soldiers lay dead around them. As he reached the hill's top, he noticed it was shaped like an egg, running generally north and south. It was approximately 400 meters wide at its northern crest and some 600 meters deep from north to south. It was triple canopy and heavily vegetated with teakwood trees. The jungle floor was generally clear, as the sun could not penetrate the treetops. There were well-traveled trails leading off to the north and south sides of the hill.

Bittrich spotted CPT Tucker. Bullets were flying, and Tucker was in a well-dug-in position with his RTOs and his 2nd platoon leader, 1LT Waller. They yelled for Bittrich to get down, but his immediate concern was what he saw less than 100 feet to his front: an M-60 machine gun was being dragged backwards. The weapon was pointed to the north, and Bittrich was anxious to get it moving back in that direction. Once that was accomplished, he returned to Tucker's position.

From what Bittrich could determine, C Company had 21 effective soldiers left on the hill and they were taking fire. The locations of the remainder of the company were unknown. His job now was, with CPT Tucker, to locate the remainder of C Company and consolidate the position. "My stomach hurt, there had to be more,"[48] he recalled.

Bittrich's early assessment was that they had a mess on their hands and that they must initially try to secure their position. The firing was very intense from the north, and he had no idea what was between the paratroopers defending the hill and that firing. At this point, Bittrich ordered 2LT Thurston to attempt to make contact with any C Company personnel by extending his position north of Hill 65. He was to maintain his tie with 1st platoon on his right. 1LT Robert Frakes, 2nd platoon leader, was to extend the perimeter to the right of 1st platoon. Immediately, 1st and 3rd platoons reported that the enemy had moved behind them and they were receiving fire. Bittrich's first thought was that the enemy had deliberately let them in and was now closing off all escape routes. Thurston reported he was receiving .50 caliber fire from two locations. Bittrich could hear it from three locations.

PFC Ross Redding was with 1st platoon, B Company. He and another soldier were administering first aid to one of their comrades when a wave of Viet Cong charged directly toward them. Since they only had one rifle, the men picked up the wounded soldier and ran with him in an attempt to join the rest of the platoon. When it appeared that they might be caught and overrun, Redding told the other soldier to continue dragging the wounded man and he would stay behind and try to hold off the enemy. Taking the rifle, he gallantly covered their withdrawal. He then rejoined the other two and they continued their move to their platoon. They came to a small clearing in the jungle, and when they reached the middle of it, two enemy machine guns opened fire and pinned them down. PFC Redding ordered his buddy to continue moving with the wounded man while he executed a flanking maneuver to draw the enemy fire. Redding ran in a zig-zag pattern toward one of the machine guns and silenced it with a well thrown grenade, destroying the machine gun and its crew. He then directed suppressive fire against the remaining machine gun until reinforcements arrived and the evacuation of the wounded soldier completed.[49]

PFC Bill Delia was a forward observer attached to 2LT Thurston's platoon. He remembers the platoon moving rapidly towards C Company. They crossed a small creek that ran behind a hill, and as they moved they began to receive small arms fire. A couple of paratroopers were wounded, and then the unit fired back and all was quiet for a moment. Thinking they had killed whoever fired on them they began moving again. They hadn't gone too far when "all hell broke loose." To Delia it seemed as if the firing was coming from all directions. The gunfire was so intense that small trees and limbs were severed and falling all around 2nd platoon. Delia thought they might be between C Company and the enemy and nobody knew. He tried to rise up and all of a sudden he felt like someone had hit him with a baseball bat in the shoulder. He could feel the warm blood running down his arm and back and realized that he was hit and losing blood very fast. Delia thought, "I've got to get out of here before the enemy finds me."[50]

SP4 Joe Diaz now moved to PFC Delia, who had a bullet wound through his right triceps. Delia sat on the slope of a hill while Diaz dressed his wound. Suddenly, the firefight erupted again and both dropped to the ground. As they did so, Diaz took cover behind Delia. Delia looked at him and asked, "Doc, why are you hiding behind me?" Diaz replied, "Ain't no need in both of us getting shot, is there?" Shortly afterward, Diaz was wounded above his left lung while treating yet another wounded trooper.[51] Able to move and continue his duties, Diaz reached the top of the hill. Delia recalls:

> Doc said, "Stay here, I'll be right back," and he moved up the trail to see if there was anyone else. I went down to gather ammo clips and grenades off the bodies and shake them to see if any of them might be breathing. I sat back down by the tree, ammo clips and grenades piled up next to me, to wait for Doc. It wasn't long when I heard someone coming through the jungle. I wasn't sure who it was, friend, foe or Doc, but I could tell it was more than one person. I just sat still with my fingers crossed, my rifle up, finger on the trigger, and then I heard that yell I will never forget, "Hey, over here, hey Sarge, over here." I knew it was our people by the voices, I let them get a little closer until I saw the fatigues on one guy and the M-16 he was carrying and I yelled to him, he yelled back and the next thing I knew I was among friends. I jumped up, yelled for Doc and moved toward them.[52]

At this point, Bittrich reported to battalion that he had a very confusing situation on his hands. He could not determine exactly where all elements of C Company were located, and he could be facing up to three VC battalions or a main line PAVN regiment. He based this conclusion on the fact that the enemy only deployed .50 caliber machine guns at the regimental level and that the guns were firing from distinct and well-dispersed directions. In addition, Bittrich reported that C Company had taken severe casualties, maybe as high as one-third of the company.[53]

"As soon as it became evident that this was a large VC force, the decision was made to commit 2/503 to the northeast of the VC positions to relieve pressure on 1/503 and to cut off VC escape routes. The request for personnel carrying helicopters could not be honored because adequate numbers of helicopters were not available, therefore, 1/503 continued the fight without additional ground support."[54]

As Bittrich worked to consolidate the paratroopers' position, 2LT Thurston reported that he had spotted one of the machine guns and was going to take it out. What he did not tell his company commander was that he was going to do it himself. As he made his personal assault against the enemy position, he was shot in the head and killed by machine gun fire.

SP5 John Moore and SP4 Davis Uptain, 173d Engineer Company, were assigned to 2LT Thurston's platoon. They were lying about five or six yards from Platoon Sergeant Rucker when Thurston was hit. Since Thurston carried his own radio, the platoon sergeant yelled at Moore to get his attention, and then said, "Go out and get the radio." Thurston's body lay some 20 yards to Moore's front. SP5 Moore turned to Uptain and said, "Go ahead and keep an eye on me and if I need some help, come forward."

At that, Moore jumped up and went about 10 yards, hit the ground and rolled. Uptain came up immediately and as soon as he came to Moore's position, was hit and went down. As he fell, Uptain's last words were, "John, I'm hit." Blood foamed from his mouth; he closed his eyes and went silent. Moore tried first aid, but Uptain had been shot in the chest and was dead in about a minute. Moore low crawled to Thurston's body, grabbed the radio, and crawled back to the platoon sergeant's position and turned over the radio.[55]

For Bittrich, the death of 2LT Clair Thurston made the fight personal. He had lost one of his best officers and now the enemy would

First Lieutenant Bob Biedleman, Operation HUMP (courtesy Colonel Walter B. Daniel)

have to pay. At this point Bittrich called for as much artillery fire as he could command. The 3/319th responded and brought a steel curtain forward of the beleaguered troops. They initially placed them north and northeast of the hill and walked them in. Although the barrage was initially devastating, the enemy would adjust.[56]

The steel curtain bought Tucker and Bittrich time to locate the lost elements of C Company. All but 17 were found, and they would be discovered the next day. Now B and C Companies formed a defensive perimeter around the hill that extended from the southeast to the northwest. The south side was not covered, so Bittrich ordered his 2nd platoon to extend as far south as possible. As the two companies consolidated their position, the wounded and dead were recovered. Both companies' medics worked feverishly.[57]

As the firing began to die down, PFC Jaime found some of his friends wounded and began pulling them to an area that seemed secure. It was a small shaded clearing where there were some rickety structures built from trees, branches, twigs and leaves. Although not good for cover, it did offer a clearing where the men could regroup. Tired, weak, 18 years

Captain Walt Daniel (courtesy Colonel Walter B. Daniel).

old and 145 pounds, Jaime began dragging fellow troopers through sporadic enemy fire to the clearing.[58]

At Charlie Company's defensive position, Chaplain Hutchens moved among the wounded, dead and dying men, looking for the faces that made up the initial left file of LT Waller's platoon. Some were there, but most were not. They had been the closest to the enemy during the initial outburst. Only four men from the left file made it back. All but one was seriously injured. The other eight were missing. They were presumed dead, but that had to be confirmed. Someone could still be out there

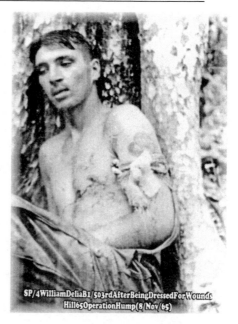

SP/4 William Delia B1/503rd After Being Dressed For Wounds Hill 65 Operation Hump (8/Nov/65)

Specialist 4 Bill Delia, Operation HUMP (courtesy John Holland).

Extraction, Inbound Operation HUMP (courtesy Colonel Walter B. Daniel).

Extraction, Outbound Operation HUMP (courtesy Colonel Walter B. Daniel).

alive and in need of help. "Throughout the morning during lulls in the fighting we could hear the screaming pleas of the wounded to the left and front of us. 'Help me ... help me ... somebody please help me,'"[59] recalled Hutchens. He approached C Company's first sergeant and told him some of their wounded were still out there on the left front. Without a word, 1SG Board moved toward the area where the cries for help sounded. He returned and reported that of the eight

Private First Class John Holland (courtesy John Holland).

men out there, all were dead but one. The survivor had two broken legs and had dragged himself behind a tree for cover. 1SG Board had a hammock that could be used as a makeshift litter to carry the wounded man. He asked for volunteers. "I need three men," he said, placing a full magazine into his M-16.

Chaplain Hutchens battled with his conscience. To go or not to go? Where was he needed most? Here with the wounded and dying, or out there? "That's right, Lord, you are sovereign. You alone control the circumstances. There is a purpose in it. All right, Lord, I'll go."[60]

One of the volunteers was an RTO who was scheduled to leave for the States to attend Officer Candidate School immediately after the end of this operation. The other was an engineer who loved a good scrap. Hutchens recalled that the four of them moved cautiously, running and crouching from tree to tree until they reached the wounded man. "Around him were his dead buddies. Most of them had been hit in the head. It was an awful sight. Their helmets were overflowing with what resembled cauliflower mixed with mucous and blood—the remains of their brains."[61]

Just as they placed the wounded soldier on the hammock, an enemy shot rang out at close range. Hutchens noticed, "Suddenly the young officer candidate who was on his last operation in Vietnam before going home threw his hands in the air, his face wincing with pain. He turned and fell. He was dead, his spine severed at the neck." Another shot and Hutchens noted that the engineer was hit—the bullet creased the middle of his back and lodged in the muscle next to his backbone.[62]

Sergeant Hector Membreno, Camp Ray (courtesy John Holland).

67

1SG Board found cover behind a tree. Chaplain Hutchens looked for cover and rolled towards another tree. Suddenly he felt a hot, numbing, stinging sensation. A .30 caliber round grazed his rib cage and entered the inside of his right thigh.

"Are you hit, Chaplain?" yelled Sergeant Board.

"Yes, in the leg, but I think I can move on it."

"Try to make it back if you can. I'll cover you."

Sergeant Board covered the engineer and Chaplain Hutchens as they moved back toward friendly lines, but he was also hit. When they made it back, Hutchens reported to CPT Tucker what had happened. Tucker then sent out a full squad to bring back the dead and wounded. They did, although suffering more wounded in the process.[63] The airborne does not leave its casualties on the battlefield.

The Viet Cong newspaper continued its story, "Suddenly the call to attack roared out! Our Number One Company received orders to advance. We leapt into the parapet. When they saw our gleaming bayonets lifted in their direction, the Americans scattered and ran, but whatever they did, they could not escape our hate-filled bayonets."[64]

That wasn't quite how it happened. As the artillery continued to fire, the enemy adjusted. They moved closer to the paratroopers' positions, thus negating the American artillery. "To the Viet Cong, the practice of hugging American troops evolved into a battlefield credo immortalized by the slogan 'Grab the enemy's belts

Staff Sergeant Theodore Shamblin (courtesy John Holland).

to fight them."[65] This was obviously a well-trained and highly disciplined enemy force. Bittrich reported to LTC Tyler that they were surrounded, but would hold. They were, however, going to need help. LTC Tyler answered that he was working on it.

Then came the sound of three bugles. When asked if he had heard them, Bittrich said he hadn't, but in fact he had. His mind just didn't want to accept it. Bittrich moved fast. He called for more artillery as B and C Companies reacted to the threat. Platoons responded quickly, almost without direction, repositioning machine guns as well as men to meet the assault. Leaders seemed to appear everywhere, knowing what was about to happen.

Second Lieutenant Clair Thurston, United States Military Academy (courtesy United States Military Academy).

The enemy came at the paratroopers shoulder-to-shoulder. It was unreal, like something from films of the American Civil War. They made it halfway up the hill before the American fire broke them. The enemy backed down the hill slowly and then made a second attempt, more desperate than the first. It met the same fate. This time they were in retreat. But it wasn't over just yet.[66]

SP5 Moore remembered that every time they moved, they received sniper fire. During this period someone in the company threw a smoke grenade and yelled, "Let's get the hell out of this fire lane." So they started moving again. Moore hooked up with PVT George Pappas, an M-79 grenadier. He and Pappas kept searching for the defensive perimeter, but it was difficult to find as it continually shifted. They would try to adjust by listening to the M-16 fire. Pappas and Moore were together for two or three hours that afternoon, constantly engaging the enemy, constantly receiving sniper fire. Then they heard bugles and whistles, and Pappas said to Moore, "Goddamn, they're coming by the hundreds." Moore thought, "This is it!" But the enemy went in another direction, and right after that the firing stopped where they were. At this time, Pappas and Moore joined up with the rest of Bravo Company and waited.

1LT Waller's forward observer (FO) began to "walk" the artillery barrage in as the enemy was immediately to the platoon's front. Dust and shell fragments filled the air. And then, above all the noise, came a spine-tingling screech resembling a bugle. The FO, Sergeant (SGT) Lloyd Greene, called in the artillery strike on his own position. He gave his coordinates to the artillery battery and they said, "Wait a minute, that's your position." He said, "I know, I know! They are all over us, goddamn it! Put that shit in here right now on top of us!" He was killed, of course, not by artillery, but by the enemy.

Chaplain Hutchens turned to a grizzled old sergeant lying next to him to ask what the bugles were for.

Lieutenant Colonel John Tyler standing on two lane trail which became our landing zone. Operation HUMP (courtesy Colonel Walter B. Daniel).

"That means they're going to eat us alive, if they can," he answered.

"What do you mean?"

"I mean, you'd better get ready, Chaplain. That's the signal for sending in the human waves … just like Korea."

"Quickly the platoon moved three M-60 machine guns in the direction of the enemy's most likely avenue of attack. The M-79 grenade launchers reinforced the machine guns. Shortly, Hutchens heard the frenzied screams of the charging enemy."[67]

Robert Blango remembered, "You don't think about anything except killing. You know you have to fire because they are out to kill you, too. You lock your mind into getting off as many rounds as you can. If they get

Second Lieutenant David Ugland, United States Military Academy (courtesy United States Military Academy).

around you, you're dead. That's how it works. I know what they are going to do with me."[68]

The paratroopers held their ground and with supporting air strikes repulsed the enemy charges, but it would be after 1500 before CPT Bittrich would be able to secure his company perimeter and tie in with C Company.[69] At this point CPT Bittrich again radioed battalion to report more than 40 Americans dead from Bravo and Charlie, approximately 70 wounded and 20 others missing. There was a long pause on the radio and then CPT Bittrich heard a pained "out."

As the battle raged near Hill 65, it became apparent that not only were Bravo and Charlie pinned down, but that the artillery and air strikes could not get close enough to dislodge the enemy force. They were surrounded. The situation was grave, and reports from the company commanders were vague, as neither wanted to broadcast his actual dilemma

First Sergeant Bill Workman, Operation HUMP (courtesy Colonel Walter B. Daniel).

in case the enemy was monitoring the frequency. LTC Tyler had good reason to believe that CPT Tucker was wounded or dead, as most radio traffic was with CPT Bittrich.[70]

1110 DCO rpts that 1/503 still heavily engaged. Receiving indirect fire in CP. Est VC Bn.

1150 CG directs that air relay for 1/503 internal net be put on station ASAP.[71]

5

8 November 1965
1200–2400

Accurst be he that first invented war.
—Christopher Marlowe,
Tamburlaine the Great

When the fighting started on the morning of the 8th, D+3, Alpha Company was sweeping to the east towards the Song Be. LTC Tyler immediately ordered us to return to base camp. Before noon, Alpha had reassembled and was ready to join the action.

One thing none of us thought about was that the battalion CP was by itself on a little hill as two companies were in contact and one was returning from patrolling to the east. As 1SG Workman said, "Well, they [VC] could have took that hill any time they wanted it. They could have. They could have took the old man early that morning before A Company got back."

The "Old Man," as LTC Tyler was affectionately called by his men, though he was barely 40 years old, had seen it all, this being his third war in a little over 20 years.

With A Company now back, LTC Tyler decided to commit us. His orders to CPT Walter B. Daniel were short and to the point: he "must take the pressure off B and C Companies. I want you to establish physical contact with the two Commanders and open a corridor so they can evacuate their wounded…. There is no help on the way, do not, I repeat, do not become decisively engaged. Do you have any questions?"[1]

LTC Tyler's list of options was short. The 1/RAR was in contact with the enemy across the Song Dong Nai and at least one to two days' march away from us. The 2/503 was in base camp at Bien Hoa, but there were no helicopters available. They were at least two days away, plus they were the designated general reserve force for all of Vietnam. Alpha Company was it; the battalion was on its own. If A Company lost its freedom to maneuver, we were stuck. The battalion would likely have to fight to the last bullet and the last man.[2]

CPT Daniel issued his frag order to his platoon leaders and then gave us time to issue ours to our men. We were to move on line up Hill 65 and relieve pressure on B and C Companies so that they might move back towards friendly lines. We were to move in column formation until we made contact with the enemy or linked up with Bravo or Charlie Companies. 2LT Dave Ugland had 1st platoon, 1LT Bob Biedleman had 2nd, and I had the 3rd. CPT Daniel directed us to saddle up and move towards the west with 1st leading, 3rd next, and 2nd in the rear.

Dave and I began moving our platoons from our defensive positions towards 2nd platoon's command post (CP) to pick up Bob's unit. But just before we reached Bob's CP, mortar rounds landed inside the battalion perimeter. The volleys fell on the battalion CP and 2nd platoon, A Company. It was devastating. In seconds the platoon sergeant and two squad leaders were killed and 1LT Biedleman and two other squad leaders were wounded. The platoon medic, RTO and FO were also killed or wounded.[3]

1215 1/503 request help from H-43 ASAP. Contact Diesel Stamp 1.
1220 Message to Danger TOC: Friendly casualties- 16 walking WIA.[4]

LTC Tyler then told CPT Daniel, "Leave the survivors of your beat-up platoon in the Battalion Base and attack with two platoons."[5]

I remember moving by 2nd platoon's position and seeing nothing but broken bodies and blood, and hearing moans, screams, and medics yelling orders. The colors red and white flooded my mind. I took red to represent blood and white to represent bandages. CPT Daniel left 2nd platoon in the battalion base area under the command of a buck sergeant (Sergeant E-5) and continued the approach to Hill 65 with 1st and 3rd platoons.

The mortars that hit the battalion CP wounded the S-3, the S-3 operations sergeant, the S-2 operations sergeant, the battalion sergeant major, and one of the battalion commander's RTOs.[6] SP4 Jack Fleming was a 20-year-old RTO for the S-3. He remembers the command group's being hit: "After an uneventful night the command group was shaken ... by a significant explosion. To this day I am not sure what happened. It was either a booby trap in the trees above or we were hit by a well-placed mortar round."

Fleming dove for the ground and was stunned by the concussion. There was great confusion and several men had received shrapnel wounds. The trees had been shredded by the blast, and he could smell the smoke. Wounded soldiers screamed for assistance. Thinking all the medics were forward with the line companies, Fleming took off running to bring some medics back to treat the wounded. He quickly directed them to the command group to attend those in need. "My adrenaline was flowing and I was both thankful I was okay and concerned that if it were mortar fire we might get hit with additional rounds."[7]

On Hill 65, CPT Bittrich heard that mortar rounds had hit the battalion headquarters. "That came as a surprise as we had not experienced any mortar fire on the hill."[8]

During the fight for Hill 65, there were approximately 35 airstrikes. There has been some disagreement about who called them in. All of the airstrikes were directed by LTC Tyler as battalion commander and he had CPT Bittrich choose the targets. Bittrich specifically concentrated on Hill 75 and Hill 78 (Hill 78 was approximately 2000 meters north-northeast of Hill 65 and Hill 75 was approximately 1000 meters north of Hill 65) as he had a gut feeling the enemy was on both hills. Bittrich explained his reasoning in an email May 25, 2015.

> When I took B Company out that day I intended to take a look at hill 78. When C Company got into trouble on 65 I stopped our movement to 78 and went to 65. There was another hill (75) between 65 and 78. If time permitted that day we were also going to check hill 75. We never got to 75 or 78. For some reason, which I can't explain, I felt that the three hills were being used by the enemy and thus wanted 75 and 78 hit. We didn't attempt to put any air strikes on or near hill 65 because we didn't know where all C Company people were located and frankly we just had very poor visibility. We used artillery to hit all around hill 65 but we put it further out than I would have liked for the same two reasons. Some of my guys told me it was still too damn close. I know my FOs were very concerned. At that time all airstrikes were controlled at the Battalion level. Later in the war that would change and we could call for air strikes at the Company level. Even then they had to be approved by the Battalion level.

75

Meanwhile, the troops settled in waiting for the enemy to charge. They came in human waves firing from the hip.

As we again moved towards the contact area, anxiety and doubt gripped me. This was my first action under enemy fire. It is one thing to be on patrol searching for the enemy. It is quite another to attack up a hill knowing that he knows you are there. How would I act? Would I do my duty? Would I lead or panic? Would I remember my training? Would one of my men die today? I was responsible for them. Decision time was here. These questions shot through my mind, not from a fear of dying, but because I *had* to do my duty. I needed to earn the acceptance of my fellow officers and respect of my men. I needed to know that I really belonged to this elite unit. This would be my rite of passage. I still ask myself those questions today. I can logically conclude that I did my duty, but somewhere deep inside, doubt remains. I have no closure as I can't remember anything but what CPT Daniel told me.

Not long after clearing the battalion perimeter, we encountered some enemy dead and some wounded stragglers from Bravo and Charlie Companies. CPT Daniel brought our platoons on line with Dave on the right flank and my platoon on the left. We advanced up Hill 65 towards B and C and the enemy.

Rick Lyons was with 3rd platoon:

> We mounted up as quick as we could and had to pass through the 2nd platoon area while they were being treated. Things were happening fast and we didn't have time to let the sight have an impact.... We moved as fast as we could and found ourselves in a gully at the base of the hill. I seem to remember the hill being to our right. We continued following the gully until we were somewhat spaced out in an assault line. The noise of the battle had continued since it started. Now we were close enough to be able to distinguish the small arms from .30 caliber machine guns, and you couldn't miss the sound of a couple of .50 caliber machine guns. We must have been spotted. The level of fire we were receiving increased dramatically. We returned fire and prepared to make the assault.[9]

As we neared Hill 65, CPT Daniel halted the company and ordered one patrol from each platoon to go forward to find out what was to our front. Here, CPT Daniel admits to committing a classic error that Rangers are taught to avoid: he did not tell the patrols how far to go and when to come back.[10]

Dave's patrol returned first and indicated that there was an enemy machine gun position approximately 30 meters in front of 1st platoon. The patrol leader stated that the machine gun was aimed in the direction of Hill 65 and that it was not dug in. My patrol returned later and reported making contact with a large number of troops from B and C. The way to Hill 65 seemed to be blocked by the machine gun in front of 1st platoon and open all the way in front of my platoon. CPT Daniel's plan was to take out the machine gun as quickly and quietly as possible, then slip to the left and up the hill and make contact with B and C. The plan did not work.[11]

As the platoons began moving forward again, I don't recall seeing or hearing anything. It was quiet; it was eerie. Was I following or leading? Were we receiving fire? Were my men firing? Were we close? My only recollection was that everything was green, and I felt claustrophobic. CPT Daniel was right behind me. He told me what he saw and what I did. I reacted automatically. Thankfully, two years of infantry training kicked in.

Unaware of our presence, the enemy assaulted Hill 65 with their backs to us. While enemy bugles blared in the jungle, 1st platoon mowed them down by the dozens. Dave led his platoon forward to maintain contact and attacked the machine gun position, killing all but one of the crew. That one enemy soldier lived long enough to shoot 2LT Ugland. He was killed instantly. One of his NCOs later reported that Dave had commented just before being hit: "What a beautiful place to die."[12]

1SG Workman took out the machine gun position with a grenade, and the whole hillside opened up. The bulk of the enemy fire was directed up the hill into Bravo and Charlie Companies. Only a few Viet Cong realized we were behind them and fired in our direction. 1st platoon accounted for a large number of enemy KIAs in the short time it took for the enemy leaders to recognize that our threat was to their rear.

1SG Workman recalled: "We came in on their flank. The jungle opened up, and we could see almost the entire length of their battle line. How the Colonel figured it out, I don't know, maybe it was luck, but we caught them just as they were blowing bugles to make an attack. Our M-16 and M-60 fire rolled up their line, and took 'em out like ducks in a shooting gallery. The rest of the VC melted back into the jungle."[13] The volume of enemy fire, combined with the number of machine guns and bugle calls, suggested to CPT Daniel that he was taking on a superior force.

He reported such to LTC Tyler, and his orders were to break contact and return to the battalion patrol base.[14] LTC Tyler had a quick decision to make. He reevaluated the current situation and reminded himself that the mission was to destroy the enemy and not to seize and hold ground. He needed Alpha Company to assume the responsibility for the battalion defensive perimeter, and he was concerned that it continue to hold the ground surrounding the 2-lane trail should it become critical. And it would in the next 24 hours.[15]

Rick Lyons remembers that his team leader, SGT Howard Oliver, ordered him, as the grenadier, and Dave Santilli, as the automatic rifleman, to start up the hill.

> I was on the left and Santilli was on the right with Oliver in the center and slightly behind us. We were about 5 yards apart and going through a standard fire and maneuver drill except we were crawling or diving to our next position instead of running. I don't think we had gone more than 20 or 25 yards when, I guess, PSG Maxie ordered us to come back. I wasn't aware until that point that we were the only ones moving. The unit was considered pinned down and was being ordered to return to the battalion perimeter.
>
> It was no picnic getting up there and it was even worse trying to get back. I didn't even attempt to return fire. I just awkwardly crawled backwards with me or my loose pack hanging up on every bush and vine on the hill. Eventually we slithered back into the gully. If anybody was scoring, I got a zero for style. It was ugly coming back down, but it would've been worse if we had kept going. I don't know what I would've done when I got too close to use the grenade launcher and only had a .45 with one magazine. The other two were in my pack.[16]

Quickly, the enemy leaders turned their men around to fire on us. Green tracers flew in our direction. The stunned 1st platoon, learning of 2LT Ugland's death, either let up fire or went to full automatic. The platoon NCOs restored fire discipline immediately, increasing it when it went slack and controlling it when it was too fast to be aimed. My platoon engaged the enemy with consistent fire. But now, CPT Daniel radioed to me, "Papa Lima Delta," which meant "platoon leader dead," and the order to break contact.

CPT Daniel began an orderly withdrawal. My platoon was given the mission to support by fire as 1st platoon moved towards the rear. We laid down a base of fire as the 1st withdrew approximately 75 yards and then took up firing positions. My platoon then fell back with 1st platoon, and with both platoons on line the enemy assaulted us. A single wave attacked, taking two steps and stopping to fire; two more steps and stopping to fire. CPT Daniel stated they were easy targets for about three or four minutes and then they went to ground and out of sight once more. We continued to "leapfrog" to the rear, and twice more the enemy assaulted us when we were on line and prone in the jungle. It was imperative that we not lead the enemy into the battalion patrol base; that the VC not learn its exact location because it held the only hope for creating a landing zone. It would be our only pipeline for evacuating our wounded and dead and getting the battalion out.

CPT Daniel said that he could see our tracers as the squad leaders marked enemy automatic weapons for concentrated fire. He could also see the green enemy tracers passing by. None seemed to be doing much damage to us.[17] When we repeated this maneuver the second time the enemy went to ground and the jungle grew silent. The enemy had left the battle. We finally broke contact and by 1320 both platoons returned to the battalion perimeter. There was still sporadic fire from Bravo and Charlie, but for the most part it sounded like the main battle was over.

1320 1/503 sitrep—B & C Co at 105307. Broken contact getting out cas at this time. A Co closed obj 2.[18]

After we broke contact, one of my sergeants told me that it was probably a good idea we had, as the enemy was getting ready to turn his .50 caliber machine guns on us.

When I reached the company area, I went to see Dave. 1SG Workman had carried his body back, and it lay under a poncho near the company CP. I slowly walked over, kneeled, and raised the poncho, but I could not see him. To this day I cannot recall what he looked like under that poncho. I could see him alive; I could not see him dead. This was a surreal moment for me: I could only see myself from the rear, as if a camera was photographing my movements as I moved towards Dave's body. And still today that is the only memory I have. He was my roommate, and now he was the first American soldier I saw killed in action.

Dave was a graduate of West Point, class of 1964, just like 2LT Clair Thurston of B Company. When Dave's body was brought back to the battalion patrol base, the brigade chaplain, Father John McCullagh, wanted to remove his West Point class ring to ensure "that some ghoul in Graves Registration didn't get it." Because of the confusion, however, it has never been determined if Father McCullagh did what he set out to do.[19]

One of the weapons platoon sergeants shared his feelings. He was a qualified squad leader and also trained as a forward observer. He had fulfilled both roles in Vietnam. He had set up earlier with Weapons Platoon on the logging road that snaked through the battalion perimeter. Expecting to go out as 2LT Thurston's forward observer, he was infuriated to learn that as punishment to another soldier, his platoon sergeant was sending that soldier in his place.

His fury built as he listened to the battle unfold. He was trained to be with his fellow paratroopers, not to sit in the rear and monitor the battle. He remembers the rifle fire as just a blur, a roar. He had mortars, but he was not allowed to fire them. He had rifles, but he could not use them. The battle continued and the orders did not come. Men he had trained with, worked with, fought with were taking fire, and he could do nothing except listen. They were out there getting slaughtered and everything he was trained to do wasn't happening. He heard when 2LT Thurston went down. He heard when various members of his unit went down. And he listened.

The reports were frantic, as was his internal battle. He was 19, and this most important moment in his life was forever altered because his platoon sergeant was angry at someone else. So he listened, and it was agony. He recalled, [T]hey wouldn't let me register my mortars, they wouldn't let me fire … they wouldn't let me be part of the team to go out there and rescue these poor bastards and be part of the battle." He wasn't an FNG, he had been on Okinawa for a year, had seen Thurston when he first came in. He had sergeants he worshipped. He looked up to them, wanted to be a paratrooper just like them. He did not want to go out there for the glory, but for who they were. They were Bravo Company, they were 1st Batt, they were the 173d.

"We didn't function like any other asshole unit in the Army. We were different than everybody. One fought, everybody fought. One died, we all risked. Nobody got left behind. And here I am sitting on this fucking hill listening to this whole thing go down and wondering what insanity is this?"[20]

Now Captains Bittrich with Tucker set about to secure their position on the battlefield. They began to get the critically wounded out, receive more ammunition, and prepare their defense. To accomplish this mission, Bravo and Charlie began to clear an area for an LZ. It quickly became apparent that this would not be accomplished before nightfall with the means at hand. Mike DeFrancesco recalls that more than one Army UH-1D attempted to make the descent into their position. The crew chiefs stood on the outside skids giving directions to the pilots, who had no room to maneuver. They tried, but they just could not do it.[21]

Now the Air Force came to the rescue:

On Nov. 8 at 12:30 p.m. the Rescue Coordination Center received a request for several medevacs. A large-scale operation was in progress and over 100 casualties had been reported. Det. 6 Air Rescue Service at Bien Hoa Air Base (AB) scrambled one HH-43F with a high bird. The other HH-43s were down for maintenance. "Pedro 1[qm] was crewed by Capt. Edwin Henningson, co-pilot Capt. Ronald Bachman, HM Alc Alex Montgomery, and PJs SSgt. George Schipper and SSgt. Dave Milsten. [PJs are parachute qualified survival medics who jump into remote places to rescue wounded or injured personnel.] As they departed they did not know that this mission would continue for two days.

Pedro 1 arrived overhead the battlefield at 1:15 p.m. and was instructed to orbit at 2,500 feet. The casualties were located in a heavily wooded jungle, with trees 150 to 180 feet high. There were no clear areas, so all the wounded would be hoisted from a high hover. U.S. ... gunships were attacking VC positions very close to the casualties. The ground force commander radioed that they were in continuous contact with the VC. SSgt. Schipper was lowered by hoist. On the way down he was inadvertently slammed into a tree. Severe pain radiated from several of his ribs. He did not contemplate his pain for long because he was soon on the ground. A raging battle was being fought all around the recovery zone. SSgt. Schipper treated casualties and prepared them for hoisting. He radioed his pilot to leave him on the ground between pickups. A stokes litter was lowered and after hoisting up casualties Capt. Henningson flew to a nearby landing zone. The patients were then transloaded [sic] onto Army UH-1 Dust Off choppers, which were unable to recover casualties from the battle area because they did not have a hoist. The Pedro crew made six of these short trips before it had to depart for fuel. While refueling, they were requested to re-supply the ground troops with ammunition.

When the HH-43 returned to the pickup zone, two cases of ammo were lowered in the stokes litter. They hoisted two more casualties and then flew to the transload [sic] point. Three of these sorties were completed when they were again requested to re-supply the ground troops. This re-supply consisted of 6 cases of ammo, 2 cases TNT, 2 power saws, 10 cases of medical supplies and water. While they were hovering to hoist down the supplies the HH-43 came under ground fire. The hoist overheated from continuous use and the crew smelled a strong burning odor. Capt. Henningson used the loud hailer (loudspeaker on the front of the chopper) to order SSgt. Schipper to get on the penetrator that was now being lowered. After his PJ was back onboard, the Pedro returned to Bien Hoa Air Base (AB) to repair the hoist. After landing, SSgt. Schipper finally told his pilot that he had injured his ribs. This took him out of action for a few days. Darkness terminated medevac operations until the next morning.[22]

1525 Sit Rep from 1/503: 26 WHA & 1 KIA have been evacuated.[23]

By now CPT Bittrich estimated that he had received more than 900 artillery rounds and 35 air strikes in support. And although fighting continued throughout the day, there were indications that the enemy was trying to disengage. His estimate up to the point of three major attacks was that the enemy had more than 110 KIA, with unknown numbers of wounded. With the last action completed, Bittrich estimated that more than 220 enemy soldiers had been killed.[24] All bodies had been stripped.

Around 1600, SSG Billie Wear from 3rd platoon approached CPT Bittrich and asked if he could lead a patrol to recover 2LT Thurston's body. SSG Wear knew where Thurston fell. Bittrich approved the request, but stated that he was going with them as a rifleman. He later realized that this was probably not the wisest decision he had ever made, but he felt compelled to go. So finally, at 1630, an improvised squad from 3rd platoon consisting mostly of NCOs was able to recover 2LT Thurston's body.[25] Thus, all members of Bravo Company were accounted for.

1605 1/503 repts B Co repts 60 VC KIA by body count. All bodies stripped. C Co after action report incomplete at this time.[26]

There were still 17 members of Charlie Company missing, but they would not be left on the battlefield either. A group of NCOs with two medics went out and quickly pulled in the dead directly in front. Then they moved to the left and found Specialist 4th Class (SP4) Gary Gratz and Private First Class (PFC) Arthur Holmes, who were still alive, and SP4 Thomas Turnage and PFC Valentine Marquez and others, who were dead.

As the companies regrouped, each unit attempted to determine its strength and casualties. Robert Blango was reported KIA, as were others from different squads.[27] One soldier who was evacuated was the sergeant SP4 Diaz had administered to earlier with multiple gunshot wounds in the abdomen. Diaz later received a letter from the sergeant's mother thanking him for saving her son's life. Diaz remembered that when treating the sergeant he had told him, "Don't worry, Sarge, I'm not going to let you die on me."[28]

Returning from Saigon in the late afternoon, BG Williamson became aware of the battle when he turned on his helicopter command radio. He was baffled why GEN Westmoreland's staff had not interrupted discussions and permitted him to rejoin his unit sooner.[29] He flew directly to the battle area, but could not find a place to land. He then went back to base camp and got parachutes for himself and his aide. He was going to jump in. Fortunately, common sense intervened. The general realized that even more casualties would be taken just trying to get him and his aide out of the trees.[30]

1717 1/503 sit rep—C & B Company still using Dust Off. Dust Off status at this time–33. Unit locations no change. Neg enemy contact.[31]
1719 CG directs chain saws go to 1/503 ASAP.[32]

In between the Air Force flights, Army helicopters dropped resupply to the beleaguered troopers. At this point it began to get dark and CPT Bittrich had a painful decision to make. Did he continue or end the rescue operation? To continue would mean he would not be able to hear the battlefield with the choppers hovering above. As it was, he could not see far to his front. The risk was too great. It was a painful decision for him, but Bittrich called off the rescue attempts.[33] By this time LTC Tyler had put CPT Bittrich in charge, as he thought CPT Tucker had been killed.[34]

Bittrich moved the remaining dead and wounded to the rear of his position on the top of the hill. He felt he could better protect them from this position than at the bottom of the hill. Chaplain Hutchens remembers, "Men with torn, mangled bodies lay quietly as the pounding rain splashed mud on their bloody hands and faces. Patiently they waited for the dawn of a new day."[35] Through the night only one of the wounded died, a tribute to the extraordinary efforts of the company medics.[36]

Robert Blango described the scene this way: "They had their dead and everything. We sat there and ate chow. You know, C-rations because,

I mean, dead here, dead here, dead and flies, you know. Blood and guts all over the place. But you see, we got to the top of the hill and we took their positions. And then it started to rain, the rain made it miserable. Good grief, the rain and the stench from the dead bodies, the blood, next the flies."[37]

John Holland's memory of that night was that he was keyed up and almost came unglued at every sharp noise, especially recon by fire. At daybreak he realized just how brutal the battle was as he lay among the wounded and the dead.

As darkness set in, the medics gathered at the top of the hill and treated the wounded who lay there and those who were continuously brought in by the uninjured troops. Except for Joel and Diaz, who were wounded during the firefight, the other 6 or 7 medics attached to B and C Companies were uninjured. They all were busy treating the wounded. Joel, with serious leg injuries from machine-gun fire, went from patient to patient, dragging himself over the ground. Diaz moved with a bullet wound over his left lung.

"With darkness upon us, minimum enemy activity, and medical supplies almost completely exhausted, we settled down to a night of rest. As a light rain fell, Joel and I huddled together under one poncho to stay warm and free from the rain. Throughout the night we heard sporadic small arms fire from the enemy and every time it occurred, I'd mention to Joel that I didn't think we were going to make it out of there alive. Joel would counter by saying that we were. After the sporadic fire was silenced with a barrage of friendly artillery, he'd say, 'We'll make it out of here, don't worry.'"[38]

Juan Jaime also remembers that night:

Night began to creep up on us, so I made a perimeter with Robles, Spenceley, Tallbull and the others. I could see many were missing. I was not hungry, but thirsty. Night came and Charlie attacked our foxhole. We held off returning fire because we had very little ammo left and did not want to give our position away. Although Charlie was throwing grenades at our perimeter, no one could stay awake, we were all so tired. [There were no other reports of enemy attacks against our perimeter.] Later that night in the foxhole, Spenceley was on watch and wanted to sleep so he turned the time on the watch forward so that it showed time for Robles to go on watch. Robles caught on to the trick and they began fighting. When Robles hit Spenceley with a steel pot, it made a big commotion and Washington in the next foxhole shouted, "What the fuck is going on? Tell me or I'm going to shoot!" I shouted back, "It's only Robles and Spenceley fighting." Washington yelled to "Keep it quiet, dammit!" Things settled down again.... It was a dark night, but the moon gave small night vision. All that night we could see V.C. walking around, trying to get our positions, so we didn't fire at them.[39]

Recalls Blango: "We stayed there all night. We didn't leave. We stayed there, the platoons, and protected the dead. We got our wounded out. And then we stayed there, this was an opportunity to stay there and protect the dead, which we did. I remember fixing bayonets for the night, but no one came that night, did they? They didn't try."[40]

I rejoined my platoon at our previous position and reestablished our defensive perimeter. Since we did not know how badly we had mauled Charlie, we were concerned that a counterattack would come during darkness. That uncertainty, plus a healthy dose of fear and the unknown, kept me anxious and unable to sleep. To make matters worse, it began to rain. It came in driven sheets all night, but no one complained.

2110 Called info to First Div TOC: 42 KHA, 59 WHA.[41]

Throughout the night CPT Bittrich paced the area and tried several times to rest on an enemy crafted log table and he listened. He wanted to hear the sound of the battlefield, but it was quiet even with the suffering of the wounded. He and CPT Tucker began to formulate plans to get the remaining dead and wounded out of this location. They could not walk and carry them out. They had no idea what the situation was at the battalion base site. There were too many wounded for the Air Force to continue the basket operation. There was not very much progress in cutting a landing zone. Finally Tucker and Bittrich came up with a plan: at dawn they would request chain saws and explosives to help cut a hole in the jungle for the helicopters.[42]

LTC Tyler recalled, "The day that seemed to be never ending came to a close with the 1/503 occupying two perimeters separated by several hundred yards of thick jungle containing an unknown enemy force."[43]

2220 Received call from Brig Gen DePuy, who wanted a description of today's action. Told him 1/503 was in contact from 0800 until approx. 1430, that casualty figures were incomplete but that 110 VC KIA had been reported.[44]

6

9–12 NOVEMBER 1965

Only the dead have seen the end of war.

—Plato

The enemy usually attacked just before dawn. He had a great ability to sneak up undetected on American lines, penetrate defensive wire, reposition Claymore mines to detonate on friendly locations, and pinpoint defensive positions with deadly accuracy. One of our countermoves was to have a "mad minute." At a designated time, usually just before dawn, the whole perimeter would open up with small arms fire for exactly 60 seconds. If Charlie was out there, he was in a world of hurt.

The early morning of November 9, D+4, was designated as a "mad minute" for the units around the battalion perimeter. Just before dawn the whole perimeter erupted with a torrent of fire. For 60 seconds we raked the area to our front so that no living thing could survive. Clearing patrols followed this "mad minute." Fortunately for him, Charlie decided not to counterattack. Or we had administered such a beating to him the previous day that he could not attack. Either way, there was no enemy to our front.

0720 CG directs that 12 axes be sent to 1/503 ASAP.

0815 Bde surgeon reports that HU-1 can now get into 1/503 area for evac.[1]

As dawn broke that morning, LTC Tyler, with BG Williamson's concurrence, made another important decision. With no reinforcements available, he decided to break contact and evacuate the area. In order to do so, however, it would be necessary to cut out by hand a landing zone on that portion of the Ho Chi Minh Trail that bisected the perimeter. Decades of uncontested growth had allowed the trees in the jungle to overgrow the area above the road so that choppers could not penetrate without damaging their blades. We had to cut down enough trees to allow at least three Hueys into the improvised LZ. LTC Tyler had power saws dropped to us, and units not in contact with the enemy selected men to clear the landing zone. Artillery, gunships, and air strikes continued to suppress and harass the enemy.

We began right after dawn. We had a twofold mission: to clear the LZ, and do it fast enough to give us time to evacuate the complete battalion before dark. It would be close.

At the same time LTC Tyler made his decision, gunships, medevacs and BG Williamson were above Bravo and Charlie's position. But first, Bravo and Charlie had three tasks to accomplish: first, to probe forward of their position to determine if the enemy was still there; second, to find the missing paratroopers from C Company; and third, to blast and cut a hole in the jungle.

The first was answered quickly as it was determined the enemy had fled the battlefield, leaving many of their dead. Second, C Company found the missing 17 troopers in different locations, although only one was alive—he had spent the day on the battlefield surrounded by the enemy and playing dead.

Cutting the hole in the jungle proved more difficult. The saws proved useless against teakwood trees. Dynamite accomplished the job, but created a mess that had to be cleared. Medevacs were there, but the area was still too small. The choppers would need twice the opening to get on the ground.

At 0605, Pedro 2 (crewed by pilot Capt. Charles Nadler, copilot Capt. Maurice Kessler, HM TSgt. Kenneth Perkins, and PJ Alc Henry J. O'Beirne) returned, hoisting casualties and lowering supplies. Later that day ground troops managed to cut down enough trees to allow the HH-43 to land when recovering casualties. O'Beirne would stay on the ground for about 3 hours, helping load the choppers with wounded and giving aid. He was on the ground when BG Williamson came in.

By the end of the operation, 71 sorties had been flown by the HH-43s. The two Pedros recovered 50 wounded soldiers and provided essential resupply to the ground troops. SSgt. Schipper was awarded the Silver Star for heroism. The rest of the crew members on this mission received the Distinguished Flying Cross.[2]

After the Air Force, BG Williamson attempted to have his C and C (command and control chopper) land near B and C Companies. Additional trees, however, had to be felled before his bird could get into the LZ. He dropped smoke grenades from his Huey to mark the area. He then directed his chopper back to LZ Ace where the artillery support position was located. There, Williamson dropped off the copilot, artillery officer, two door gunners with their machine guns and ammunition, and his radio operator. In addition, he had fuel drained from the helicopter to make it lighter. BG Williamson, his pilot, and the general's aide would attempt the landing.[3]

At the landing zone, the brigade commander's pilot, Warrant Officer (WO) Charles Smith, began a 250-foot straight descent through a hole in the jungle. One small error on his part and the chopper would be down for good, as there was hardly a foot of clearance between the helicopter blade tips and the trees. But skill and daring prevailed, and they made it down.[4]

General Williamson and his aide jumped from the chopper and told CPTs Bittrich and Tucker to load it up with as many wounded as possible. WO Smith then started his slow, vertical climb out of the jungle. This was even slower than when he came in, but he cleared the trees. "Dust Offs" (medical evacuation helicopters) followed. In two hours all the wounded and dead were evacuated.

"Early the next morning we were awakened by the sound of a UH1 helicopter engine hovering over the treetops of the makeshift landing zone and carefully descending down to the ground. As it landed, an individual exited the aircraft and we immediately recognized him as the brigade commander, BG Williamson. Seeing him there among us lifted our spirits and it was then that I finally convinced myself Joel had been correct the night before."[5]

BG Williamson was a tough, distinguished looking, white-haired, highly decorated, 47-year-old professional soldier.[6] He was greatly respected by his officers and men and his presence on the battlefield comforted them. "Everything was going to be all right."[7]

Russ Roever was a medic with B Medical, Support Battalion. He remembers walking a wounded soldier to the helicopters for evacuation. The soldier was bent over holding his side and his cheek. Sitting in the gunner's seat in the chopper was BG Williamson. As they approached

1/503d, Headquarters & Headquarters Company, Medical Platoon. Front row: 1st from left Specialist 5 Lawrence Joel, Medal of Honor; 3rd from left Specialist 4 Joe Diaz. Fifth row: 1st from left, arms crossed, Specialist 4 Thomas Marrinan. Last row: under platoon banner, Albert Rascon, awarded Medal of Honor for later action (courtesy Joe Diaz).

the chopper, the soldier saw the general, pushed Roever away, and stood up straight and saluted. Williamson sat up, his chest went out, and he saluted back. He then got out of the seat, put the young soldier in, lashed his seat belt and said, "Okay, son, where's the war now?"[8]

Roever also recounted:

> We had a forward aid station and all we could do the first day was just listen to this battle. And listen to one RTO talking to another screaming, "We're coming, we're coming. We're losing men as we're coming." There's just a help-less thing to just sit and listen to this. I remember one guy saying, "There's nobody left." Then the next day [9 Nov] when they were finally able to extract the wounded, so many guys that came out, there wasn't a lot really, all had

leg wounds. And we kept asking them, "Why are you hit from the ankle to the knee?" It just didn't make sense. You don't stand out in the field of fire. They said, "We fell down. We suddenly realized the bottom two feet of the jungle was cut away and you could see the gun turrets."

In the two years that I was a medic with the 173d, that's the only operation I ever remember when the wounded came, or the dead came out, we were told to open the [body] bags and try and ascertain how many head wounds. Apparently the NVA were overrunning our wounded and killing them. Just shooting them in the head... They were literally assassinating the guys as they were going back and forth.[9]

Juan Jaime also remembered the next morning:

The whole place was a stinking mess, bloody bodies all over, covered with the flies that attack the dead. Helicopters came in to drop power saws; we began cutting a clearing to evacuate the wounded. The smell of blood, dead bodies, gunpowder, shattered trees and mosquito repellent was intense. Slowly the mess began to take shape as we gathered in the dead and wounded and secured the area. Once we had a landing area cleared, a chopper came in. To my surprise, there was Gen. Williamson. He looked like God—clean, starched fatigues, polished boots and a big shining belt buckle. He was wearing a pistol. It made us all feel secure, like the whole thing was over with. We were brought chow and then evacuated. I saw some men cry. Some were brave, some were confused and sick, some were so cool and clean I thought they must have changed clothes on the field.[10]

As BG Williamson moved among his men, he was somber and unsmiling. "He paused for a long time before the rows of lifeless bodies wrapped in ponchos.... Then, lifting his head, he looked about. He raised his hand to his helmet and saluted."[11]

0910 Capt Hammett reports 3 walking wounded & 29 dead left to evac from 1/503.

0940 CG directed that Dust Off be speeded up.

1000 CG notified DO to complete current evacuation before diverting ships to any other unit.

1033 CG requests 2 D models be at 1/503 loc ASAP for final evacuation.[12]

The evacuation begun earlier continued as the LZ had been enlarged. By 1100, all the wounded had been evacuated and all the men accounted for. At this point CPT Bittrich expected one more helicopter to come and get BG Williamson. But Williamson said no, he was walking

Unknown wounded paratroopers receiving medical aid while awaiting helicopters for evacuation (courtesy John Holland).

out with his two companies. Now Bittrich was very concerned. He did not know the situation between his position and the battalion base. How the hell was he going to protect the general? Why take the chance? He called LTC Tyler seeking his assistance to convince the general to fly out. LTC Tyler's appeal fell on deaf ears, as he knew it would. BG

Williamson "did what all 300-pound gorillas did—exactly what they wanted to do." In this case it was for the good of the unit: BG Williamson was walking out with his two companies.[13] LTC Tyler's orders were to take it slow and to get the general back to battalion base safely.

1130 1/503 reports 102 VC by body count for total of 206. Uniforms consisted of green shirts, blue pants, white scarf with a red dot.

1200 1/503 reports 391 VC KIA by body count. Three types of uniforms—1. black pajama, 2. Fatigues with steel pots, no cover and packs, 3. Khaki pants and green shirts.

1235 S3 reptd fol info: 1. Recon in area of B/1/503, complete; 2. All friendlies accounted for; 3. VC body count in 3 locations now 391; 4. One portion of one hill where major action took place has not been counted yet. 5. 4 different enemy uniforms: A. Khaki, B. Gray, C. Green, D. Peasant; 6. Will move to area of 1/503 as soon as body evacuation completed.

1255 Msg to Col Duddy—CG will not return to this location at this time. Will extract 1/503 today.[14]

Knowing Bittrich's concern, BG Williamson looked at him, smiled and said, "Let me know when you're ready." At that point, Bittrich left him with CPT Tucker and began to organize the march back to battalion base. He ensured all the troopers knew that the brigade commander was with them, that they would move slowly and would not be taking any chances. With that, Bittrich asked BG Williamson to stay with his command element and ordered his men to move out. They spread out and moved slowly, followed by Charlie Company. Within an hour, Bravo and Charlie closed on the battalion base area. Bittrich put his company on the perimeter and then stood on that perimeter until the last man from C Company closed the position. That last man straightened up and said, "All the way, sir." Bittrich responded proudly, "Airborne."[15]

Doc Marrinan watched as B Company moved back into the perimeter. He told Bittrich, "I should've been with you." Bittrich responded, "You would have been dead." Doc then made him a cup of coffee.[16]

The young weapons platoon sergeant watched as the men from Bravo and Charlie Companies returned to battalion base. He recalled, "I watched these men that I have drunk with, fought with, knew really long. I saw them come in out of the jungle and it was like they weren't even hardly alive. They'd left part of themselves behind. One of the finest captains you could have ... big, tall Lowell Bittrich. He looked like he was sunken eyed. And I was counting heads. What the fuck is going on here? Where are these guys? And they weren't coming back."[17]

1345 Msg from CG—1. Enemy wore helmets similar to ours but not as deep. 2. Enemy pack uniform and precisely camouflaged with wire net and natural foliage. 3. Several new types of weapons being evaced. 4. Enemy def positions had 30" log and dirt overhead cover, consisted of 2 man fighting position, rather long trenches. 5. One camp complete with picnic type tables and reasonably sophisticated latrine system. 6. Although some contact CG believes main force has withdrawn. 7. Spirits high.[18]

The battalion worked continuously under a hot, blazing sun to prepare the main landing zone. Only with the help of photographer and ex-logger Chuck Keen was the LZ finished before nightfall.[19] Keen used a method he called the "Arkansas Drive." You get a bunch of trees in line ready to fall, then fell the first one and it takes the others down with a domino effect. Keen's actions influenced the brigade to recommend that a special team be trained to cut landing zones in the jungle, as he produced five times the results of anyone else.[20]

When the area was large enough, evacuation began. First the wounded were evacuated and then the dead. And after the dead, B and C Companies were flown back to Bien Hoa.

1438 1st lift 1/503 on way.
1600 1/503 requests extraction be speeded up if possible.[21]

The pickup went smoothly until one of the Hueys went down on the LZ with a damaged rotor blade. There was some discussion about what to do with the chopper. For whatever reason, the decision was made to repair the helicopter and fly it out rather than destroy it on the ground. At this time, units guarding the extraction and protecting the downed helicopter crew reported enemy movement near the LZ. Until the chopper could be repaired, the pickup zone capacity was reduced to only two birds.[22] A replacement blade was available only in Saigon and had to be flown from there to the battle area to repair the downed helicopter. Valuable time was lost, and it was later recommended that in future operations a decision be made immediately whether to evacuate the damaged chopper, attempt to repair it, or destroy it on the spot.[23]

The lull in the activity on the LZ while the helicopter was being repaired had attracted the enemy to move forward and investigate. He obviously thought the extraction was complete. Our security element killed several of the enemy during this time. In addition, a door gunner was able to claim three enemy kills while sweeping the area with fire on departure of his lift. No friendly casualties or damage to helicopters was inflicted.[24]

After the Huey was repaired, there remained only 14 men on the LZ, all but two from A Company: CPT Daniel; XO, 1LT Gene Krause; 1SG Bill Workman; three NCOs; two company RTOs; the 3/319th Arty LNO, CPT Gary DeBausch, and his RTO; three troopers and me.[25]

It was close to 1745, dusk, and I was getting a little anxious. After all, there were only 14 of us, and out there were an unknown number of enemy soldiers, an inhospitable jungle, and no choppers. To make matters worse, we were taking sporadic small arms fire from enemy patrols searching for their dead and wounded or fleeing to Cambodia. We huddled behind logs, large rocks, or anything else we could find for cover. We did not have much firepower—mostly M-16 rifles, .45 caliber pistols and one M-60 machine gun. Our one machine gunner had been hit earlier, so one of CPT Daniel's RTOs manned the gun.[26] But we did have CPT DeBausch, the artillery forward observer. He called in fire from 18 105mm howitzers to support our little perimeter.[27]

At this time, 1SG Workman led two others to the far end of the extraction zone where the abandoned helicopter blade lay. He connected commo wire to the blade, placed a hand grenade under it, pulled the pin and ran back to the company CP. The blade held the grenade handle. Some minutes later, CPT Daniel observed movement near the helicopter blade and 1SG Workman pulled the wire. There was an explosion, but it was not determined if any VC were killed or wounded by it.

I looked around and knew it would take some luck to get us out of this mess and back to Bien Hoa safely. My mind could imagine that there were VC behind every tree in that jungle just waiting to kill us. And each VC had a machine gun and 1000 rounds just waiting to use it on us.

But the wait finally ended. Suddenly we heard the most precious sound to an American soldier: the "whoop, whoop, whoop" of chopper blades cutting the heavy, humid air. Three beautiful UH-1D troopships, with supporting gunships, appeared out of nowhere and descended into the hastily constructed LZ. A fantastic sight!

The door gunners fired into the jungle at the edge of the landing zone while the gunships used rockets and machine guns to shoot even deeper into the jungle.[28] CPT Daniel yelled out to everyone to head for the nearest bird when it landed and to do it "double time." As the three Hueys touched down, we scrambled for the nearest one. I remember running as hard as I could with two of my squad leaders in pursuit, diving through the open door of the Huey, and nearly sliding out the other end as I skidded on my stomach on the compartment's floor. The two NCOs were on my tail and jumped in right after me. The pilot did not wait for any signals, but immediately pulled the stick and began to ascend. I prayed we'd make it up and over the jungle's triple canopy without taking any hits from the enemy snipers. Luck and alternating artillery and gunship fire allowed all three choppers to rise above the jungle floor and head south towards Bien Hoa and home.

Major Don Bliss was brigade aviation officer and the pilot on the last Huey into the LZ:

> I can well remember Walt and his crew continuing to fire back into the woods as we loaded and pulled pitch. I have no idea how many troopers we had on board. All I know is that I had to redline everything in that chopper to get it off the ground. The pickup was on a road, and when we started the takeoff run we had to follow the road for a distance to get above the trees. The road made a slight turn to the right as we were trying to gain altitude, and I followed it to the right. Just as we made the right turn of about 20 degrees, we encountered about eight or ten black pajama–clad troops, obviously enemy as they were shooting at us. They must have been just as surprised as we were, as they missed with everything they threw at us.[29]

It was a short flight before we landed within the confines of Camp Ray. We had made it! A small reception committee from Company A welcomed us back. 1LT Bobby Oakes, who commanded our weapons platoon, was one of the greeters. He never looked better. He told me that when the radio message "Papa Lima Delta" was first transmitted, everyone listening on the company net thought it was me, not Dave, who had been shot and killed. That brought an empty feeling to my gut; first, the loss of Dave and then knowing how lucky I had been. Only by the grace of God was I now still alive.

1900 Notified 1st Div that 1/503 extraction completed approx. 1835 hours.

1904 1/503 repts all elements closed & all pers accounted for at 1845.[30]

Earlier, upon closing base camp, CPT Bittrich reported all personnel and weapons accounted for and headed for the hospital. He wanted to get there as fast as possible to let the wounded know they were uppermost in his mind and that they were wanted back as soon as possible.[31]

Sam Scrimanger remembers arriving back at battalion base. "As we disembarked the Hueys, which brought us in behind our company, and as the Hueys departed, there was complete silence. No one talked or said anything—we just filed through the concertina wire where there was a gate. There was a chaplain at this point. He spoke to a few of us.[32]

SSG Harold Dale was new with the battalion. He had arrived two days before HUMP began, and since he did not have all of his equipment he was left behind. When the troops from Bravo Company began arriving back at the helipad, Dale went to meet them. "They all had their head hanging down, tired and I said, 'Talk to me.' And they all said, 'Later.' Except Don Seavey. He said, 'I think I'm lucky for being here. We all thought we were going to die. I took my magazines out, I stacked them all up and I was going to fire every one of them until they were all gone. And then I'll be ready to go, too. But I'm going to take a lot of them out with me.'"[33]

CPT Bittrich returned from the hospital to learn that GEN William Westmoreland was due to visit his company on the 10th. Tired, dirty, and with no sleep for two days, Bittrich called his platoon leaders and platoon sergeants together and issued his instructions: get a shave, a shower, some chow and sleep. The next morning they would prepare for the general's visit.

The next day GEN Westmoreland, accompanied by BG Williamson and LTC Tyler, inspected Bravo Company. Bittrich led GEN Westmoreland to each soldier in his squad tent. As the officers entered each tent, the soldiers were called to attention and then instructed to continue working on their equipment. The officers then approached the individual soldiers. Each came to attention and stood toe-to-toe with the general.

Westmoreland then asked each man if he was in the battle and if he fired his weapon. All responded to the affirmative, except one. When asked why he did not fire his weapon, the soldier responded, "Sir, I'm a grenadier. I was so damn busy firing an M-60 machine gun, an M-16 rifle and my .45 I never got to my grenade launcher."

One soldier with a speech defect felt pushed to the point that after several questions, the last of which was, "How do you know you killed the enemy?" responded without a stutter, "Because I got his blood all over me."[34]

LTC Tyler remembers as he and GEN Westmoreland walked away, the general whispered to him with a chuckle, "I asked for that."[35]

Operation HUMP found a well-trained and disciplined enemy force. First, the enemy moved his forces as close as possible to the American troops to minimize his vulnerability to our artillery and air strikes. This tactic was later described as "clinging to the belt." Second, once the enemy "fixed" our positions, he quickly moved to the flanks to bring us under fire from all directions and to conduct human wave attacks to overrun the position.[36]

There were two strange findings during HUMP. The first was the enemy's uniforms: they were a mix of khaki, gray, black, and dark blue. A number of dead were also stripped of uniforms in an attempt to hide their identification. Second, some of the dead did not appear to be Vietnamese or Cambodians. It was subsequently reported that a significant number were Chinese.[37]

American newspapers picked up the story of those five days in War Zone D. The *New York Times* wrote that the Sky Soldiers inflicted major losses on the Viet Cong, reporting 391 enemy killed.[38]

The *Los Angeles Times* reported a smashing American victory in the "first large-scale, stand-and-fight battle between nearly equal-sized Viet Cong and American forces."[39]

The *Washington Post* reported that the "toll of Vietcong known dead is one of the heaviest since American combat units were committed in March."[40]

The *San Francisco Chronicle* wrote the enemy "employed, for what is believed the first time in the Vietnam War, flame-throwers and thermite grenades."[41]

For the troops overseas, the *Pacific Stars & Stripes* also credited the 1/503rd with 391 enemy killed and reported that it had defeated an enemy regiment.[42]

On November 12, 1965, the battalion held memorial services for its fallen comrades.[43] Those of us who were left stood in formation, at attention, to salute our departed colleagues. Chaplain Hutchens recalled, "The sky again was dark with angry clouds. A gentle breeze across the open field played with the fluttering flags in their standards. It was time for solemn reflection, a time to worship, a time to remember. And then the roll call began."[44]

The adjutant, CPT Dick Chegar, read the name of each man killed:

Aguilar, PFC Rudolph Rene, 19
Los Angeles, CA
C Company

Belton, SP4 James, 22
State Park, SC
C Company

Brayboy, SFC Bryant Jr., 33
Philadelphia, PA
B Company

Brown, PFC Herman, 18
Richlands, VA
B Company

Campos, SSG Magno, 32
Lahaina, HI
B Company

Cannon, SFC Henry Tucker, 31
Jacksonville, FL
B Company

Carlton, PFC Lavalle Ernest, 18
Cleveland, OH
B Company

Eidson, SSG Samuel Arlan, 32
North Birmingham, AL
A Company, 2nd Battalion, 503rd
Infantry

Elmore, PFC Gary Lewis, 23
Garden City, MI
B Company

Foster, PFC Byron James, 23
Detroit, MI
C Company

Goias, SP4 Everett William, 20
San Francisco, CA
B Company

Goldman, PFC Harold, 17
Ocala, FL
C Company

Graham, PFC Kenneth Errol, 21
Defiance, OH
B Company

Greene, SGT Lloyd Vincent, 29
Paterson, NJ
C Battery, 3rd Battalion, 319th
Artillery

Hamilton, PFC Joseph Thomas, 20
Philadelphia, PA
C Company

Hannigan, PFC John Edward III, 20
Antioch, CA
A Company

Harden, SP4 Robert Wesley, Jr., 21
Waycross, GA
C Company

Harrington, SSG Clifton W., 34
Aberdeen, NC
C Company

Hill, PSG Leroy, 34
Washington, D.C.
A Company

Holcomb, SGT Rebel Lee, 38
Wichita, KS
B Company

Howard, SGT Lawrence Paige, Jr., 26
Philadelphia, PA
B Company

Hughlett, SGT John Albert, 23
Brighton, TN
C Company

Humphries, SP4 Wayne Warren, 21
Shawnee, OK
B Company

Jones, SGT Theodore R. Jr., 33
Auburn, NE
C Company

Keel, SGT David Latimore, 26
Houston, TX
B Company

Lockett, CPL Cleo, 22
Birmingham, AL
C Company

Marquez, PFC Valentine, 21
Wiley, CO
C Company

Mathison, PFC Michael K., 19
East St. Louis, IL
C Company

Medley, PFC Michael Milton, 18
Jackson, MI
B Company

Mitchell, PVT Charles Leroy, Jr., 22
New York, NY
B Company

Nathan, SP4 John Arthur, 19
San Francisco, CA
HQ Company

Orris, PFC Steve III, 19
Wayne, MI
C Battery, 3rd Battalion, 319th
Artillery

Potter, PFC Jerry Lee, 18
Englewood, CO
B Company

Russo, PFC Michael Phillip, 21
New York, NY
B Company

Rutowski, PFC Dennis David, 22
Waterford, WI
HQ Company

Smith, PFC Harold McRae, 19
Sumter, SC
C Company

Sobota, PFC Daniel James, 18
Peoria, IL
C Company

Spencer, SP4 Cordell, 24
Bessemer, AL
C Company

Tate, SP4 Scip, 19
Newark, NJ
C Company

Thurston, 2LT Clair Hall, Jr., 23
Thorndike, ME
B Company

Tolliver, PFC Samuel Stanley, 18
Richmond, VA
A Company

Turnage, SP4 Thomas Alfred, 21
Texarkana, AR
C Company

Ugland, 2LT David Leonard, 23
Minneapolis, MN
A Company

Uptain, PFC Davis, 21
Fayette, AL
173d Engineer Company

Vincent, SP4 George, 23
Los Angeles, CA
C Company

Ward, PFC Danny Russell, 19
Beauty, KY
B Company

Whitaker, PFC Kelly Eugene, 18
Memphis, TN
B Company

Williams, SGT Troy Byron, 29
Mt. Hope, WV
C Company[45]

These names are inscribed on Panel 3E of the Vietnam Veterans Memorial in Washington, D.C., from line 29 to line 39. Theodore Shamblin (B Company) died on November 11 from wounds suffered on November 8, 1965. His name is on line 41.[46]

The 1/503 did not fight this battle alone. Supporting artillery units fired 5352 rounds.[47] Army aviation flew heliborne assaults and provided armed helicopters, aerial resupply, airborne radio relay, command and liaison assistance, and medical evacuation support—a total of 1747 sorties. The Air Force flew 117 tactical air sorties and expended 158.5 tons of ordnance. In addition, Air Force HH-43 helicopters flew 60 medical evacuation missions.[48]

For this engagement on November 8, 1965, the 1st Battalion (Airborne), 503rd Infantry, 173d Airborne Brigade was awarded the Presidential Unit Citation for extraordinary heroism by President Lyndon B. Johnson.[49] We had officially killed 403 enemy soldiers. "The largest kill, by the smallest unit, in the shortest time in the war in Vietnam to date."[50]

"About three months later, the 1st U.S. Infantry Division captured the records of an enemy field hospital that recorded that the November 8 battle was backed up by not one but TWO field hospitals and that just one of those hospitals had received over 700 bodies, dead on arrival."[51]

In Saigon, a few days after the battle, selected members of 1/503 attended a news conference known as the Five O'clock Follies. The following quotes came from that conference.

SSG Billy Wear, B 1/503, was with a platoon that knocked out two machine gun positions. "I don't know what VC unit was there, but I know the other side knows we were there and won't want to tangle with the 173d again for a long time."[52]

Captain Walter Daniel remembered that SSG Wear "picked up an SKS rifle that had been captured in the battle and in his most expert Fort Benning instructor style voice told the newsmen, 'This is a 7.62mm, hand held, shoulder fired, gas operated, clip fed, air cooled, semi-automatic weapon that fires a 150 grain projectile at 2800 feet per second and is capable of a sustained rate of fire of XXX rounds per minute.' All

Captain James Hutchens delivers prayer during Battalion memorial services, November 12, 1965. Lieutenant Colonel John Tyler is at right (courtesy United States Army).

true, but if you substitute a .30 Cal for 7.62mm, you have just described the U.S. M-1 Rifle. Everyone was impressed by our knowledge of enemy weapons, and LTC Tyler remained silently hopeful that none of the newsmen were old enough to know anything about the M-1."[53]

PSG Sylvester Bryant, C 1/503, probably articulated the American victory best. He was asked about the number of enemy killed. "I don't know how many they lost," he answered wryly, "but I can tell you one thing, old Charlie could hold his morning roll call in a phone booth."[54]

American casualties were 49 killed and 83 wounded. Within 30 days three more major battles would be fought by the 1st Infantry Division between War Zone C, the Iron Triangle and War Zone D: November 12 at Ap Bau Bang, November 20 at Trung Loi, and December 5 at Ap Nha Mat.[55]

Only years later it was learned that Charlie's "whole purpose was the destruction of a 'Named or Identifiable Unit of the U.S. Armed Forces.' He wanted this victory for the psychological effect that it would have on the civilian population back in the U.S."[56] In addition, MG Williamson wrote, "There is no doubt in my mind but that the enemy high command issued orders to their forces to stand and fight and that we were the first to stand toe to toe against such instructions. Prior to that time they would cut and run as soon as we learned their location well enough to zero our weapons in on them."[57]

As Robert Blango said, "We went in, we came out. They said it at first: If you go in with 900 you are going to take out 900. If you go in with 500, you are going to take out 500. No MIAs, no POWs. We have a very good record on that."[58]

One footnote to the HUMP: "In 1967 the U.S. 25th Infantry Division recovered a VC document referencing the combat achievements of the 9th Viet Cong Division. 'The document,' said the official American military accounting of it, 'states that Cong Truong 9 has never been defeated.' Word of the 9th Viet Cong Division's untarnished combat ledger would have undoubtedly amused the American veterans of Hill 65."[59]

And maybe the final comment on HUMP should come from the young sergeant who never got in the fight: "We all made it back. Those of us who could make it back made it back. And the next several days, man, were like hell ... the whole formation in the morning, I'd look around and not see guys who been there standing with you all the time. To go to the beer hall and look up and not hear the same bullshit from the same guys that occupied the same bar stool for day after day and everything. And the routine things, man, 'Let me go over and see how Goias is doing.' And he ain't there. And the meetings that we'd have with Thurston. There ain't no meeting with Thurston any more."[60]

Only five days later the 1st Battalion Seventh Cavalry's battle at LZ X-Ray in the Ia Drang Valley began, and America quickly forgot the HUMP.

7

THE IA DRANG VALLEY

> This story, then, is our testament, and our tribute to 234 young
> Americans who died beside us during four days in Landing Zone
> X-Ray and Landing Zone Albany in the Valley of Death, 1965.
> —LTG Harold Moore and Joseph Galloway,
> *We Were Soldiers Once ... and Young*

After HUMP the heavy fighting moved to II Corps and the Central
Highlands. Whether planned this way or not, the enemy now moved
against the 1st Cavalry Division in the Ia Drang Valley.

The 1st Cav was, of course, the offspring of the 11th Air Assault
Division (TEST). In November 1964 the 11th completed its final six week
exercise in North and South Carolina. With the air assault concept now
proven to be a viable combat option, the Department of the Army moved
to integrate it into the Regular Army. Therefore, on July 1, 1965, the 11th
was redesignated the 1st Cavalry Division (Airmobile) and became a
Regular Army division.

As the new air-mobile division moved toward being a reality, South
Vietnam deteriorated both politically and militarily. Still President Johnson
resisted the recommendations of his advisers for a massive escalation
of the American presence there. Once he had beaten Barry Goldwater in
the '64 election, Johnson was certain he could cut a deal in the best Texas
tradition with the North Vietnamese.[1] With Operation Rolling Thunder
underway, however, GEN Westmoreland requested U.S. Marines to guard
the American Air Force base at Da Nang. Thus, on March 8, 1965, the
3rd Battalion, 9th Marines splashed ashore at China Beach.

On April 1, LBJ approved GEN Westmoreland's request for two
more Marine battalions. So on April 10 the 2nd Battalion, 3rd Marines
landed in Da Nang with its regimental headquarters, and the reinforced
3rd Battalion, 4th Marines arrived on April 14.[2]

On May 5, as previously mentioned, the Army's 173d Airborne Brigade from Okinawa arrived in country and took over security of the Bien Hoa Air Base just northeast of Saigon. Shortly thereafter, high-ranking officers from the 1st Cav were receiving secret briefings and map exercises on the Central Highlands. And finally, in a televised address to the nation on the morning of July 28, 1965, President Johnson declared: "I have today ordered the Airmobile Division to Vietnam."[3]

When the 1st Cavalry Division landed off the coast of Qui Nhon in mid–September 1965, PAVN commanders in the south became very nervous and very worried about what they were hearing about this strong, mobile unit so well equipped with helicopters. The PAVN moved mainly by foot and were poorly equipped. Their hospital and food services were not very good. PAVN military historian LTC Hoang Phoung wondered, "How can we fight and win against the Cavalry? ... We had to study how to fight the Americans."[4]

LZ X-Ray

The North Vietnamese planned a variety of operations to draw the ARVN and then the Americans into combat. Phase I was to attack the Plei Me Special Forces Camp just south of Pleiku and then ambush the ARVN unit that would be coming to rescue the survivors. In Phase II the PAVN expected the Americans to come, and they would also attack them. In Phase III the North Vietnamese commanders expected the Americans to drop troops behind them, so they prepared to attack the Americans in those rear areas.[5]

In late October 1965, elements of the 1st Brigade along with LTC John Stockton's 1/9th Cav had been pursuing enemy forces involved in the attack on the Plei Me Special Forces Camp on October 19. The PAVN, however, realized they didn't have enough troops, so they broke off their attack on Plei Me and abandoned the ambush attempt. With only small skirmishes the 1st Brigade returned to the division base camp at An Khe on November 6 and the 3rd Brigade took to the field on November 10.

Intelligence indicated that an enemy base camp was located on the 2,400-foot-high Chu Pong Massif above the Ia Drang Valley. The Chu

Pong is located in the Central Highlands of South Vietnam, west of Plei Me, and it abuts Cambodia. Physically it has mountains, valleys, ravines and ridges. It runs west for more than 15 miles, with the last five in Cambodia, and it runs 10 to 13 miles from north to south.[6]

On November 13, the 1/7th moved into the Ia Drang to "find and kill the enemy." The North Vietnamese, meanwhile, had sent the 320th and 33rd regiments back to the Chu Pong base area to rest and regroup. The 66th PAVN regiment had just arrived at the massif from the north. The Ia Drang offered an ideal staging area for them, with ample water, wooded and jungle-covered valleys, and excellent training areas. But best of all was its closeness to the Cambodian border.[7]

At 1048 on November 14, 1965, the 1/7th, under LTC Hal Moore, air assaulted into Landing Zone X-Ray amidst three PAVN regiments and right in the middle of three battalions of the 66th Regiment: the 7th, 8th and 9th battalions. The 66th had 1600 officers and men.[8]

The North Vietnamese command on the Chu Pong observed the assault on LZ X-Ray and began to move troops forward to meet the Americans. At 1215, with only a portion of the 1/7th on the ground, contact was made. The battle for LZ X-Ray had begun.[9]

By 1338 about 250 of Moore's 450-man battalion were on the ground, and the intensity of the firefight had multiplied. He decided to move his LZ from the larger clearing to a smaller one to the east, as the larger one made the helicopters especially vulnerable.

By 1430 additional units had begun their air assault into X-Ray. And by 1445 all three rifle companies were heavily engaged with the enemy and wounded were streaming into the battalion aid station.

Nearing 1500, Moore requested an additional rifle company for reinforcement. Twenty minutes later the rest of the battalion began arriving. By 1545 Moore had all his men in and had a company of replacements on the way. In addition, the small landing zone was secure and most of the wounded had been evacuated.[10] The battle continued.

By 1700 the reinforcements from 2/7th arrived. The 120-man strong unit now gave Moore a battalion reserve force. It was time to pull all his companies in tight with artillery and mortar fire registered for the approaching nightfall. Also, he called his companies and requested a casualty report. He had 85 men killed or wounded and one platoon cut off from the battalion.

Shortly after 2100 the 1/7th received a final resupply for the night as ammunition and water were brought in. As the helicopters approached, those onboard saw an elliptical northwest-southeast stream of tiny, twinkling lights more than a half mile long and 300 yards wide move down the hillside. They were no more than a half mile from the 1/7th perimeter. Artillery and air strikes were brought to bear in the area the lights were spotted. Moore kept his troops on 100 percent alert all night.[11]

At 0650, November 15, the enemy attacked. As the fighting intensified, 1LT Charlie Hastings, the forward air controller (FAC), made an immediate, instinctive decision. Sensing disaster, Hastings used the code word "Broken Arrow," which meant an American unit in contact was in danger of being overrun. This call meant that the unit would receive all available aircraft in South Vietnam for close air support. The Air Force responded and aircraft were stacked at 1,000-foot intervals from 7,000 feet to 35,000 feet.[12]

Again Moore requested reinforcements from Brigade Headquarters and at 0928 units from A 2/7th began landing. And by 1000 the North Vietnamese began withdrawing from the battlefield.

Help was also on its way by land. The lead elements of 2/5th Cav, led by LTC Bob Tully, made their way into LZ X-Ray at 1145, and by 1315 2/5th with B 1/7th attacked towards the lost platoon. LTC Tully's men collected the survivors, dead and wounded and started back towards X-Ray. By 1615 they passed through the perimeter.[13]

At 0422, November 16, the enemy attacked again in human waves. The PAVN used screams, whistles and shouts to move their men to the attack. The first rush by at least 300 enemy soldiers was beaten back in less than ten minutes, but they came back again. The intensity of the attack increased as the PAVN swept down the mountain into the killing ground. The attacks persisted against various parts of the perimeter.

During the two and a half hours of the attack against the south-southeastern sector, the rest of the perimeter had been quiet. So at 0655 LTC Moore ordered a reconnaissance by fire for two minutes. Immediately a force of between 30 and 50 PAVN arose from cover 150 yards to the front. The "mad minute" had triggered the attack prematurely.

Now at 0746 Moore ordered a cautious and deliberate sweep by his troopers on their hands and knees inside the American lines to search for friendly casualties and enemy infiltrators. Twenty minutes later the units reported negative findings. At 0955 the Americans began a search and clear operation 500 yards to their front. At 1030 they found three American bodies and brought them back to friendly lines.

Near noon, 2/7th Cav with A 1/5th attached approached LZ X-Ray. With the 2/7th and 2/5th at X-Ray, the brigade commander, COL Tim Brown, ordered 1/7th to pull out for a much needed rest. Once Moore had determined that every American casualty had been found and was accounted for, he ordered the evacuation to begin.

Realizing that higher headquarters would want a body count of enemy killed, LTC Moore quizzed his company commanders for their best estimates. The total was 834 killed by body count and an additional 1,215 estimated killed and wounded by artillery, air strikes and aerial rocket artillery. On his own, Moore cut the 834 figure back to 634 and let the 1,215 stand. The 1/7th also evacuated six prisoners. American casualties were 79 killed, 121 wounded and none missing.

LZ Albany

Due to the lack of available helicopters the decision was made that the 2/5th and 2/7th would have to walk out of the valley rather than be flown out. B-52 bombers from Guam were already airborne and on their way so friendly forces would have to be well outside a two-mile safety zone when the bombs began raining down. At 0900, November 17, LTC Tully's 2/5th led out first in a northeasterly direction towards LZ Columbus. LTC Robert McDade's 2/7 would follow and then split off and move in a northwesterly direction towards LZ Albany.

As the battalions moved out they found themselves in surprisingly clear terrain, a scrub forest with small trees, ankle high ground cover and very little undergrowth. Visibility was good. Around 1100 the 2/5 and 2/7 split up with the 2/7 moving northwest towards LZ Albany and the 2/5 continuing east towards LZ Columbus. For the 2/7 the terrain began to change. After crossing a small stream the terrain turned to jungle: tall, triple-canopied trees towered overhead, shutting out the sun. The undergrowth changed to the in-your-face, heavy, broad-leafed vegetation of a tropical rain forest. The battalion's progress slowed to a crawl.[14]

At 1157 two PAVN soldiers were captured. They had new weapons, gear and hand grenades and claimed to be deserters. LTC McDade ordered his companies to hold in place and he would move forward to interrogate the prisoners. The men, exhausted after more than 48 hours without sleep and four hours of marching, fell to the ground or just lounged around. They were in tall elephant grass. At this point in time McDade called his company commanders forward. Since McDade was moving his battalion in column formation (one company following the other), the last company was more than 500 meters to the rear.

After the interrogation the battalion began to move again. After less than 100 yards the pace began to quicken. All of a sudden a quick burst of small arms fire erupted from the jungle. One platoon had made contact. Then the entire jungle exploded into an incredible symphony of small arms fire. Two platoons were now surrounded and taking casualties.[15]

Sometime between 1315 and 1320, enemy mortars began exploding on the column and an infantry assault began. The most savage one-day battle of the Vietnam War had just begun. The 2/7th had walked into the 550-man 8th Battalion of the 66th PAVN regiment. In addition, the 1st Battalion of the 33rd began moving towards the head of the American column and the 2/7th recon platoon had marched to within 200 yards of the headquarters for the 3rd Battalion of the 33rd.

As many of LTC McDade's troops lay in the grass resting, hundreds of North Vietnamese soldiers swarmed toward them. To the enemy commanders this fight was just an extension of the battle at X-Ray, only at a new location a short distance away. They remembered GEN Giap's dictum, "You must win the first battle."[16] The PAVN troops began hitting the Cav troopers on their flanks. With the tall elephant grass making it difficult to see, the Cav companies were having a difficult time organizing a defense, as the soldiers couldn't find each other and the North Vietnamese were mixing in between the units.

The North Vietnamese commander ordered his battalions to divide themselves into small groups when they made contact and to attack the Americans from all directions and divide the American column into many pieces. He further stated he wanted his men to move inside the column and "grab the Americans by the belt" to avoid casualties from artillery and air strikes.[17]

As the Cavalry troopers attempted to regroup, they found that their company commanders with their radio operators were still up front at the battalion CP. They would remain there for the rest of the battle. Only the A 1/5 commander, Captain George Forrest, whose company was the furthest away, was able to run back to his unit and organize a defense.

The 2/7th literally had been reduced from a full battalion in column line of march to a small perimeter defended by a few survivors and stragglers from three companies, the recon platoon, and the battalion command group at the Albany clearing. And 500 to 700 yards to the south was another small perimeter held by the last company, A 1/5th. In between, dead or wounded or hiding in the tall grass, was the bulk of the 2/7th: the fragments of two rifle companies, a weapons company and Headquarters Company.[18]

Every man still alive on that field, whether American or North Vietnamese, was fighting for his life. In the tall grass it was impossible to identify friend or foe except at extremely close range. The battle had become hand-to-hand. Chaos ensued.

At this point the battalion S-3 called in A-1E Skyraider air strikes on the enemy: napalm, bombs and guns. The individual units threw smoke to outline their positions to assist the pilots. Hidden enclaves of PAVN were cleared out by the napalm. At each pass the Skyraiders came in a little closer, flew a little lower and dropped their ordnance a little more accurately.[19] This was probably the event that would turn the course of the battle in the favor of the Americans. And at the same time, the battalion fire support coordinator began bringing in artillery strikes around the LZ on visible clusters of North Vietnamese in the tree line.[20]

In relief, B 1/5th arrived at 1630 but was only able to reinforce the last company due to the distance between that company and the rest of the battalion. CPT Buse Tully deployed his company to secure a one-helicopter landing zone at the tail of the column to bring in medevac helicopters. At 1700, when the majority of the wounded had been evacuated, CPT Tully and CPT Forrest moved their units toward the 2/7th. Within 400 yards the units came under mortar and small arms fire. Bravo Company routed the enemy and CPT Forrest radioed that he had picked up more wounded and needed to evac them. By 1825, orders were received for the two companies to form a perimeter and prepare to sweep north at daybreak and make contact with 2/7th. They still had 22 wounded in their perimeter.[21]

Sometime afterwards, B 2/7th began air assaulting into LZ Albany. Not all of the Hueys made it into the LZ, but most of them did, and they brought 80 fresh troopers, a resupply of ammunition, and water jugs.[22] Bravo Company moved between A 2/7th and the battalion CP and pushed the perimeter out a little. Then the two companies formed defensive positions and waited for nightfall.

On the morning of the 18th the 2/7th and 1/5th began searching for survivors, rescuing the wounded and eventually bringing in the dead. This would take the better part of the 18th and 19th. At one point in the morning a rescue party found PSG John Eade. He had been wounded in the legs early in the fight when the mortar rounds dropped on the unit. He managed to prop himself against a tree when a PAVN soldier found him, raised a pistol to his face, and pulled the trigger. The round entered his eye, passed through his skull and exited through the back of his head. The PAVN left him for dead, but Eade survived. He was conscious when found and placed on a stretcher. His legs and head were wrapped in bandages and he was smoking a cigarette when the rescue party brought him in. SGT Eade boosted everyone's morale.[23]

Also on the 18th, GEN Westmoreland visited Pleiku and requested a briefing from LTC Moore, his staff and company commanders regarding LZ X-Ray. All went well until CPT Matt Dillon, the battalion's operations officer, mentioned a report by some of the troops that they had seen the body of an enemy soldier they suspected was Chinese. He was large and dressed in a uniform different from that of the PAVN. The body disappeared before it could be retrieved. Westmoreland reacted angrily: "You will never mention anything about Chinese soldiers in South Vietnam! Never!"[24]

Finally, on November 20, Third Brigade turned over control of the Ia Drang operation to the Second Brigade.[25] The Third Brigade's responsibilities for the Ia Drang had temporarily ended.

Total American casualties from the fight at LZ Albany were: 151 killed, 121 wounded and four missing in action.[26] On April 6, 1966, the new brigade commander, now Colonel Hal Moore, SGM Plumley, and CPT Dillon took a platoon of the 1/7th into the Ia Drang to search for the four missing soldiers. They found four sets of remains which were positively identified as the American MIAs.

Prior to 1965, American combat deaths in Vietnam had *totaled* 267. In 1965 that number reached 1,369. Of that number, 49 were killed at HUMP, 79 at X-Ray and 151 at Albany, for a total of 279 killed in action. Within a two-week period, American deaths had already surpassed the total number of deaths for all the years preceding 1965.[27]

The Vietnam War was now a whole new ball game militarily, politically and diplomatically. No longer were we fighting a ragtag guerrilla band of peasants. The level of fighting had intensified. For the first time since Dien Bien Phu, the North Vietnamese Army had taken the field in division strength.

As soon as it became abundantly clear that the United States had embarked on a policy of "limited war" in defense of South Vietnam, Communist Vietnamese military leaders and soldiers wondered: How should we fight the Americans? Communist field commanders pondered the same question during the opening period of big-unit battle, and some even broached the subject at COVSN. While attending military meetings ... the commanders requested that "the COSVN Military Party Committee" provide them "with combat formulas...."

General Thanh (Nguyen Chi Thanh was COVSN party secretary and political commissar) heard these appeals and offered a terse reply. "You have to go out there and find them...." The Viet Cong and the NVA would learn how to fight Americans by fighting Americans. Hence the closing months of 1965, and the battles fought therein, were a period of tactical trial and error for the Viet Cong and the NVA. Battles would be fought, outcomes would be reviewed, and tactics and techniques would be revised and refined.[28]

8

AFTERTHOUGHT

More than an end to war, we want an end to the beginnings of all wars.

—Franklin Delano Roosevelt

The battle for Hill 65, followed by the 1st Cav's engagement in the Ia Drang, marked a turning point in the war. For the first time the enemy chose to stand and fight rather than break contact and melt back into the jungle.

The American Army may have lost a golden opportunity to inflict further casualties on the enemy by not following through with its advantage. In both battles the Americans chose to leave the battlefield rather than pursue the enemy through the jungle.

COL Walter B. Daniel's recollections of the battle for Hill 65 were written on November 30, 1996. His account included some thoughts regarding the change of enemy tactics:

> Shortly after the battle, there were assertions from the press about being ambushed and about falling into a Viet Cong trap. These were quickly put to rest on the spot by the leaders at all levels. There was no trap and no ambush. Nevertheless, something had changed. What was it? Employing the advantage of hindsight, I offer the following:
>
> As late as September 1965 the strategy of the enemy seemed unchanged. Control the population, build up supplies, and avoid decisive engagement. The tactic was to disrupt the economy, interdict lines of communication, and discredit the central government (collect taxes, confiscate crops, destroy bridges, and assassinate local political leaders). Our challenge was finding and fixing the enemy. We were always good at finding. Our training had taught us that the jungle was neutral. We could, and did, live there just as easy as the enemy. We could patrol (search and destroy) for days or even weeks, and we could find the enemy before he knew we were there. When we fought we won. But, we could never seem to fix the enemy long enough to bring him to decisive battle. They were always able to escape.

Sometime in September we heard rumors that units of the 1st Inf Div had fought long jungle battles and rumors that they left the jungle before they occupied the terrain defended by the enemy. We passed these off as either false or the result of inexperienced troops. I now think that the enemy strategy (or at least his tactic) had changed. He was now willing to stand and fight if he could do so on his terms. Our failing was that we did not recognize this opportunity to pile on (mass our forces) and bring meeting engagements to a decisive battle.

In October my company again found the enemy. As in the past we deployed and assaulted. As in the past the line of enemy outposts collapsed and withdrew, leaving their dead behind. Unlike the past, when we advanced we did not find a supply cache or an abandoned camp; instead we encountered a dug in enemy force. Pausing just long enough to bring our mortars and artillery to bear, and to find the flanks of the position, we continued our fire and maneuver to close with and kill or capture the enemy. For the first time in my experience the enemy had parity in machine guns. The attacking platoons slowed and finally stopped.

The balance of the Battalion was not engaged and the Battalion Commander led them to the fight. The first to arrive was the Recon Platoon with four machine guns. With this added firepower we gained fire superiority and I decided to continue the attack. This time the two platoons in contact and the Recon Platoon provided a base of fire while the reserve rifle platoon maneuvered to the flank of the enemy position. En route, the maneuver platoon ran into the nose of an enemy counterattack. They deployed, fought through the enemy formation, and gained a position on the flank of their objective (the small hill occupied by the enemy). My FO shifted the indirect fires and we assaulted. In minutes we were on the objective with one platoon. The enemy withdrew, barely escaping the arrival of Company B. As the rest of the Battalion neared, Companies A and B consolidated the objective, and A 1/503 reorganized and redistributed ammunition. The balance of the day was spent replacing ammunition and other supplies and evacuating our dead and wounded. Even though we had piled on by massing the Battalion, the new enemy tactic to stand and fight and even counterattack, went unrecognized. The next day we continued our routine search and destroy mission.

In November we found the enemy again and once more experienced his willingness to stand and fight.[1]

Daniel continued:

There is little doubt that the enemy knew of our presence in War Zone D because it's hard to miss a helicopter assault. But, I find no evidence that he knew exactly where we were or that he suspected we had located his command post. For example, Lt Ben Waller, 2nd platoon, C/1–503, discovered and cleared a deserted enemy position (a primitive VC village). Forty yards away his platoon was engaged first by command-detonated mines and later by automatic weapons fire. My assessment is that Waller had walked in on the enemy regimental headquarters and that he was taken under fire by support troops providing local security for that element. Not far away, and at almost the same time, Lt Russ, 1st platoon, C/1–503, engaged a small group of enemy soldiers that were talking as they moved along a jungle trail. While they were quick to return fire, they were totally surprised at the presence of Russ's platoon and seemingly unconcerned by the fighting going on near them. Were they also support troops that thought they were so near the headquarters that they were safe? I think so. I think the rest of the regiment was up and about trying to find us. Perhaps they thought we would go join the Australians and that they would intercept and ambush us along the way.

On hill 65 there was no clever enemy trap and no ambush, simply an enemy force that decided (or was ordered) to reassemble and fight. When the fighting started I doubt that any enemy, with the exception of headquarters troops, was in a fighting position. If the enemy did have a preconceived plan to conduct some sort of mobile defense on hill 65 (there was no indication of a static defense) it was thwarted by the arrival of B Company. I think that when they encountered C Company the enemy threw up some covering fire and tried to get back to their foxholes and bunkers. Some made it, a large number did not. For the second time in about a month the timely arrival of Captain Bittrich and his always-ready B Company had turned the tide. B Company had to fight hard. After all, they were outnumbered 4 or 5 to one, but fight they did. Most of the enemy force was kept in the jungle and away from their prepared positions.

The larger force made more than one attempt to overwhelm the two paratrooper companies on hill 65 but were repulsed. Moving away to regroup and to plan their next move, the now mobile enemy force was hit from the rear by A/1–503. By now the enemy regiment was a spent force. My vision is that tactical communications (from regiment to battalion and from battalion to company) failed and the subordinate enemy commanders, reverting to their last sure tactic, chose to leave the battlefield to the paratroopers of the 1/503.

The next test of the enemy's will to stand and fight was in the Ia Drang. This time the Americans had the ability to mass a superior force but failed to do so. By not recognizing this new ability to bring the enemy to decisive battle an opportunity to destroy a Main Force regiment was lost. Over the years there were other missed opportunities to destroy Main Force regiments. Meanwhile, North Vietnamese reinforcements swelled the ranks of the enemy in the South. In the end a weak South Vietnamese Government failed to consolidate hard-won victories. As the will of American political leadership failed, the North Vietnamese recaptured unoccupied territory. Eventually they won control of the entire country.[2]

LTG Hal Moore, who co-authored *We Were Soldiers Once ... and Young* with Joe Galloway, commanded the 1/7th Cavalry, 1st Cavalry

Division in the Ia Drang. In his book he also wrote about the American strategy not to pursue the enemy:

Those of us who commanded American soldiers in the opening days had already undergone one crisis of confidence in the political leadership's commitment to the struggle when President Johnson refused to extend enlistments and sent us off to war sadly under strength and minus many of our best-trained men. Now, in the wake of the Ia Drang, America political determination was tested again, and again found wanting.

We knew for a fact that the three North Vietnamese regiments that we had fought in the Ia Drang had withdrawn into Cambodia. We wanted to follow them in hot pursuit, on the ground and in the air, but could not do so under the rules of engagement. Washington had just answered one very important question in the minds of Hanoi's leaders.

General Kinnard [1st Cavalry Division Commanding General during the Ia Drang campaign] says: "I was always taught as an officer that in a pursuit situation you continue to pursue until you either kill the enemy or he surrenders. I saw the Ia Drang as a definite pursuit situation and I wanted to keep after them. Not to follow them into Cambodia violated every principle of warfare. I was supported in this by both the military and civilian leaders in Saigon. But the decision was made back there, at the White House, that we would not be permitted to pursue into Cambodia. It became perfectly clear to the North Vietnamese that they then had sanctuary; they could come when they were ready to fight and leave when they were ready to quit."

General Kinnard adds, "When General Giap says he learned how to fight Americans and our helicopters at the Ia Drang, that's bullshit! What he learned was that we were not going to be allowed to chase him across a mythical line in the dirt. From that point forward, he was grinning. He can bring us to battle when he wants and where he wants, and where's that? Always within a few miles of the border, where his supply lines were the shortest, where the preponderance of forces is his, where he has scouted the terrain intensely and knows it better than we do."[3]

9

BACK TO 'NAM

I wake to sleep, and take my waking slow.
I feel my fate in what I cannot fear.
I learn by going where I have to go.
                                —Theodore Roethke

New Year's Day, January 1, 1992, was a typical cold, clear winter morning in Northern California. I boarded the American Airlines flight to Seattle at 8:45 a.m., and began the first leg on my trip back to my past. Just before takeoff the stewardess handed me a cup of coffee and without warning my hand began to shake. Why? Why now would I have uncontrollable tremblings? Whatever it was, it ended at 9:04 as the Boeing 737 left the tarmac at San Jose International Airport and began the two-hour flight to Seattle.

I had not been in the Seattle-Tacoma International Airport (Sea-Tac) since my return from Vietnam more than 23 years earlier. On a warm, muggy July night in 1968, we had landed at McChord Air Force Base in Tacoma, just south of Seattle. We grabbed our duffel bags, jumped into a cab, and headed for Sea-Tac and the first flight home. On that flight from Cam Ranh Bay, I had vowed never to return to Vietnam. Never again did I want to step back into that country with its oppressive heat, unmerciful jungle, blood-sucking leeches, biting red ants, bone-soaking monsoons, and inscrutable people. But now I was going back. Now I was retracing my steps. First Sea-Tac, then Bangkok, and then Vietnam. How did I get myself into this?

It had started two years earlier. I had decided to return to San Jose State for my master's degree in history. The first class I signed up for was History 161, The Vietnam Wars. I needed to take this class in order to find out what really happened some 25 years ago. Maybe this class would help me understand why I had continual flashbacks and intrusive memories.

Midway through the semester I asked the professor to be my thesis advisor because I wanted to write about the war. He agreed and suggested I go back to Vietnam and record my thoughts, feelings, and perceptions and compare them with my memories from the war itself. At the time I said to myself, "Are you kidding? Go back? There is no way in hell I would go back!"

But time changes one's attitudes, and as the months passed, so did my opposition to the idea. It started to make sense, then an urgency began to surround it. I had to go back! I had to go back and confront whatever it was that was eating away at me. Maybe I could find that young captain and tell him his war was over; it was time to go home. Maybe then the flashbacks and intrusive memories would finally fade.

But first, I must inject an odd occurrence that surrounded this trip back to Vietnam. Some weeks before I was to leave I received a call from my professor. He said, "There's someone I want you to talk to." He then put on a Vietnamese woman who began to ask me questions. "When are you going back to Vietnam?" "How long are you staying?" "Where are you staying?" "Would you like to meet some POWs while you are there?" Gulp 1. I said, "Sure." "Can you secure funds to have them released?" I replied, "Yes!" (At this time, a former POW and retired naval officer, CPT Eugene Baker "Red" McDaniel, had started the American Defense Institute to look into the possibility of American POWs still being held in Indochina. He had also raised funds to secure the release of any of those POWs. His organization had dropped flyers along the Mekong River from Laos down through Vietnam stating that they would pay $3.4 million for any POW.) She closed by saying she would get back to me. At this point my prof got back on the phone and said, "What do you think?" I replied, "Hell if I know." He said, "If this meet with the POWs happens, call me and I will fly out to Vietnam." "Okay."

So nothing happened until a few days before I was scheduled to depart. She again called me and confirmed that all the information I had given her previously was still true. I assured her it was. She said she would meet me in Ho Chi Minh City. The only people who knew of these two phone calls were my professor, her, and me. I did not tell anyone else.

On the flight from Bangkok to Ho Chi Minh City there were two Americans sitting a couple of seats over from me. One said he was a pig farmer from Iowa and the other was a minister from Georgia. The pig farmer was going to meet with some farmers in the Da Nang area to teach them some new ideas on raising pigs. The reverend was going to connect with some underground Christians in the same area. They were going to stay four days longer in Vietnam than I was.

As we were filling out customs forms before landing at Tan Son Nhut, the pig farmer leaned over and whispered to me, "There are no POWs in Vietnam. Plus, if there are, neither the Vietnamese government nor the American government will let them out of the country. Also, there could be CIA personnel on this flight who are watching you." Gulp 2. I turned around and noticed a couple of white guys with round eyes sitting a few rows back of me. CIA?

So we landed and went through customs. As I finished with that, a Vietnamese who looked official approached me and said he wanted my passport, visa, and return flight tickets. I refused. He explained to me that I had no choice. He won the argument. As I turned them over, I asked, "When will I get them back?" He said, "Don't worry. You will have them before your flight home." Boy, that was encouraging.

I checked into my hotel and a few days went by with no contact from anyone. Then one day I finished eating lunch in my hotel and got in an elevator to go back to my room. There were three Asian gentlemen in the elevator, but they were definitely not Vietnamese. Turns out they were Taiwanese in Vietnam for business. One of them turned to me and said in perfect English, "Are you American?" I replied, "Yes." He said, "Why are you in Vietnam? Looking for POWs?" "No, no, of course not," I stammered. Gulp 3.

A couple of days later I was in Tay Ninh at the Cao Dai Temple. Guess who is also there? The pig farmer and the reverend. For those not familiar with Vietnam, Tay Ninh is nowhere near Da Nang. We didn't discuss anything but the Temple.

I finished my trip to Vietnam and was never contacted by anyone regarding POWs. I then boarded the plane to go back to Bangkok. And who was sitting near me? The pig farmer and the reverend. I asked why they were here and they said that the reverend couldn't make contact with the underground religious group and the farmer pretty much finished what he needed to do. So they were going home early.

Was all of this a coincidence?

I would not believe this story if I were not part of it. And I don't fault anyone for questioning my sanity or recall. But this is the truth, and I have carried it with me for more than 20 years and I can't shake it. What the hell was that all about? And how did anyone know about my interest in POWs?

But right now I was on a jet bound for Seattle and trying to cope with my emotions. Forty minutes into the flight, with no warning or apparent reason, I began to cry. Cry? I don't cry! Why now? I didn't know, but I hoped I was on my way to confront whatever was out there.

I met my cousin Barbara at a coffee shop in Sea-Tac. She reminded me how upset Kathy had been in 1967 because I was going back to war. I had volunteered for Vietnam and had not told her. I had felt it was my duty to return, but could not express my survivor guilt feelings to her. The first time I had come home after only five months in country and had remorse for leaving my troops and not fulfilling my obligation to them. I was an infantry officer trained to lead men in combat. I had to go back and finish what I had started. But I hadn't told Kathy that.

Kathy understood my sense of duty; she did not understand being left out of the decision-making process. I had hurt her and she was angry with me. She decided to return to school, finish her bachelor's degree and get a teaching credential. While at Cal State-Northridge, she became an antiwar advocate. She mailed me antiwar literature, including excerpts from the speeches of Robert Kennedy and Eugene McCarthy. In addition, she sent me *The Arrogance of Power* by Senator William Fulbright and *The Bitter Heritage* by Arthur M Schlesinger, Jr. I was still pro-war, fiercely anti–Communist and a believer in the "domino theory." Also, I was in the midst of the war fighting for what I believed in. The chasm developing between us reflected that which was dividing the country in 1967 and 1968.

I never did apologize or explain my actions to her before she suddenly died on June 4, 1974, at the age of 31 from a brain aneurysm.

So I said goodbye to Barbara and boarded my flight to Thailand. The flight was long and uneventful and I landed at Bangkok International Airport at 10:00 p.m. on January 3. I checked into my hotel, but slept very little. By 8:30 I was on my way back to the airport. Then it was wait, move; wait, move. Wait in line to have your baggage X-rayed, move quickly to the check-in counter; wait in line to check in, move quickly through customs; walk a long distance to Gate 46, then wait for 80 minutes for the plane; hurry up and board, then wait on the tarmac. It reminded me of the Army: "hurry up and wait."

I arrived at Gate 46 and waited and by 10:40 a.m. we took off for Ho Chi Minh City. I was really going to go through with this. But, at least, it would not be like the first time.

Twenty-seven years earlier I was on the troopship *General Simon B. Buckner* sailing from Charleston, South Carolina, through the Panama Canal to Long Beach, California, to Vietnam. We were the first American Army infantry division to be committed to the conflict. We had no idea what lay ahead.

I was with a few thousand other GIs armed, cocky, and feeling in control of the situation. We had set sail on 15 August 1965 intent on winning the war by Christmas. It was an adventure for most of us. We were America's finest: charter members of the 1st Cavalry Division (Airmobile). We had spent the previous four weeks packing our equipment for movement and searching Army surplus stores in Columbus, Georgia, for individual weapons such as K-Bar knives in case we had to kill Charlie close up. We had been organized originally as the 11th Air Assault Division (TEST) at the recommendation of the Howze Board report of 20 August 1962.[1]

The test unit was activated on 15 February 1963 at Fort Benning, Georgia.[2] We had trained for two years just waiting for the opportunity to demonstrate our prowess. On 1 July 1965, the 11th was officially activated into the regular army as the 1st Cavalry Division (Airmobile). And on 28 July, President Lyndon B. Johnson announced on national television that he was sending the 1st Cav to Vietnam.[3] Now it was our chance.

Thirty days at sea had us infantrymen eager to get off that rusting, World War II bucket of bolts and get ashore. We were bored with the lack of meaningful activity, stuffed with too much rich food, tired of the confinement, physically out of shape, but mentally ready to go. We were foot soldiers and we wanted our feet on terra firma, now!

Forty-eight hours from the coast of Vietnam, we began preparations for a "hot" beach landing. We were ordered to take the beach with necessary force, then air assault along Highway 19 to secure it for movement of our logistical support to the division's new base camp at An Khe. We were very aware that on the same road the Viet Minh had destroyed the French Mobile Group 100 on 24 June 1954.[4] Now we were going to secure it so that our road-bound vehicles would not meet the same fate.

At 0600 on the warm, clear morning of 13 September 1965, the first elements of the 1st Cav disembarked off the coast of South Vietnam, near Qui Nhon. Similar to World War II landings, the troops maneuvered down rope ladders and into assault landing craft. Most of us carried more than 50 pounds of equipment on our backs and we were ready for anything the enemy might throw at us. The assault boats filled with their human cargo and headed for the beach. We passed the line of departure and locked and loaded our weapons. This was our hour, our moment. My pulse felt like it was beating 1,000 times a minute. The adrenaline was flowing. I was tense, I was anxious and I was nervous. I was scared.

In what seemed an instant, the landing crafts edged up to the beach and lowered their ramps, and then thousands of America's finest charged forward amid shouts, screams, curses, and anticipation. As we surged forward looking for somebody to kill, anybody to kill, we were met by General William C. Westmoreland and the United States Army band. A collective groan could be heard as we were lined up and channeled onto waiting Chinook helicopters and flown to An Khe. Highway 19 had been safeguarded, An Khe was secure, and we meekly filed in and out of Chinooks to await further orders. It was our first day in Vietnam, but none would ever be this easy again. I had not even seen a Vietnamese.

All my built up emotions dissipated in minutes. I not only expected to assault a "hot" beach, I wanted to. I wanted that brutal introduction to war. I wanted to test my courage; I wanted to prove to myself that I was capable of leadership. Instead we flew to An Khe and began building our base camp, pulled perimeter security, acclimated to the countryside, and prepared to meet the enemy.

But for now I was on a Thai Airlines jet heading for Ho Chi Minh City. One hour and 45 minutes after take off, the plane's tires made contact with Vietnamese earth and I was back. Unlike my first landing with multiple battalions, now I was alone, unarmed, apprehensive and definitely not feeling in control. I did not have the protection of the United States Army and government behind me. I was an American citizen in a country not recognized by our government, and not authorized for visit by our citizens. An uneasiness set in. I was alone in a Communist country ruled by my former enemy.

We disembarked the aircraft at 12:31 p.m. and I had returned after 23 years. Vietnam was still very hot and very humid, the way I remembered it. And the other thing that remained the same was the smell. The smell of Vietnam was unlike anything I had ever experienced before or since. I recalled it from my first two times in country and now it returned to me in a rush: it was the smell of something rotting, of everything rotting.

Tan Son Nhut Airport was desolate, dilapidated and dirty. It looked like it had not seen any maintenance for 20 years. There were scores of uniformed Vietnamese, male and female, just sitting around talking while we went through customs and waited for our bags. There were more of them than us, but most of them were doing nothing. The process of entering the country was tedious and long, with an endless list of forms to be completed. When that was accomplished, there was a delay in getting our baggage off the aircraft and through X-rays again. Automation had not yet replaced manpower here.

There was a remarkable lack of activity at this facility considering it was the main hub into the southern part of the country. No other aircraft landed while I was there and no foreign airliners could be seen on the tarmac. Only a few Russian-made Air Vietnam jets lingered on the ground. The last time I had been in Tan Son Nhut was in 1965, and then the airport bustled with American servicemen coming from and going to all parts of the country, or arriving from and departing for home. American and South Vietnamese fixed-wing and rotary-wing aircraft were continuously taking off and landing. It was hectic. But now there was nothing. The only reminders of an American presence were some unused helicopter revetments I spotted as we were making our runway approach.

An hour and a half after landing I exited the terminal area and was met by my guide for the trip into the city and to my hotel. The drive through Saigon, or rather Ho Chi Minh City, was uneventful, yet deeply significant to me. I had been here before; part of me may still be here.

The city was teeming with people, more than 6,000,000 of them. Motor scooters, bicycles, and pedicabs were the major forms of transportation.

My initial impression of Ho Chi Minh City, as we drove to the hotel, was that it had certainly seen better days. There was an apparent lack of maintenance; the buildings were filthy and in bad disrepair. The outskirts of the city were dirty and decaying. I wondered what the main downtown area would look like. But there was no visible battle damage from the city's fall in April 1975.

I checked into my hotel, unpacked, and thought of the last few days. I had left home in California, flown more than 10,000 miles, crossed the International Date Line, and just like the war years, landed in another country and another culture, without any transition period. I had to stop, take note of the past 72 hours, and sort out my feelings and impressions.

My first response was, "It's Saigon, it's Vietnam, but it's not the Vietnam I remember." The Vietnam I remembered was a Vietnam with a jungle, a Vietnam with hills, a Vietnam with the rhythm of war and endless patrols and air assaults. I didn't remember a Vietnam with Saigon and bars and restaurants and city noises.

10

Back in 'Nam

No war, or battle's sound
was heard the world around.
The idle spear and shield were high up hung.
—John Milton

After I decided to make the trip back to Vietnam, I listed the areas I most wanted to see: An Khe, Bong Son, War Zone D, and the Iron Triangle. But the most important was Bien Hoa, the former home of the 173d Airborne Brigade. Bien Hoa, some 30 kilometers northeast of Saigon, had been the site of a major American air base, and the 173d occupied a portion of its northwest perimeter.

At this time, however, the Vietnamese government was not letting Americans roam the countryside by themselves or with anyone else. So my chance of getting into Bong Son, War Zone D, or the Iron Triangle was zero. And the chances of getting up north to An Khe weren't promising. Plus I had a driver and guide, who I was sure reported where I went and when back to a headquarters.

So the three of us drove to Bien Hoa. Since I had no recall of Saigon, I was sure that once we left the city and headed for Bien Hoa it would be different. I would find that Vietnam I knew: rice paddies, water buffalo, villages, thick vegetation and jungle. Now I expected to find my past, my Vietnam.

As we entered Bien Hoa, however, I could not find any familiar sights. The Bien Hoa I remembered was a small town with a village square. It was not here now. This Bien Hoa was a bustling small city with multiple construction projects going on. So we drove to the air base and walked inside. Nothing was familiar except a couple of old, rotting conex containers left by the American Air Force. In 1965, the air base had been barren, all vegetation having been destroyed in order to give the security excellent fields of fire. Now everything was overgrown. We drove completely around the air base searching for Camp Ray, but nothing matched my memories. All my signposts, guides, landmarks, and beacons were gone. Nothing was the same; nothing was familiar. I left Bien Hoa disappointed. For some reason I expected everything to be the same after 27 years. Of course, it wasn't. But then neither was I.

On January 6, I went to Cu Chi with my guide to see the tunnels that the Viet Cong had built right under the nose of the 25th Infantry Division. There were more than 250 kilometers of tunnels, first constructed by the Viet Minh against the French in 1948. It took 20 years to complete them. As we neared the complex the sign out front should have been an indication to me of something peculiar. It was like going to an amusement park in the States.

RESTAURANT
CU CHI TUNNEL REMAINS
LOCAL SPECIALTIES
by THE RIVERSIDE, WITH
FRESH AIR, NATURAL,
ROMANTIC ATMOSPHERE
WELCOME

The sign was only in English. We paid an admission fee of 2000 dong, or about $.17 American each. The first thing we did was sit through a 15-minute lecture in Vietnamese on the tunnels: their history, construction, layout, size, location of the 25th and ARVN units, and battle sites. Then we went on a tour of various tunnel construction styles including a mess hall, conference room, water storage area, and a general's quarters.

But the most interesting episode happened next. As the end of the tour we sat eating fruit when I noticed a stack of shoulder weapons next to some PAVN soldiers. I asked my guide to inquire if I might handle the weapons. The soldiers in turn asked me if I wanted to fire them. Hell yes, I did!

As we walked to the rifle range they had built away from the tunnel complex I was hit with a flashback. The trail leading to the range was exactly like the hundreds I had walked in my previous tours: narrow with heavy vegetation on both sides. I was carrying an M-16 when all of a sudden I began scanning my front and both sides of the trail. I stealthily moved, I scanned, I listened. For a few moments I was back in 'Nam during the '60s. It was real and I was there.

As we closed on the range I came back to the present. And for $1 U.S. per round I was allowed to fire the M-16 and an AK-47.

I fired 10 rounds from each rifle. As I did so, it struck me that here I was in Vietnam, with a rifle in my hand and my former enemy standing only a few feet from me. I could just as easily have turned the weapon on him. Up to now this whole tunnel area had had a carnival atmosphere: the sign, the admission charge, the tour, and now a firing range. But with this rifle in my hand and my former enemy close by, this was reality! What if I shot him instead of the targets? What if I went back and killed them all and stole their weapons and ammunition? Thankfully my common sense didn't let these thoughts linger long.

During my 10-day stay in Vietnam I walked all through Ho Chi Minh City and Cholon. The people were friendly. Some approached me to make sure I was an American. Others stopped me and told me they had relatives in America. Some in vehicles yelled and waved a greeting. One caught me on a street and tried to sell me Military Payment Certificates for $200 U.S. By the end of the discussion I bought them for $2 and I had no idea what I was going to do with them.

In Ho Chi Minh City I found the War Crimes Museum. It was obviously constructed by the government as a propaganda tool. There were numerous captured American vehicles featured in the courtyard, including an M48 tank and an armored personnel carrier (APC). Inside the museum were hundreds of pictures of Americans mistreating the Vietnamese. There were other foreigners there, including some Europeans. As I walked through and looked at the pictures, I became very pissed. They were so anti–American I wanted to yell at the top of my lungs that these pictures were false, staged, and not representative of the American forces. There were obviously no pictures of any VC assassinations or killings, or the torture they brought on captured ARVN soldiers. I was boiling.

As I fumed, four young Vietnamese approached me. I think they were in their early 20s. They spoke a little English so we communicated as best as we could. They were interested in my reactions to the museum. I told them. Then the conversation turned to other things as they wanted to know about America. We talked for quite a long time and at the end agreed to meet up the next day and go to Tay Ninh and see the Cao Dai temple.

The next day they came by and picked me up from my hotel. We stuffed ourselves into their car and off to Tay Ninh we went. The Cao Dai religion and temple were interesting. Cao Daism is a mixture of Confucianism, Taoism, Christianity and Buddhism. The partial list of their holy people include Buddha, Jesus, Joan of Arc, Muhammad, Sun Yat-sen, Julius Caesar and Victor Hugo. The temple itself was brightly colored and almost garish. It was an interesting day. Most of my time in Vietnam was spent trying to find a memory: something that was still the same, something I could relate to. I had come back to Vietnam after 23 years searching for that young captain, but he was not there. He had gone home.

11

LESSONS LEARNED

> We had a strategy of people's war. You had tactics, and it takes very decisive tactics to win a strategic victory. You planned to use the cavalry tactics as your strategy to win the war. If we could defeat your tactics—your helicopters—then we could defeat your strategy. Our goal was to win the war.
> —General Vo Nguyen Giap

At the end of every major battle the Army looks for lessons learned. And hopefully, these lessons are then transmitted to all units so that the same mistakes are not made again. In my opinion the battle for Hill 65 in War Zone D marked a turning point in the Vietnam War. For the first time the enemy chose to stand and fight rather melt back into the jungle.

Some of the lessons learned from official records regarding HUMP were:

- The enemy stood his ground and his front line did not withdraw upon receiving artillery and TAC air fire.
- Keeping a formation in dense jungle is virtually impossible unless continuous eye contact is maintained.
- In order to develop a combat situation, it was determined that breaking contact and striking the enemy with artillery and air strikes was most desirable.
- After contact is established, any timetables should be discarded and the battle adjusted to the pace of the local commander.
- It is best to set up a battalion base and operate from it rather than move as a whole battalion.
- Use blocking forces more. As a substitute for using personnel, artillery or mortar fires can be used.
- When scout dogs are used with ARVN forces on a continuous basis

and then brought into the operation with American forces, it disrupts their sense of smell.

• The M-16 performed well during the battle. There is a need for chamber brushes and a ruptured cartridge extractor.

• In several instances flame throwers could have been used.

• An investigation of the 81mm mortar rounds that exploded in the CP area revealed cleat marks on tree trunks. It is recommended that tree trunks be examined in the future.

• During the extraction, high-angle artillery fire could not be employed due to flight corridors.

• It is necessary to use firepower at the commander's disposal. It may be necessary to stop everything in order to carefully adjust artillery fire where it is needed.

• The man on the ground must be able to identify his location. It is recommended that a marking round for the M-79 be developed.

• Armed helicopters are excellent reconnaissance vehicles.

• Armed helicopters need a marking round in the form of a smoke streamer to identify forward ground elements.

• There was some confusion in obtaining and directing USAF rescue helicopters. Request for air force helicopters should be treated the same as an immediate tactical air request.[1]

As it can be seen, the above are tactical lessons learned. Although we didn't realize it immediately, strategically the whole nature of the war had changed.

We learned that the VC and PAVN could and would move large units into a set-piece battle with us at the location and time of their choosing. This was no longer a hit-and-run guerrilla war fought by a peasant army against a technologically superior American Army. We found that the enemy, whether Main Force VC units or PAVN, were well trained, well equipped, tenacious and motivated. In the jungle especially, where our superior firepower and mobility were often hampered, they proved to have superior light infantry units and very professional soldiers. But at HUMP we also learned that we could hold our ground with them, even with our relatively green troops versus their superior experience.

Tactically, we learned that the helicopter and the air-mobile concept really did work in intense combat; it was our lifeline. Our scout helicopters would seek out the enemy and bring fire upon him from following gunships. Our Hueys and Chinooks could move troops over forbidding terrain and land almost anywhere we wanted. This saved the foot soldier from humping nearly 70 pounds of equipment up and down hills. During HUMP, choppers brought in water, ammo, and chow, and took out our dead and wounded. Gunships gave us fire support and another weapon besides artillery and small arms.

Attaching an Air Force Forward Air Controller (FAC) to the 1/503 proved very effective. The ground FAC was able to provide close air support to LTC Tyler and communication with the air FAC to increase tactical air response (TAC) and enhance friendly troop safety from TAC air fires. The same was true for the Ia Drang.

We learned to use our resources rather than field jackets to recon an area. The 173d refused to sacrifice men to recon areas when artillery or observation helicopters were more effective.

At HUMP and X-Ray we found that indeed Chinese advisers were working with the VC and PAVN, contrary to what the Communists might have indicated or GEN Westmoreland wanted to hear. During this war Chinese advisers would be noted continuously by various units in contact.

Just as we learned lessons from HUMP and later operations, so did the enemy. The VC and PAVN developed tactics to negate our superior firepower in War Zone D. They learned to "hug our belts," causing difficulty for our ARA and artillery to give fire support to units in contact.

The enemy learned that he could cross an imaginary line in the dirt and we would give him sanctuary. We would not follow him; we would not go after his supply depots in the rear areas. In the context of the whole Vietnam War, HUMP and later X-Ray and Albany would demonstrate that the above lesson would be adhered to by all American combat units assigned to the country. This had to give the enemy a sense of confidence when confronting American units. He could now plan his offense with complete confidence that we would not follow up, would not hold ground and would not chase him into Cambodia or Laos. He now understood the strengths and weaknesses of air mobility and he could build his strategy around that. He now had a better idea of how to fight us.

We learned that the enemy was willing to sacrifice men to meet his objectives: kill ratios of 10–1, 12–1, and higher meant nothing to him. It did not affect his ability to continue the fight. After HUMP, LZ X-ray and Albany, when more than 1500, and possibly closer to 2,500 VC/PAVN were killed, the enemy fell back to sanctuaries, regrouped, brought in fresh troops, retrained, and went back on the offensive. We would literally wipe out enemy forces only to see the same units months later, still in the same area of operations and still effective.

We learned that by not holding ground we had already won we would have to go back and fight for it again and again. The 173d would go into War Zone D five times in the first six months it was in country. The 1st Division would also pull operations in that forbidding jungle. And neither unit held the ground it had occupied. We would not follow up on our successes. Instead, we would leave the battle area and return to base camp. And it wasn't just the 173d that did this. The Marines left Khe Sanh after 77 days, the Iron Triangle was attacked over and over again by different units, Hill 881 was assaulted again and again, the Ia Drang Valley was attacked and then left only to be attacked again, the same for the Plain of Reeds and War Zone C. Bong Son had to be fought for more than once before the 1st Cavalry finally decided to put a permanent camp there.

After HUMP we came to realize that we would have to fight the enemy with one hand tied behind our backs. We could not invade the north and we couldn't follow the VC and PAVN into Cambodia or Laos. As CPT Walt Daniel said to me after HUMP, "What are we doing here [South Vietnam]? We should be making a combat jump into Hanoi and attacking the North Vietnamese in their own backyard."

And finally, maybe, just maybe, if our political and military leaders had read and understood books such as *Street Without Joy* (1961) or *The Quiet American* (1955) or *Last Reflections on a War* (1964), or listened to French leaders who warned us not to get involved, it would not have been necessary for American troops to fight in Vietnam in the first place. At the very least, our military leaders should have been able to define a strategy to win. A strategy that was definitely better than attrition.

We learned that not one American life was worth sacrificing if we as soldiers were not going to be allowed to win. Fighting to a draw is not viable strategy. Losing American soldiers for a stalemate was against all rules of warfare.

We learned more than 20 years later that there was a more frightful price to pay for our participation in that war: PTSD. I have fought that war for nearly 50 years and still do today.

And with the restrictions placed on us by the White House, Congress and the Joint Chiefs of Staff (JCS), we realized we were not supposed to win this war. We were only there to ensure one president didn't lose Vietnam on his watch and another would somehow achieve "peace with honor." The American soldier was caught up in the middle of this political mess and let down by the White House, Congress, the Joint Chiefs of Staff, and our generals.

He deserved better.

12

BIG & RICH

We are not weak if we make proper use of those means which
the God of Nature has placed in our power.... The battle, Sir, is
not to the strong alone; it is to the vigilant, the active, the brave.
—Patrick Henry, speech to
Virginia Convention, Richmond

In 2005 country duo Big & Rich wrote and recorded "The 8th of
November" in honor of Niles Harris (C 1/503) and Operation HUMP.
The song is a testament to the courage and professionalism of the air-
borne combat infantryman. And we definitely appreciated it.

In fact, in June 2006 Big & Rich were part of a country concert tour
that came to Seahawks Stadium in Seattle. I and three others were
brought on stage just after they sang "The 8th of November." We were
welcomed home by the crowd of more than 50,000.

When Big & Rich flew to Vietnam with Niles in September 2005,
their in-country production crew found a villager, actually a village
patriarch, who claimed to be a VC spy during Operation HUMP. His
village was supposedly the closest to Hill 65. He stated on camera that
he was forced by the VC to spy on the Americans because his family
had been threatened. He indicated also that his job was to be the liaison
between the local VC forces and the PAVN, as the two units had poor
communication. Although he was not at the battle site—in fact, he was
forbidden to participate—he did lead the enemy forces to where the
Americans were.

His recollections were that our forces moved along a trail and the
VC/PAVN set up an ambush for us. He said that many Americans died
in the battle.

It is hard to determine if this "spy's" story is true or not. It is possible
that this villager may be confusing HUMP with another engagement,

as there are inconsistencies between his story and the remembrances by the veterans who were there.

For example, I saw no villages during our movement from November 5 through November 7 or after contact on the 8th. He said he saw Chinooks bringing resupply into our positions and yet no Chinooks were used. Of course, he may have mistaken the Air Force H-43s for Chinooks. He also mentioned burning tanks, but there were no tanks in the battle. It is possible that he might be thinking of a later 1st Division incursion into War Zone D. Most likely this man was a VC spy and liaison. He probably did at one time spy on American units, but I doubt he did so during Operation HUMP.

But if it was an ambush, then a newly found website report seems relevant. Pham Xuan An was a journalist with Time magazine in Vietnam. He was the most Americanized of the Vietnamese working for various American magazines and newspapers in Vietnam. This allowed him to develop close relationships with many writers who were there reporting on the war and gave him unlimited access to classified and

Chapter XVI concert. Back row: Steve Konek, Sr., Big Kenny, Cowboy Troy, Niles Harris, Mike Lovelace, Ray Lockman. Front row: Thai Phan, Craig Ford, Al Conetto, John Rich, Two Foot Fred.

unclassified reports. An was also North Vietnam's top spy. At face value, this is of no significance, but when combined with the practices of GEN Westmoreland it becomes very significant. "General William Westmoreland ... had the most liberal press policy of probably any general in American history. He tried to woo journalists by being open and candid. He told them classified information, with the understanding, of course, that it was either off-the-record or would be used only for background.... Westmoreland's headquarters always gave ... advance notice when a major military operation was scheduled to take place." An had access to that information. Were the VC aware of Operation HUMP ahead of time? Who knows?[1]

Was the 8th of November an ambush? I don't think so. It probably was a matter of two opposing units who met on a battlefield and decided to stand and fight. Neither one backed down until the casualties were overwhelming. Hundreds upon hundreds of young men died defending their fellow soldiers that day. Neither victory nor defeat will help those who no longer walk with us.

So who won? The unit that inflicted the most casualties on the enemy or the unit that would eventually regain the ground lost? By definitions made by the opposing armies, perhaps both sides won. Or maybe both sides lost.

Who knows?

13

PTSD

And so, my fellow Americans, ask not what your country can
do for you; ask what you can do for your country.
                                        —John F. Kennedy

In late January 1966 my two year obligation to the Army ended and
I left Vietnam and active duty. I returned home to my wife and daughter
and entered the civilian world. But I became overwhelmed with guilt.
The intensity and frequency got worse and I realized that I had survivor's
guilt: guilt that I was alive and so many others who fought beside me
were not. Guilt that the men I served with were still there and I was safe
at home. Guilt that asked "Why me?" "Why was I spared?" "Why me
and not Dave?" "Why couldn't I have died on that hill?" The guilt continued daily and wouldn't leave me alone. It was driving me nuts. Finally,
after being home for only a few months, I volunteered for active duty
again. I had to go back to Vietnam and finish what I had started. I had
to fulfill my obligations to my country, my men, but especially to myself.

In October 1966 I was sent to Fort Lewis, Washington, to run a
tactics committee for the Advanced Infantry Training (AIT) group
there. One month later I was promoted to captain. By the end of December I had volunteered to return to Vietnam and a combat unit. I volunteered for the 173d, the 1st Cav, and the 101st Airborne. In July 1967 I
was sent to the 1st Battalion, 8th Cavalry, 1st Cavalry Division stationed
at LZ English in Bong Son, II Corps. I was initially the Battalion Logistics
Officer (S-4) and then in October 1967 I was given command of
Delta Company. But before LTC Jenkins gave me command, he admon-
ished me: "You are not getting this command to become a hero at
your men's expense. You will take care of your men and ensure that as
many go home safe as possible. Do you understand?" He did not once
mention killing the enemy. I began to wonder if he didn't believe in the

war. Over the months under his command I developed a deep respect and affection for this man. He was a leader like CPT Daniel. And he even found time to chew my butt once in a while.

I would find out that being a company commander was the best job in the infantry. Working with troops and having the responsibility for them would bring me unbelievable satisfaction. This was the best job I ever had. I would stay in command until March and then be sent to division headquarters as the assistant G-2 (Intelligence) briefing officer to the commanding general.

Let me digress for a moment. When LTC Jenkins left Vietnam in December 1965 to return home, his replacement was a former staff officer who had, in my opinion, no skills as a troop leader. He and I clashed often. In March 1968 he sent me to division. My company shortly thereafter was sent into the A Shau Valley. Six of my men were killed. I was furious as I felt he should have let me lead them into the A Shau. I had the experience and knew the troops. I was stuck at Division and they died. I have held that anger against that Battalion Commander ever since. I still do.

But, I would leave Vietnam in July 1968 completely disillusioned with the war and its leaders. We were not going to be allowed to win and our sacrifices were only to please stateside politicians. I left active duty in January 1970 and again returned to civilian life. I had accomplished all my goals. I had graduated from college, become an infantry officer, gone to jump school, and commanded a platoon and then a company in combat. And I was only 28 years old. But the guilt still did not go away and it still hasn't.

Sometime in the late '70s or early '80s I began to notice that I was having trouble sleeping, I was having intrusive memories and flashbacks, I was hibernating and I could not concentrate. In addition I began having nightmares, suicidal thoughts, depression, and an increasingly short temper. And I began to have an insatiable appetite to read anything that concerned the Vietnam War. Without realizing what was going on, I just ignored the above signs and attempted to live a "normal" life.

I also began having memories that would stay with me for a time until I wrote them down. Once I had written the memory down it would vanish and another one would pop up. This continued on for some time until I had written nearly 50 pages of notes. But I still paid no attention to what was happening to me.

Finally, in May 1994 I found out, through my friend Phil, that the San Jose Vet Center offered therapy for Vietnam veterans. I really didn't think I needed any help, but he insisted and I went there with him. He introduced me to his counselor and she took one look at me, listened to a couple of comments I made regarding the VC, and immediately suggested I join a therapy group at the Center. I said, "No, there's nothing wrong with me." After much intense lobbying by Phil, I decided I would try it and see what might happen. I made an appointment to see her the following week. At that meeting I began to tell her my story of 8 November. At the end she said, "Look at your body language." I did and I was all wrapped up like a pretzel. Maybe I did have some problems. So I joined a group, but four months later I moved to Seattle. I found the Vet Center there and joined another group.

At this point let me digress and further delve into PTSD as related to combat.

Most people have heard of Post-Traumatic Stress Disorder (PTSD). It was the Vietnam War that really put PTSD on the psychological map of the average person in the street. Veterans of that war became increasingly vocal about the after effects of the war, not only the physical, but psychological. The disorder slowly became recognized, both by the health community and the general public alike...

Of course, PTSD has existed from the time humans first roamed the earth. After the First and Second World Wars, it was referred to as "shell-shock" and most people are familiar with this term...

Essential to developing PTSD is having experienced a traumatic event, or series of traumatic events. There must also exist a belief that as a result of that trauma, one is going to die...[1]

Another authority notes:

The symptoms can range in severity from mild to devastating, and not everyone will have all of the symptoms at the same time:

• Loss of authority over mental function—particularly memory and trustworthy perception
• Persistent mobilization of the body and the mind for lethal danger, with the potential for explosive violence
• Persistence and activation of combat survival skills in civilian life
• Chronic health problems stemming from chronic mobilization of the body for danger
• Persistent expectation of betrayal and exploitation; destruction of the capacity for social trust

- Persistent preoccupation with both the enemy and the veteran's own military/governmental authorities
  - Alcohol and drug abuse
  - Suicidality, despair, isolation, and meaninglessness

Such unhealed PTSD can devastate life and incapacitate its victims from participation in the domestic, economic, and political life of the nation. The painful paradox is that fighting for one's country can render one unfit to be its citizen.[2]

I believe my own symptoms came from three separate incidents. First, the events of 8–9 November 1965. Second, escaping death at the last second when rockets crashed into a tent I was sleeping in when stationed at Division HQ at Camp Evans. And third, seeing one of my troops decapitated by a helicopter.

The Seattle Vet Center is where I really began to deal with my PTSD. The group consisted of seven combat veterans. Our counselor, Bill, was also a combat Vietnam vet. These sessions began to get very intense as we told stories of our experiences in the war. Bill reminded us that we would all get worse before we began to get better. He also told us that his goal was to get all of us into the in-patient PTSD therapy program at the Seattle VA Medical Center. Into 7 West, as it was known.

As Bill had prophesied, I began to really hit the dumps. As the months dragged on, my relationship with my girlfriend, Melody, that had been ongoing for 3 years was unraveling. I was unable to do my job and then I was unable to hold one. I was unemployed more than employed. She finally had enough and threw me out of her condo. I was on my own, period. And I wasn't doing very well. More than once I tried to "swallow my gun." I would stay in my apartment with the blinds drawn for hours on end. I didn't venture out unless absolutely necessary. I was hibernating and isolating. Everything hurt. It hurt to raise my head in the morning, I had headaches, the sun bothered my eyes and I could not shake the funk. I didn't laugh anymore. I was angry, frustrated and sad. I had excuses for anything and everything. Everybody was after me; everybody was trying to hurt me. It was everyone else's fault I was like I was. I had all but given up; there was no hope. I was dead inside.

And then the holidays hit. I had noticed ever since returning from 'Nam in 1968 that I had major problems during the holidays. I just did not like them. I despised the commercialism, the phoniness, the crowds, the happiness, the religious element, and the beauty of the season. I just hated the whole thing. I suffered through them, and it was tough. I kept reflecting back to 24 December 1967 and that we were in the field searching for enemy soldiers to kill. By February 6, 1995, I had collapsed psychologically: suicidal depression, guilt, feeling sorry for myself and the pain. "I am so down. All I can think of doing is killing myself. I am not going to make it at this rate. I am on the verge of ending it all. Fuck it, this isn't living. This is fucking suffering. I don't need any of this shit anymore." In addition, the guilt really built up. "Why couldn't I, instead of Dave, have died on Hill 65? It would have been so much better. I would trade my life for Dave's. Why the fuck was I chosen to live? To live in pain? Why me?"

I had dropped as far as I could. There was no bottom below where I was now. By 3:30 p.m. I had called Bill and asked that he get me into the PTSD program at the Seattle VA immediately. He called back and told me to be there at 5:00 p.m. he had arranged a place for me.

I was there by 4:45 p.m. but waited for four hours to be checked in. After finishing a meeting with staff at 11:15 p.m. I was finally admitted to 7 East, the psych ward. I was put in with three other vets experiencing what I was going through. I said "hello" to them and then went straight to bed. But before sleep, the insecurities came: "Do I belong here? Am I really this sick? Can I survive being bottled up inside a hospital for a month? I am scared. What have I got myself into? These people are fucked up; am I? Am I that fucked up?"

It would be a few days before I would be moved to 7 West, as the staff needed to bring me back to some sort of normalcy before moving me. I immediately began to relax. On the 7th I attended a class on depression. Everyone was so depressed the instructor could not get a reaction from any of us.

Finally on the 13th I was moved over to 7 West. My treatment team would consist of a psychologist, a psychiatrist, and a primary nurse. We would be on a pretty rigid regimen: meals, classes and medications, all scheduled at the same time each day. First call was at 6:15 a.m. lights out was at 10:00 p.m. Every Monday at 8:30 was Opening Group and every Friday at 3:00 was Closing Group. Television hours and visiting hours were set up, as were telephone hours. A patient government was organized. The staff was going to keep us as busy as possible with classes and meetings. Weekend passes were available if they were earned. The biggest thing as far as staff was concerned was that we learn to manage and control our anger.

In addition, Buddy Status was implemented to award a veteran for attending and participating in all groups, keeping his area and himself clean, and abiding by the expectations of the ward. Buddy Status would allow one, with another Buddy, to be gone for up to 90 minutes on hospital grounds.

The classes offered were health education, psychotherapy, anger management, relaxation therapy, PTSD Education, stress management, war trauma, and coping with depression. They were all for an hour and some were twice a week. I was ready to jump in with both feet. I needed, more than ever, to get a handle on this PTSD, as it was slowly killing me.

Before the end of my first week in 7 West I was beginning to feel claustrophobic. I had been in the hospital for nearly 10 days and the walls were starting to close in. I needed some fresh air, but I had not yet earned "Buddy" status, and that was necessary to be able to get off the ward. To do that I had to earn points. I started off at the bottom and if I was a "good boy" I would gain a point, a change in status. For example, if I was a "B" I could leave the ward with another vet. When I earned an "I" rating I would be on "independent" status. Within 24 hours I experienced feelings ranging from being institutionalized, to being comfortable in my surroundings, to claustrophobia. This was going to be a long 30 days.

The classes began on Monday and my first one was anger management. The instructor explained the physical, emotional and behavioral symptoms of anger. This was a good start on my rehabilitation and hopefully the beginning of the end my stress.

Within 7 West I became part of a 3-man group that started to push back on some of the rules that were being applied to us. The first thing we decided to go against was Buddy Status. The three of us felt that this was just a sham procedure. Supposedly one had to take a request to the patient government and be questioned on it. Then the patients voted on the request. If approved, it went to staff, who had the final decision. We protested that the patients' vote meant nothing, as all the power was held by the staff. We had our righteous indignation up and decided not to apply for Buddy Status. At this point, our senior officer (a retired naval lieutenant commander) had decided to leave the program on his own. He was fed up with the rules. After much consultation with staff he was finally convinced to stay. So he applied for Buddy Status and I still refused. It was on principle, of course.

By now I began to try to get back at Melody any way I knew. I was going to play one of her daughters against her. I was going to hit back as hard as I could. I was going to show her.

So the classes continued, my fight against the staff continued, and my stand on "principle" continued. The classes began to dig up lost memories: Hill 65, the day one of my troops walked into the helicopter blade, and my need for my father to be proud of me. My emotions were lost for a while, but slowly they began to surface in different classes and with different stories. But as the emotions returned, so did the guilt. Mostly survivor's guilt. Again it was, "Why Dave, why not me?" It became difficult to try to understand why I was allowed to survive.

The memory of the day my soldier walked into the helicopter blade brought a different type of guilt. It was guilt for failure to act and for failure to realize the difficult position we were in as the helicopter approached. This cost my soldier's life and I can't do anything but blame myself. After all, I was responsible. I was the officer in charge. And responsibility had been beaten into our heads as officers from day one. We were responsible for everything our troops did and didn't do. Period.

The need for my father to be proud of me became harder to accomplish as I was sitting in a hospital ward with PTSD and not out in the world doing something positive. So the emotions flowed and I tried to gain some control.

The claustrophobia returned. That and the feeling of being institutionalized. During the weekends it became acute. Especially a 3-day weekend. I tried to fight it, but I couldn't leave the hospital and the walls were closing in on me. "Can't sit still, can't concentrate. Don't know if I can make 2 more weekends of this. I feel like a confined animal. All I do is pace." And, of course, boredom reigned supreme during the weekends. But I was too bullheaded to apply for Buddy Status and a solution to the problem. That Saturday night I cracked. I was in the TV room with another patient when a nurse walked in. She introduced herself as our primary nurse during the weekend and then began asking questions.

Before I knew it I was on the "Buddy System." "At this point I really became agitated and began explaining to her the stupidity of the rules.... I told her I was an adult and expected to be treated as such. Right now with these stupid, inane rules I feel I am being treated as a child. I became angry and said, 'Fuck it, I don't need this,' and stomped out of the room. I felt I held my temper in check very well, but she just pissed me off."

The next morning I awoke feeling a little better than last night. "I am, however, still bothered by the stupid rules in this place. Must give much thought to staying and making this work for me. I will talk to my treatment team Tuesday and express my displeasure concerning the restrictions."

The 3-day weekend finally ended and Tuesday was here. "Meeting with my team this morning. Going to bitch about the 'B' system."

At Opening Group I got into it with the psychologist regarding the "B" system. He took it personally when I called the patient government vote a "sham." The staff, obviously, didn't agree with me. They want us to discuss it among ourselves.

At this point my other buddy in the 3-man group fighting the system had applied for "Buddy Status." He was denied, got pissed and walked off the ward. Now I became irritated with the staff for making him angry enough to leave. "To deny him 'B' status is ridiculous. Their 'excuse' is that he has drug and alcohol problems." By now I was spiraling down again. I was lashing out at anything.

At our next anger management class we discussed whether we stuffed our anger and did we escalate it to rage. It was brought out that stuffers can deny anger. Of course, that wasn't me. "We escalate anger into rage because we feel we have no other choice, to demonstrate an image of power or strength, to avoid expressing the underlying emotions, fear of getting close to someone, lack of communication skills, and stuffing is a learned behavior."

My anger towards the system continued to grow. I was becoming more vocal about it and didn't care who heard me bitch. I had obviously not absorbed the teachings from the anger management classes yet.

On February 22 I met with my treatment team: my psychiatrist, psychologist and two nurses:

> They are going to release me on March 2 because my anger is getting in the way of my treatment. They feel my anger is directed at each of them and

they take it personally. I mentioned that some of the guys would rather talk to me than them and they took that as another dig at the team. In other words, I said that to hurt them or put them down. They felt I was attacking them and they didn't want to be subjected to my barbs and digs anymore.

Wow! I slowly walked back to my room. I felt like someone had just kicked me in the stomach. I don't know how to react, what to say. I felt scolded, put down, knocked back on my heels, and like I had the wind kicked out of me all at once. I don't know what to think. This was definitely not what I was expecting. I was the one planning to take the offensive; instead I had been attacked first. I don't want to be released early. I don't want to be kicked out of the program. Right now I do not feel very good about myself. I feel like a bully who has just been given a dressing down by his elders. Is that me?

I feel lost, hurt, and ashamed by my behavior. I don't want to be kicked out like a spoiled, little boy.

I discussed this with my two other protagonists against the "Buddy System" to try to find an answer to this mess. Our senior officer recommended that I apply for "B" status. It sounded as if the Treatment Group had nailed him, too. After much thought, I decided to apply for "B" status and for a weekend pass, also. The fight had been taken out of me.

"Whatever the reason for the Treatment Team's handling of my situation, I was now questioning myself. Maybe I was the problem. Maybe I have more to do with my healing than others. Maybe I need to look hard at my actions and what effect they have on other people. Maybe I better get my shit together."

As I continued to attend classes, the effects of the mental beating I took from the Treatment Team still affected me. I looked at myself and saw a very angry and stubborn person. I needed to learn to use my head, to think, to use logic and to use common sense. Get away from the anger.

At Closing Group on Friday I thanked the Treatment Team for hitting me across the head with a 2 × 4 to get my attention. I needed that. It feels so much better not carrying the anger around. It felt like a giant load had been lifted off my shoulders.

On February 26 I talked to one of the nurses about the March 2 release date and my desire to extend it. She asked me why I felt I should stay and I told her because after the meeting with the Treatment Team my anger had subsided. I no longer carried that weight inside me and I wanted to get better. She indicated to me that the March 2 date on the calendar was followed by a "?" and that March 8 also had my name. She would talk to the Team tomorrow.

Finally at Opening Group on February 27 my psychologist said they would move my discharge date to March 7. Great!

I attended my classes with a new vigor. I had been given the opportunity and now it was up to me to take advantage of it. I had 8 days left to get everything I could out of the program. I continued to attend the classes and to participate. As I did, more memories of Vietnam came to the surface and I had to look at each one and attempt to deal with it. I specifically remembered the times when one of my soldiers was hurt or killed. Those thoughts just never went away. They were always lurking somewhere in the back of my mind, just waiting for the opportunity to come forward and nail me.

March 7, 1995, was my last day. I had been in the Seattle VA Medical Center for 30 days and had formed some very strong relationships with the guys. Now I had to leave and face the outside world and I knew it would not be easy.

I returned to my apartment and again felt the loneliness and emptiness of it. It was cold outside, but my apartment was colder. The walls immediately began to close in. I needed to find something or someone to get my mind off this. I began to take it "one day at a time." I began to look for a job. I needed to get back to work. And I again checked in with the Seattle Vet Center. Of course, the six other guys were still there, as was Bill. And I made contact with Melody.

The days drifted on. March blended with April and I was still searching for a job and watching my relationship with Melody slowly move in a positive direction. But as the job search continued with no positive results, I saw my mental state sliding down. The apartment walls began closing in again. And again my relationship with Melody went south.

Then a breakthrough. My very good and longtime friend Larry found an opportunity for me with a basketball equipment manufacturer in Michigan. They were looking for a national sales manager with no experience in the sporting goods industry. Larry talked to the owner, touted me and then gave me his name and number. I called and secured an interview at the home office in late May. I flew out, toured the facility, interviewed with the president, met some of the employees, and liked what I saw. He offered me the position and I accepted. I was on my way back. It was June 5, 1995.

I moved to Michigan ten days later and looked forward to the challenge of the new job and a new state to live in. I hoped it was the beginning of some positive changes in my life. I hoped. And as my professional life took off in a new direction, my personal life began to look up as now Melody saw me in a new job with new responsibilities. We began a cross-country relationship. The new guys in the company were a fun group. They worked hard and partied hard. We argued the positive traits of Michigan vs. Washington, the rain vs. the snow. We argued Seattle Seahawks vs. Detroit Lions, Mariners vs. Tigers, Wolverines vs. Huskies, Spartans vs. Cougars. Beers after work added to the discussions. I also began to travel. I was in states I had never seen before: Wisconsin, Illinois, Texas, Minnesota, Indiana, Missouri, Kansas, Massachusetts, Rhode Island and Ohio. I was having a ball and loved the work. I was dealing with sporting goods dealers, with our distributors and salesmen, and with universities. And I sought out and found a veterans' group that met on a weekly basis.

But in the back of my head a thought began to germinate that all was not right. In my own inimitable way I ignored it and continued the march.

In this new vet group I began to look at spiritual healing. Initially I scoffed at the idea. Me, spiritual? Come on, I don't believe in that babble. But I listened. I began to search to see if there was more to this world than what I could touch, feel, see, hear or smell. Maybe there is something else out there. But where?

At the same time my relationship with Melody improved. She flew out to Michigan to see me in August. In November I flew to Washington to spend some time with her. For the first time in a long time I began thinking that she and I could have a future together. I had this unique sense that I could feel Melody's love and presence even though we were 2000 miles apart.

Sometime after New Year's Day 1996 I became uneasy with my relationship with the company president. It was obvious to me that our ways of doing business and our ideas were counter to each other. Things became strained. We had a few philosophical and operational clashes along the way and our relationship spiraled downward from there. As spring approached I knew my time with the company was winding down, even though I enjoyed it and the employees very much, loved the industry and relished the challenges and opportunities. Finally, in June I quit or I was fired. Either way, it was mutual. So in July, I rented a truck, loaded it with all my possessions, hitched my car to the rear and headed west. It was time to go home.

By October I had a new job and had moved in with Melody again. Although I had initially rejoined my old Seattle Vet Center group, by October I had dropped out. After all, my life was on track: I was living with the woman I loved, I had a great new job and I was back in Washington. Everything was great! What could go wrong?

As I continued to write this book, I was going in and out of depression. Sometimes it would be a deep drop, sometimes not so severe. Either way, it affected my relationship with everyone, but especially Melody and her daughter Carrie. When I finally noticed I was depressed, I had to work hard and concentrate to get myself out of it. I would think positive thoughts, exercise, get out into the sun or try to be around people. I struggled with the depression, as it was usually a slow decline and I had difficulty recognizing my descent. But as I look back, I realize that at best, I was in a continual state of mild depression all the time and had been since my return from Vietnam in 1968. So, even though I had gone through peer group therapy and the in-patient program at the VA Medical Center, I still had PTSD and I was still affected by the associated depression. I had to come to grips with the fact that it would be with me for the rest of my life and I had to learn to deal with it on a daily basis. Or it would ruin me and all my relationship.

Fortunately my relationship with Melody continued to grow and strengthen. We were married on August 29, 1997. But I was still in that mildly depressed state. I could not experience joy, or laughter with the same intensity as I had before Vietnam. I would be at parties or with friends and feel isolated and alone. I was an observer, not a participant in life. There was an imaginary barrier I could not break through to the highs of life. My joy was always immersed below this barrier. The happiness I did enjoy was tempered by the limited access I had to it. Depression and anger, on the other hand, I could experience to the fullest. There was no barrier to them, except me.

In late November 1998 my depression worsened. A succession of personal stresses had overwhelmed me. Melody and I were not getting along, and our marriage was going to hell fast. My mother was in the hospital and we didn't know how serious it was. Krissy was pregnant and expecting in February. I had been informed that my plant was closing and sales and production were moving to Iowa. I was effectively laid off as of March 12, 1999. At my age (57), looking for another job was not a welcome prospect. Now I was in a constant state of deep depression. I was going downhill fast.

In early February I sought help. I found an independent contractor in Everett that the VA recommended. PTSD still had control of me. At the same time the VA approached me to join a test program called Project Mood. They started me with literature and Sertraline (Zoloft). I'm not into drugs, but what the hell. I gave it a try.

The Sertraline began to work almost immediately. My mood lightened. And my sessions with my new counselor were very productive. We discussed seasonal affective disorder (SAD):

> Some of the symptoms that characterize SAD—especially lethargy, low self-esteem, and feelings of despair—are the same as those of ordinary depression. Other symptoms are often the reverse: While people with ordinary depression frequently have trouble sleeping, those with SAD tend to sleep more than usual—as much as four hours longer every day. And while depressed people often lose weight due to diminished appetite, SAD people are more likely to crave food (especially sweet or starchy food) and gain weight.
>
> At its worst, SAD can be just as debilitating as non-seasonal depression. Sufferers have difficulty managing personal relationships and work responsibilities; some withdraw completely or have suicidal thoughts."[3]

To combat SAD I got a bright light box from the VA. It had been shown to be an effective form of treatment.

But, whether it was the drugs, the light box or the counseling, I began to feel better than at any time since 8 November 1965. For the first time in more than 30 years I was once again participating in life, not just observing. The barrier that existed in my mind and blocked my ability to feel joy and happiness and experience laughter had been removed. That weight on my shoulders, that stress was gone. My outlook became positive. I was mellower. Situations that would have previously caused me to explode became minor irritants. I was involved with life. I once again cared for others and myself.

Within this therapy program I experimented with hypnosis. I had always been interested in this form of treatment, but I wasn't sure if I could be hypnotized. And I was interested to see if hypnosis could help me visualize the events of 8 November 1965. I am quite sure that I was under hypnosis at least three times, but I could not see the events of 8 November. Once, I thought I saw the green that I remembered beginning to lighten. I could almost distinguish between the trees and the brush. I tried self-hypnosis once on a flight from Portland to Seattle, but couldn't bring up Vietnam. The third time I thought I saw my men's positions at the base of Hill 65 and had a partial vision of Dave's face including the bullet to the head.

As I write this I still have not found those missing memories. Would I ever see clearly the events on Hill 65? I do not know. And as the months and years pass I find that it is not as important to me as it once was. It would be ideal to see those events and clear up any questions I have regarding my performance. But none of my men were killed or wounded that day; ours was the only platoon that did not suffer any casualties. Were we lucky or was it because I did my job? I will probably never know the answer to that question either, but does it matter? The results are what they are.

It's 2015 as I write, and I am still in therapy. Melody and I moved to Walla Walla, Washington, in 2003 and I joined a peer group here. I have been a member of it more than 11 years and it is still going strong. There are 10 members, all combat vets, and we see each other every week. We have breakfast, then our meeting, and then have lunch. Within those 6 or 7 hours we still help each other deal with PTSD. We are committed to stay in this group until there are no longer any of us alive. Combined with my sessions in Everett, this group has worked wonders for me. It is my lifeline. And I find that I trust each and every one of these guys with my life and love them like brothers.

I completed two stays in the Seattle VA Medical Center for the inpatient PTSD program. The first stay in 1995 was for 30 days and the next in 2005 was for 17 days. I am still in recovery mode.

During my time in therapy I have come to realize that the government should never have brought us home until we had completed our mission as we expected to: win the war. The government also did us a great disfavor with the 12- and 13-month tours and not mandating victory as our objective. We have no closure, no finality. We are still trying to win that war. I want back what was taken from me: the opportunity to win.

Group therapy has helped me put my life in order and stabilize my relationship with Melody, who has had to put up with me for more than 20 years. I can now, with medications, function in normal society. But I need that weekly visit to my group to keep me going and I need those meds. I am a Vietnam veteran with PTSD and that is okay. Actually, I have had it so long it is who I am and who I will always be and I don't know anything else.

But what I found, by accident, by delving into my PTSD was that I missed the war and my time in it. I missed it because for the first and only time in my life, I felt I was doing something important, something for my country, that the decisions I made really mattered. And at a very young age and for a very short period of time, I held the fate of more than 150 American soldiers in my hands. My decisions determined life and death for them and an unknown number of Vietnamese. I was authorized by my rank and command to take lives and preserve lives. That is power and responsibility and it is very addicting, especially for someone in his mid–20s.

And coupled with the constant fear, the unknown, the excitement, and the intensity of combat, Vietnam—and especially the Vietnam War—have been forever etched in my mind. It will always be there. The war was and is the highlight of my life. Each day was an adventure. Each day brought new doubts, new fears and new challenges. Decisions and actions were demanded immediately. Nowhere in nonmilitary life, except maybe the police, does that kind of intense relationship with life exist. My nerve ends were constantly on edge. I touched everything, smelled everything, saw everything with more intensity.

But I also miss the war because I loved it. Loved it, and hated it. William Broyles, Jr., wrote an article in the November 1984 issue of *Esquire* titled "Why Men Love War." Some of his thoughts I have quoted here because he has captured the true feelings that I still have and I couldn't have written them better:

> Ask me, ask any man who had been to war about his experience, and chances are we'll say we don't want to talk about it—implying that we hated it so much, it was so terrible, that we would rather leave it buried. And it is no mystery why men hate war. War is ugly, horrible, evil, and it is reasonable for men to hate all that. But I believe that most men who have been to war would have to admit, if they are honest, that somewhere inside themselves

they loved it too, loved it as much as anything that has happened to them before or since. And how do you explain that to your wife, your children, your parents, or your friends?

That's why men in their sixties and seventies sit in their dens and recreation rooms around America and know that nothing in their life will equal the day they parachuted in St. Lô or charged the bunker in Okinawa. That's why veterans' reunions are invariably filled with boozy awkwardness, forced camaraderie ending in sadness and tears: you are together again, these are the men who were your brothers, but it's not the same, can never be the same. That's why when we returned from Vietnam we moped around, listless, not interested in anything or anyone. Something had gone out of our lives forever, and our behavior on returning was inexplicable except as the behavior of men who had lost a great, perhaps the great love of their lives, and had no way to tell anyone about it.[4]

Boyles continues:

Part of the love of war stems from it[s] being an experience of great intensity; its lure is the fundamental human passion to witness, to see things, what the Bible calls the lust of the eye, and the Marines in Vietnam called eye fucking. War stops time, intensifies experience to the point of a terrible ecstasy.... War offers endless exotic experiences, enough "I couldn't fucking believe its!" to last a lifetime.

War replaces the difficult gray areas of daily life with an eerie, serene clarity. In war you usually know who is your enemy and who is your friend, and are given means to dealing with both.[5]

Of course, the enduring emotion of war is comradeship. A comrade in arms is a man you can trust with anything, because you trust him with your life—the defining emotion that binds us.

And last, because of that love of war and comrades, I volunteered to return to Vietnam in 1967. Because I volunteered, I have "bragging rights." To paraphrase George C. Scott in the movie *Patton*: Thirty years from now when you are bouncing your grandson on your knee and he asks you what you did in the great Vietnam War, you won't have to tell him you were shoveling shit in Louisiana. I didn't shovel shit in Louisiana. I have done something that only a very small percentage of American men have: I have been in combat, I have done my duty, and I have survived.

I do not suggest that my story is any worse than another soldier's. I am confident that many saw much more horrible things than I did. I only want to note what this soldier's search for peace has entailed.

I was fortunate to have served in combat with two of the finest units in the history of the United States Army: The 173d Airborne Brigade (Separate) and the 1st Cavalry Division (Airmobile). I served with officers, noncommissioned officers, and enlisted men of the highest caliber. They were professional, knowledgeable, motivated, dedicated and proud. They cared for their country, their unit and each other. They supported each other in times of unbelievable stress and danger. They were America's finest.

It is too bad our politicians were not of the same caliber. Many brave men gave their lives only to be sold down the river by those in Washington, D.C.

And maybe that is the great lesson of Vietnam: Do not send American troops to fight a foreign war unless you plan on using every available means to win. A tie is not a win. To risk young American lives for anything less is sheer stupidity and should be considered treasonous. Every American life is precious, and our politicians should not risk even one unless it is to protect the United States or its real interests.

Obviously, with our forays into Iraq and Afghanistan, our politicians have not learned that "great lesson."

I crossed over many humps in Vietnam. I passed the test of combat at Hill 65 and earned membership in the 1/503. I passed the test of leadership as a company commander and platoon leader. I passed my own personal tests.

I am extremely proud of my service. I did my duty, as did those who served with me. America has never really come to grips with the Vietnam War and I still am haunted by it, but I did what my country asked. I am proud that when my country called me to go and serve, I answered that call.

Appendix 1

THE MEDAL OF HONOR

All during the morning and afternoon of 8 November 1965, as Charlie Company found itself under a constant and intense enemy fire, one man distinguished himself above all others: SP5 Lawrence Joel, Charlie Company's senior medic. Wounded twice in the leg, he hobbled about in the heaviest fighting to aid his fallen comrades.

Joel "crammed battle dressings into sucking chest wounds, jabbed morphine Syrettes to comfort those already drunk with pain, gave mouth-to-mouth resuscitation amid blood and vomit as he breathed life into the near dead. Every medic out there quit [sic] himself like a man, but this one was made of superior stuff. He had that indefinable quality that separates the great from the near great. Many a man on Hill 65 on 8 November 1965 can look back and say with pride that he is alive today because of the selfless gallantry of Specialist-Five Lawrence Joel."[1]

Joel's exploits on Hill 65 were not to go unheralded. SP4 Joe Diaz and seven others initiated, LTC Tyler recommended, and 18 months later President Lyndon Johnson bestowed upon Lawrence Joel, the nation's highest and most coveted combat award: the Medal of Honor.

Lawrence Joel became the first living black man since the Spanish-American War to receive the Medal of Honor.[2] The official citation reads as follows:

Name:	Lawrence Joel
	Specialist Sixth Class, U.S. Army
Rank & Organization:	Headquarters and Headquarters Company, 1st Battalion (Airborne), 503rd Infantry, 173rd Airborne Brigade
Place:	Republic of Vietnam
Date:	8 November 1965
Entered service at:	New York City, NY
Born:	22 February 1928, Winston-Salem, N.C.
G.O. No.:	G.O. No. 15, 5 April 1967.

For conspicuous gallantry and intrepidity at the risk of life above and beyond the call of duty. Sp6c. Joel demonstrated indomitable courage, determination, and professional skill when a numerically superior and well-concealed Viet Cong element launched a vicious attack which wounded or killed nearly every man in the lead squad of the company. After treating the men wounded by the initial burst of gunfire, he bravely moved forward to assist others who were wounded while proceeding to their objective. While moving from man to man, he was struck in the right leg by machine gun fire. Although painfully wounded his desire to aid his fellow soldiers transcended all personal feeling. He bandaged his own wound and self-administered morphine to deaden the pain enabling him to continue his dangerous undertaking. Through this period of time, he constantly shouted words of encouragement to all around him. Then, completely ignoring the warnings of others, and his pain, he continued his search for wounded, exposing himself to hostile fire; and as bullets dug up the dirt around him, he held plasma bottles high while kneeling completely engrossed in his life saving mission. Then, after being struck a second time and with a bullet lodged in his thigh, he dragged himself over the battlefield and succeeded in treating 13 more men before his medical supplies ran out. Displaying resourcefulness, he saved the life of one man by placing a plastic bag over a severe chest wound to congeal the blood. As one of the platoons pursued the Viet Cong, an insurgent force in concealed positions opened fire on the platoon and wounded many more soldiers. With a new stock of medical supplies, Sp6c. Joel again shouted words of encouragement as he crawled through an intense hail of gunfire to the wounded men. After the 24 hour battle subsided and the Viet Cong dead numbered four hundred and ten, snipers continued to harass the company. Throughout the long battle, Sp6c. Joel never lost sight of his mission as a medical aid man and continued to comfort and treat the wounded until his own evacuation was ordered. His meticulous attention to duty saved a large number of lives and his unselfish, daring example under most adverse conditions was an inspiration to all. Sp6c. Joel's profound concern for his fellow soldiers, at the risk of his life above and beyond the call of duty are in the highest traditions of the U.S. Army and reflect great credit upon himself and the Armed Forces of his country.

Appendix 2

Where Are They Now?

William Acebes joined the Army in January 1965 from Sacramento, California. After his first tour with the 173d he was assigned to the Ranger Department at Ft. Benning, Georgia. He would later spend two more tours in Vietnam. After 30 years active duty, Bill retired as a command sergeant major.

Bob Biedleman, to the best of my knowledge, never returned to the A 1/503 after being wounded on HUMP. We have lost track of him.

Lowell Bittrich retired as a lieutenant colonel after more than 20 years active duty. His paper "Battle on Hill 65," written in May 1966, was responsible for much of the information I have used in this manuscript. In addition, he has been available to me by email to answer any questions I might have. In particular, he is responsible for clarifying the unit that we encountered, contrary to what others had said.

Richard H. Boland (aka Rawhide 6) saw combat in World War II, Korea and then Vietnam. He spent more than 30 years on active duty and retired as a full colonel. He currently lives in Lakeport, California. His men still love and revere him.

Al Conetto left the Army in January 1970 after six years' service and 17 months in Vietnam. He was a company commander on his second tour with the 1st Air Cavalry Division. Although he wanted to be a career officer, the frustrations from Vietnam forced him to resign his commission. He received his MA in U.S. history in 1993 and has been writing this book for more than 20 years ago.

Walter B. Daniel (aka Diesel Stamp 6) served once more in Vietnam as an ARVN adviser after his initial tour ended. COL Daniel graduated from OCS in 1960. He retired as a full colonel after 35 years on active duty. COL Daniel made more than 500 parachute jumps in his career and was inducted into the Infantry Officer Candidate Hall of Fame in 1982. He was my idol and passed away on March 22, 1997.

Michael DeFrancesco entered the Army on March 5, 1962. He took basic and advanced infantry training at Ft. Dix, New Jersey. He went to the Infantry OCS program at Ft. Benning and was commissioned a 2LT on December 14, 1963. Mike left active duty on December 7, 1968, and returned to college at the University of Rhode Island. He graduated with a civil engineering degree and went to work in Providence, Rhode Island.

William "Bill" Delia enlisted in the Army from Augusta, Maine, on September 10, 1963. After he recovered from wounds suffered on HUMP he was assigned to Ft. Campbell, Kentucky, as a basic training cadre. He was honorably discharged on September 9, 1966. Bill went back to school and spent 22 years in the plastics industry. He then started his own communications company and moved to Virginia. He finally retired on December 31, 2006.

Jose "Joe" Diaz joined the Texas National Guard on December 6, 1955, in San Antonio, Texas, and the Regular Army on June 4, 1957. After leaving Vietnam in 1966, Joe was reassigned to the 50th Medical Detachment in Fort Polk, Louisiana. From here Joe applied for and was accepted into the Warrant Officer Flight Training Program in 1967. After completion of this course, he was sent to Vietnam for a second tour. Joe retired from the Army after 26 years' service in 1981. He continued his career in civilian aviation. He is now retired back in San Antonio.

John "Dutch" Holland entered the Army in 1960 from Nicoma Park, Oklahoma. After Operation HUMP Dutch volunteered to return to the 173d in April 1966. He spent a total of six years on active duty with one break in service. He spent his last year on active duty with C Company, 1st Special Forces. Dutch's civilian career was with the U.S. Postal Service. He currently lives in Oklahoma.

Lawrence Joel was awarded the Medal of Honor for his exploits on Hill 65 on November 8, 1965. He became the first living black man since the Spanish-American War to receive the Medal of Honor. When he was told that he had been recommended for the medal, Joel thought for a moment and said: "I sure hope I get it. That means my son can go to West Point." The arena in Winston-Salem, North Carolina, was named after him.

Henry "Sonny" Tucker grew up in Columbus, Mississippi, and was a member of the undefeated 1959 National College Football Championship team from the University of Southern Mississippi. Sonny served on active duty for more than 20 years and retired as a lieutenant colonel. He served as a district senior advisor in Vietnam under the legendary John Paul Vann, who was the subject of Neil Sheehan's book *A Bright and Shining Lie*. LTC Tucker was also XO in the 101st Airborne Division to GEN Colin Powell. He also graduated from Mid-America Baptist Theological Seminary and was minister of pastoral care at the 28,000-member Bellevue Baptist Church in Memphis, Tennessee.

John E. Tyler, our gutsy battalion commander, retired as a full colonel after 32 years on active duty. He turned 40 the day before HUMP started. COL Tyler entered the Army from Winona, Mississippi, on December 29, 1943. He went to OCS and was commissioned an infantry 2LT on April 23, 1947. He assumed command of 1/503 on August 4, 1965. He was the brigade S-3 for 15 months prior to that.

Ellis W. Williamson joined the 120th Regiment of the North Carolina National Guard prior to 1941. LT Williamson deployed with the 120th to Europe. At the end of World War II he was a lieutenant colonel and moved to the Regular Army in 1946. During the Korean War he helped plan and also participated in the Inchon landing. He was promoted to BG and organized the 173d on Okinawa. He led the unit to Vietnam in May 1965. He was promoted to major general and later returned to Vietnam as commanding general, 25th Infantry Division. MG Williamson retired from active duty in 1973. He passed away on January 28, 2007.

William Workman retired to Oklahoma as a command sergeant major. Bill would later become President of the Society of the 173d Airborne Brigade (Sep), forerunner to the current Association of the 173d Airborne Brigade. He retired as chief of police of Stonewall, Oklahoma, after 22 years' service, and he retired for good after 8 years as mayor of Stonewall.

Appendix 3

KEY PERSONNEL

1st Battalion, 503rd Infantry
Operation HUMP

Title	Name
Battalion Commander	LTC John E. Tyler
Executive Officer	MAJ Albert C. Butler
S-1	CPT Richard D. Chegar
S-2	MSG Thomas Clark (acting)
S-3	MAJ William L. Mitchell
S-4	CPT Pete Sharber
Company Commander, A	CPT Walter B. Daniel
1st platoon Leader	2LT David L. Ugland
2nd platoon Leader	1LT Bob Biedleman
3rd platoon Leader	1LT Al J. Conetto
Wpns Platoon Leader	1LT Bobby Oakes
Company Commander, B	CPT Lowell Bittrich
1st platoon Leader	1LT Mike DeFrancesco
2nd platoon Leader	1LT Bob Frakes
3rd platoon Leader	2LT Clair H. Thurston
Wpns Platoon Leader	1LT Edward F. Pleasants
Company Commander, C	CPT Henry B. Tucker
1st platoon Leader	2LT Sam Russ
2nd platoon Leader	1LT Ben Waller
3rd platoon Leader	LT James B. Shannon
Wpns Platoon Leader	1LT Phil Harper

Appendix 4

COMBAT AFTER ACTION REPORT

After an operation it is Army SOP to prepare a number of reports for higher headquarters. The report discusses where the action took place, when, the mission, commanders, force organization, supporting units, intelligence, execution, results and commander's analysis.

The report that follows is the actual After Action Report filed by Headquarters, 173d Airborne Brigade on 19 December 1965.

COMBAT OPERATIONS AFTER ACTION REPORT
173D ABN BDE (SEP) OPERATION 26-65 (HUMP)

Cover sheet for Army's after action report on Operation HUMP.

DEPARTMENT OF THE ARMY
HEADQUARTER 173D AIRBORNE BRIGADE (SEPARATE)
APO U.S. Forces 96250[1]

AVAB-SC   19 December 1965

SUBJECT: Combat Operations After Action Report (MACV/RCS/J3/32)

THRU: Commanding General
           1st Infantry Division
           APO U.S. Forces 96345

TO: Commander
           U.S. Military Assistance Command, Vietnam
           ATTN: MACJ34
           APO U.S. Forces 96243

In accordance with MACV Directive Number 335–8 the following report is submitted.

173d Airborne Brigade (Separate) Operation 28–65 (HUMP)

1. The 173d Abn Bde (Sep) OPORD 28–65 was issued at 011800H November 1965 outlining plans for a Search and Destroy Operation to be conducted in Tactical Area of Responsibility 28–65 in Tan Uyen and Cong Thanh Districts of Bien Hoa Province to find, fix and destroy or capture Viet Cong personnel, supplies and equipment. "HUMP" as the operation was named, marked the fifth time that the 173d has entered the Viet Cong Dominated "D" Zone in force and produced the heaviest single day's fighting of the war in Vietnam. The reporting officer is Brig Gen Ellis W. Williamson and the Task Organization and Task Force Commanders were as follows:

a. Brigade Headquarters and Staff (Brig Gen Ellis W. Williamson, Commanding) and Airforce ALO/Brigade Tactical Air Control Group remained at Bien Hoa.

b. Task Force 1/503-Lt Col John E. Tyler
   1st Battalion (Airborne), 503d Infantry
   One (1) RRU Team
   One (1) FAC Team
   One (1) Engr Squad

DOWNGRADING AT 3 YEAR INTERVALS
AUTOMATICALLY DECLASSIFIED AFER
12 Years
DOD DIR 5200.10 APPLIES

   Two (2) Vietnamese Police

c. Task Force 1/RAR—Lt Col I.R.W. Brumfield
   1st Battalion Royal Australian Regiment

Royal Australian Artillery Battery
One (1) RRU Team
One (1) FAC Team
Two (2) Vietnamese Police
   d. Task Force 3/319—Lt Col Lee E. Surut
A Battery, 3/319 Artillery
C Battery, 3/319, Artillery
Troop E/17 Cavalry
D Company, 16th Armor
One (1) RRU Team
One (1) Engineer Squad and Water Point
Security force from Admin Company
   e. U.S. Air Force provided Tactical Air Support to the Brigade.
   f. 145th Aviation Battalion provided helicopter Support.
   g. Special Forces conducted Operations to the NE of the 173d Bde TAOR from 6–9 November.

   2. Concept of Operations: The 173d Abn Bde (Sep) conducted Operation "HUMP" in five (5) phases (See Inclosure [*sic*] 1, Operations Overlay):
   a. Phase I-Fire support base (TF 3/319) moved by convoy to Position "ACE."
   b. Phase II—TF 1/RAR conducted Airmobile assault on LZ "JACK."
   c. Phase III—TF 1/503 conducted Airmobile assault on LZ "KING.
   d. Phase IV—Task Forces conducted Search and Destroy Operations in respective TAOR's.
   e. Phase V—All forces were extracted by combined helicopter lift and motor convoy.
   The 2nd Battalion, 503d Infantry assumed responsibility for the Base Camp TAOR effective 051200H November and was prepared to provide a company sized reaction force on two (2) hour notice or a battalion sized force on four (4) notice.
   Prior to D–Day a request to use Tear Gas during Operation "HUMP" was approved by MACV.

   3. INTELLIGENCE:
   a. Intelligence Prior to Operation:
   Intelligence prior to the operation revealed that the area surrounding the junction of the Song Be and Dong Nai Rivers was a VC stronghold. Order of battle reports had placed the home bases of Q762 Regiment and D.800 Battalion in or near the TAOR. It was estimated that up to 3 VC Battalions were in or near the TAOR, and the Viet Cong had a capability of massing up to 3 Main Force Regiments and 7 separate battalions, (for a total

of approximately 8,500 men within 48 hours). Their armaments consisted of the new family of Soviet and Chicom weapons; to include 81mm and 82mm mortars, 57mm and 75mm recoilless rifles and 50 caliber and 30 caliber machine guns. In addition, interpretation of aerial photography disclosed several possible locations of bunkers, trenches, and weapons emplacements.

    b. Enemy Situation During Operation:

    On 5 November 1965, the 1/503 Infantry conducted a heliborne assault into the area (War Zone "D"). From the 5th through the 7th, only light resistance was encountered and the battalion destroyed several bunkers, huts, and booby traps. On the evening of the 7th, a SPAR report was received which indicated a VC unit of unknown size, was located approximately 500 meters west of the 1/503 Infantry's position. Patrols were dispatched and verified the presence of enemy forces in that location; exact size of these forces was not determined. On the morning of the 8th, Company C became heavily engaged when approaching this area. Initial strength of the VC unit was estimated to be a reinforced company; well armed, to include M-79's and machine guns. During the fighting which continued for 6 hours, the 1/503 Infantry reevaluated the then estimated VC strength of a Battalion reinforced, to a Regiment. Four distinct types of uniforms were observed; green, khaki, grey jungle fatigues, and black peasant dress. (This indicated that both Main Force and Local Force units were encountered.) By the next day when the battalion was able to obtain a VC body count, the VC had stripped their dead of all clothing and equipment. A number of documents were captured; one of which noted a unit designation of C505. (This designation has been previously used as a cover number by a battalion organic to the Main Force Regiment 271.) Final VC body count was 403; however, one area struck by artillery and TAC air and known to contain a concentration of VC, was not accessed.

    In conjunction with the 1/503 [words were marked over and undecipherable] 1/RAR conducted a search and destroy mission to the south of the junction of the Dong Nai and Song Be Rivers. Until 8 November, only light resistance from snipers and small groups; (estimated to be squad size) were encountered. On the 8th, the 3rd Platoon A Company encountered an estimated company of well dug in armed VC. (The VC were armed with at least 3 machine guns and 5 sub-machine guns.) Documents captured, and the statement of a dying VC prisoner, related the presence of elements of C.306, a VC Province Mobile Battalion, and a Local Force Platoon, C-270. Three machine guns were encountered, and the VC used excellent fire and maneuver.

    During this operation, the Brigade's recently formed, Long Range Reconnaissance patrols were utilized. Two-five man teams were injected into an area south of the Dong Nai River. Their mission was to observe suspected routes and report VC activity. These patrols sighted and reported several small groups of local VC guerrillas, but no large concentrations were observed in their area.

c. Fortifications:

Fortifications found in the area of 1/503 Infantry, included weapons pits, trenches terminating in hollowed out ant hills, two-man defensive positions with 30 inches of overhead cover and punji traps. The village was heavily trenched and each hut had a tunnel used as an air raid shelter. The entrances to this village was [sic] mined and booby trapped.

d. Terrain:

The terrain found in the 1/RAR operational area was open paddy land in the vicinity of the north south trail along their west flank. As the unit progressed in an easterly direction, the paddy land gave way to small hill masses seldom reaching an elevation of over 70 feet. The vegetation consisted of rice paddies on the west flank but low scrub growth was evidenced as the unit moved generally east. Once the small hill masses were reached, secondary jungle vegetation was encountered. The canopy level was approximately 30 feet to 40 feet in height but open in many places. The undergrowth consisted of thick low hanging vines and entanglements, but observation was good up to approximately 50 meters. Cover and concealment were excellent and fields of fire were generally good. The critical terrain features were the hill masses which overlooked the avenues of approach and the numerous east-west trails leading into the area. The terrain found in the 1/503 operational area consisted of low paddy land initially. As the unit progressed north and northeast, small hill masses were encountered. (These hill masses seldom exceeded 70 feet in height.) The vegetation found in the helicopter landing zone area consisted of tall elephant grass and reeds which reached a height of six to ten feet. As the unit moved generally west and northwest, vegetation changed to thick undergrowth in the vicinity [of] the stream beds which limited observation to 5–10 meters; as the streams were crossed the undergrowth became sparse and observation was good up to 50 meters. The canopy was thick, virtually without openings, and reached a height of 200 to 250 feet. Cover and concealment were excellent and fields of fire generally good. The small hill masses were considered critical terrain in that they overlooked the avenues of approach into the area. Numerous trails were found leading from the hill masses to the Song Dong Nai and Song Be Rivers.

4. EXECUTION:

a. D–Day (5 November 1965): Implementation of the 173d Abn Bde (Sep) OPord 28–65 began at 050530H when E/17 Cavalry crossed the Start

Point vicinity YT 023144 to clear the route of march for TF 3/319, the fire support element, to it's [sic] position "ACE" vicinity YT 113222. TF 3/319 crossed the S.P. at 050600H and closed into "ACE" at 050650H with negative contact. During the move forward convoy security was furnished by E/17 Cavalry, D/16 Armor, TAC Air and Armed Helicopter. The Landing Zone preparations scheduled to commence at 050715H were delayed for 1½ hours because of bad weather. As a result of an intelligence report that two VC battalions were waiting to ambush the heliborne forces going into LZ "QUEEN," it was decided that the Alternate LZ "JACK" vicinity YT 134257 would be used. The suspected VC locations were hit with the air sorties already on station for preparation of LZ "QUEEN" and by Artillery. By 050845H another twelve (12) sorties were on station and the air preparation began on LZ "JACK," followed by Artillery and Armed helicopter preparations. Commencing at 050930H 1/RAR conducted its hellebore [sic] assault into LZ "JACK," closing by 051021H with negative contact. The units immediately moved to secure the East Bank of the Dong Nai River opposite LZ "KING," vicinity YT 139275. Shortly thereafter, the Royal Australian Battery equipped with the light weight Italian Howitzer helilifted by UH-1D's into firing positions vicinity LZ "JACK."

The 1/503 Inf, also preceded by intense LZ Preparations, began the assault on LZ "KING" at 051245H. During the landing helicopter received ground fire at YT 122245, but no contact was made by the ground troops. By 051335H the landing of 1/503d was complete and they and the 1/RAR moved to secure battalion base positions. After CP's were established the two battalions used the remainder of the day to clear their immediate areas. No contact was made, however several VC camps and positions were discovered. At 051500H 1/503 found a group of fortified positions North and South of a potential LZ at YT 1328. 1/RAR discovered a VC camp with five (5) huts, tunnels, chickens and five (5) grenades vicinity YT 145278, and at 051600 entered ZAN CAY XOAI village vicinity YT 1427 with appeared to have been vacant for approximately one (1) week. At the end of D–Day unit CP's were located as follows:

1/503d	–	YT 149286
1/RAR	–	YT 139258
3/319	–	YT 115226

At 050630H two Long Range Reconnaissance Patrols (five (5) men each) were landed by helicopters on LZ's vicinity YT 153183 and YT 190235 respectively. The patrols [sic] primary mission was to observe and report VC activity and when possible direct air strikes and artillery fires against them.

b. D+1 (6 November 1965): On D+1 TF 1/503d continued to search in sector using platoon sized patrols from three company bases at YT 138294, YT129291, and YT 126286. At 060950H two VC camps with trenches and tunnels were destroyed vicinity YT 135299 and YT 144290. Two wells and a water point were discovered at YT 135295 and YT 135302, respectively, and were destroyed. At 061035H three (3) booby trapped VC huts were discovered and destroyed at YT 133305. Two (2) VC gas masks were discovered in one of the huts. At 061055 an observation tower was discovered and destroyed vicinity YT 123293 and at 061120H tear gas was used in a tunnel system vicinity YT 135307, but no VC were present. The tunnels were then destroyed.

TF 1/RAR continued to search in its TAOR East of the Dong Nai River with several light contacts during the day. At 061030H sniper fire was received vicinity YT 1426 and YT 1424 with no casualties. About the same time a VC camp of six (6) huts with a tunnel network was destroyed vicinity YT 161277. At 061330H a small VC force was encountered vicinity YT 155283 with no casualties and five (5) VC being captured. At 061515H contact was made with three (3) VC vicinity YT 139268. The VC fled to the West with casualties unknown. The heaviest contact of the day came at 061705H when 1/RAR encountered a VC force of unknown size and killed three (3) VC, capturing their weapons and one (1) claymore mine.

The Long Range Reconnaissance patrol located at YT 190235 was extracted by helicopter at 061030H. The patrol located at YT 153183 continued to observe and report VC activity.

At the end of D＋1 CP locations were as follows:

1/503	–	YT 144291
1/RAR	–	YT 135257
3/319	–	YT 115227

c. D+2 (7 November 1965): Operation HUMP continued with TF 1/503d moving to a new base position vicinity YT 110305 and continuing to search in sector. At 070955 a VC tunnel system was located and destroyed vicinity YT 140301. The portion of the "Ho Chi Minh" Trail just North-east of the confluence of the Song Be and Dong Nai River, long reputed to be a heavily-used VC supply route, revealed no indication of recent traffic. Signs of usage which had appeared in aerial photographs were actually the results of rain water erosion on the open trail. At 071650H a rice bin containing a small quantity of rice was destroyed vicinity YT 109313.

On D+3 1/RAR continue [*sic*] to search its sector vicinity YT 1626, YT 1624, YT 1522, and YT 1622 with negative contact.

Late in the afternoon the Bde S2 informed TF 1/503 that confirmed intelligence indicated that a VC force was located less than 2000 meters to the west of the battalion positions. Small patrols were dispatched just before darkness. They soon made contact with the enemy and fixed his position before returning the battalions perimeter. As the night settled the stage was set for the climatic events of 8 November. CP locations were as follows:

1/503	–	YT 112306
1/RAR	–	YT 135257
3/319	–	YT 115227

d. D+3 (8 November 1965) on D+3 the 173d Bde fought and won a major battle. The initial contact was made as C/1/503 moved toward what intelligence reports and patrols of the previous day had indicated as a VC installation. At approximately 080800H the right flank platoon came upon an enemy fortified area. The enemy and our troops exchanged a heavy volume of small arms and automatic weapons fire. The platoon was soon joined by the remainder of C Company, and it became evident as the fight progressed that they had engaged a battalion or larger size force. The fighting was frequently at eye-ball contact and hand to hand in an extremely dense jungle area. The VC attempted to envelope C Company's flanks, and B Company was immediately moved in from the Northeast. After a period of intense fighting, B Company smashed through the enemy circle around C Company and secured its right flank. C Company again found its open flank being enveloped. At this time A Company was committed, attacking toward the enemy's left flank. C Company continued to break the VC encirclement. Shortly after noon B and C Companies consolidated their position and directed intense artillery fire and air strikes against the VC. The enemy continued to make futile assaults on B and C Companies, suffering severe losses. It should be noted that during the morning, fighting was at such close quarters that supporting fires generally had to be employed in depth rather than in close support. The forward area of the enemy was relentlessly chewed up by small arms fire while his rear was pounded by air and artillery. As soon as it became evident that this was a large VC force, the decision was made to commit 2/503 to the Northeast of the VC positions to relieve pressure on 1/503 and to cut off VC Escape routes. The request for personnel carrying helicopters could not be honored because adequate numbers of helicopters were not available, therefore, 1/503 continued the fight without additional ground support.

The main battle ended about mid-afternoon with sniper fire and sporadic machine-gun fire during the late afternoon and night around the perimeter of A and B Companies. The Battalion CP, located about 1000 meters to the east, was brushed several times during the night. It was later determined that there were VC elements withdrawing from the battle area.

TF 1/RAR continued to search in sector South of the Dong Nai River with no contact during the morning. Shortly after noon one (1) VC dressed in black and green uniform was killed vicinity YT 177235 and his weapon, a Chicom carbine, was captured. At 081620H two VC were killed and their weapons captured vicinity YT 170234. Shortly thereafter, 1/RAR engaged a well dug-in enemy force estimated to number 100 men vicinity YT 1722. A heavy fire fight followed with four (4) VC killed before the VC broke contact.

At the end of the day CP locations were as follows:

1/503	–	YT 112306
1/RAR	–	YT 135257
3/319	–	YT 115227

e. D+4 (9 November 1965): During the morning of D+4, the primary concern was to determine enemy locations and evacuate friendly casualties from the battle area of 8 November. During the night and early morning of 9 November the troops of 1/503d worked feverishly to cut a helicopter landing zone out of the dense jungle. Power saws were lowered into the area and trees up to 250 feet tall and six feet in diameter were cut down. A funnel 250 feet deep and approximately 80 feet in diameter was cut into the jungle. A great feat of skill and courage was performed by Army and Air Force helicopter pilots as they maneuvered their planes in such a restricted area to evacuate casualties.

Throughout the day patrols continued to operate in the battle area, searching for VC forces and counting the enemy dead. Only light contact was made and a total of 391 VC bodies were counted in the immediate vicinity. The remainder of the VC forces broke contact.

During the morning the Special Forces Survey team was extracted from its area Northeast of the Bde TAOR. At 091300H the Recon Platoon 1/503d, which was located along the river to protect the Bn Rear, was extracted from LZ vicinity YT 139315 and returned to Bien Hoa. When this was completed, extraction of the remainder of the Bde began with 1/503 using LZ at YT 111308 and TF 1/RAR using LZ at YT 136260. During this extraction the flexibility of this organization was dramatically demonstrated. The 1/503 LZ could accept only three helicopters at a time. One helicopter damaged a rotor blade upon landing and blocked the LZ from further use. The extraction of 1/503 was temporarily delayed and the airlift was diverted to the Australian Artillery which began its lift-out in a matter of minutes. By the time the Artillery was out, a new helicopter blade had been flown into the 1/503 LZ, the helicopter was repaired, and the lift out of 1/503d continued. Pilots of the helicopter lift reported receiving light sniper fire from areas surrounding the LZ. As darkness began to fall, 1/RAR was extracted from its LZ, completing at 091900H. Immediately thereafter, TF 3/319 moved from position "ACE" back to base positions, closing at 092235H and ending Bde Operation 28–65 (HUMP). During the move E/17 Cavalry fired upon and sank two enemy sampans on the Dong Nai River, killing five (5) VC.

5. SUPPORTING FORCES:

    a. Task Force 3/319 Artillery and Royal Australian Artillery Battery.

        (1). Size of force: Two (2) six (6) gun and one (1) four (4) gun 105mm howitzer batteries.

        (2). How and When Employed:

            (a). Preparatory fires on Landing Zones "JACK" and "KING" on 5 November 1965.

            (b). On call missions from 5–9 November 1965.

            (c). Harassing and interdiction fires from 5–9 November 1965.

            (d). Quick reaction fires on VC locations established by intelligence elements from 5–9 November 1965.

            (e). Suppressive fires during and after extraction on 9 November 1965.

        (3). Results: During Operation "HUMP" the artillery fired a total of 343 missions expending 5252 rounds. Preparatory fires on landing zones and harassing and interdiction fires were very successful. Only light contacts were made during the heliborne assaults and at night. As always, the effectiveness of on call missions was difficult to assess. Effective destruction of VC camps and installations was observed but only estimates can be made of VC killed or wounded by artillery. During the height of the 1/503d engagement on 8 November which lasted four to five hours, only six (6) missions could be fired because of the close proximity of friendly troops to VC locations. However, almost 900 rounds were expended on these missions and numerous VC casualties were certainly inflicted by the Artillery.

        (4). Timeliness: Because of coordination effected in the Brigade Fire Coordination Center between Artillery, Army Air, and Air Force elements, the timeliness of Artillery fires was excellent. Rapid reaction to enemy intelligence continued to be effected during this operation.

    b. D Company, 16th Armor:

        (1). Size of force: Five (5) M-56 SPAT'S eleven (11) M-113 APC's, and four (4) 4.2 Inch Mortar Carriers.

        (2). How and When Employed:

(a). Convoy security for TF 3/319 motor march to Position "ACE" on 5 November 1965 and back to Bien Hoa on 9 November 1965.

(b). Security of TF 3/319 in Position "ACE" from 5–9 November 1965.

(c). Conducted road reconnaissance Northeast from position "ACE" to vicinity YT 133255 on 6 November 1965.

(d). The mortar platoon fired a total of 274 rounds during the operation.

(3). Results: Excellent. It is felt that the mobility and firepower of this company is a detriment to VC attack. The road reconnaissance of 6 Nov produced much valuable information on the trafficability of the road Northeast of position "ACE" and of several possible bridge by-passes.

(4). Timeliness: N/A

c. Army Air:

(1). Size of Force: The 145th Aviation Battalion, A Company, 82nd Aviation Battalion, 173d Aviation Platoon, 74th Aviation Company, 61st Aviation Company, and the 57th Medical Detachment gave Army Air Support during this operation.

(2). How and When Employed:

(a). Heliborne assault of TF 1/RAR and TF 1/503 on 5 November 1965.

(b). Armed helicopter support from 5–9 November 1965.

(c). Aerial Resupply from 5–9 November 1965.

(d). Airborne Radio Relay support from 5–9 November 1965.

(e). Command and Liaison support from 5–9 November 1965.

(f). Medical evacuation support from 5–9 November 1965.

(3). Results: During this operation Army Air flew a total of 1747 sorties for a total of 505 hours. The results produced were excellent as indicated by the following examples:

(a). Once again the flexibility and responsiveness of Army Aviation was confirmed in the heliborne assaults on 5 November and extraction on 9 November. In both cases a last minute change of plans was required. Army Air support reacted in an excellent manner and continued the mission with no delay.

(b). Unit resupply was accomplished when requested in all cases.

(c). Medical evacuation missions were accomplished as rapidly as possible. On this operation assistance was required from Air Force H-43 Helicopters (See paragraph 5,D.)

(d). Communications were maintained at all times between the Bde CP and TF Headquarters.

(4). Timeliness: See 5,C, (3) above.

d. U.S. Air Force:

(1). Quantity of Force: During Operation HUMP a total of 117 Tactical Air Sorties were flown expending 158.5 tons of Ordnance. 33 Forward Air Controller sorties for a total of 88 hours flying time were flown and 60 Medical Evacuation sorties were flown by Air Force H-43 Helicopters.

(2). How and When Employed:

(a). Tac air was utilized for convoy cover, preparations on two landing zones for the heliborne assault, and for pre-planned or on call missions throughout the Operation.

(b). Flare ships were on call nightly during the operation.

(c). An airborne FAC was available at all times either in the air over the operational area, or on strip alert at Bien Hoa. Ground FAC teams were also furnished for each Infantry Task Force.

(d). Air Force H-43 Helicopters were utilized on 8 and 9 November to evacuate casualties from the dense jungle of the operational area.

(3). Results: Air Force support during Operation "HUMP" was excellent as indicated by the following examples:

(a). The VC made no attempt to attack the motor march to and from Position "ACE."

(b). The flexibility and accuracy of the TAC air preparations were excellent. When it was decided on short notice to both delay the initial landing and then to use the alternate LZ "JACK," the TAC Air reacted quickly and efficiently. At the last moment an intelligence report indicated that a large enemy force was just south of the primary LZ. The twelve USAF planes that were aloft for the LZ Preparation were called down on the reported forces. Twelve more planes were called up from ground alert and the preparation on the alternate LZ was completed in accordance with the revised schedule. The preparations were on target and effective as only light contact was made during the assault.

(c). During the major battle by 1/503d on 8 November a total of 36 TAC air sorties were expended. Because of the close proximity of friendly forces to the VC locations, the air support was generally employed in depth, rather than inclose [sic]. On several occasions when friendly forces consolidated their positions and called the air support in close the accuracy and effectiveness was [sic] outstanding. It is not possible to estimate the number of VC killed by air, but there undoubtedly was a great many.

(d). The Airborne and ground FAC's used during this operation were very effective, resulting in timely and accurate support by the Air Force.

(e). The Crews of the H-43 Air Rescue Helicopters did an outstanding job during medical evacuation operations on 8 and 9 November.

(4). Timeliness: See 5, d, 3 above.

(5). Air Request Net Utilized: A preplanned air request net was utilized during Operation "HUMP." Requests were initiated by the commander on the ground, sent to the Brigade Tactical Air Control Group (TACG) by the ground FAC or through the Airborne FAC and then to III Corps. Direct Air Support Center (DASC). On occasion missions were generated at Bde level from intelligence information. If a strike was requested when the FAC and TAC Air were both Airborne, no further coordination was required and the strike was conducted immediately.

(6). Air-Ground Marking System: In all cases targets for TAC Air were marked with White Phosphorous rockets by the Airborne FAC.

6. ADMINISTRATIVE MATTERS:

a. Supply: At the beginning of this operation a Brigade Supply Operation Center (BSOC) was opened at Bien Hoa Air Base and the Brigade Logistical Operations Center (LOC) was opened in the Bde Base position. Representatives from each unit engaged in the operation were located at the BSOC and LOC to act on resupply requests and to prepare the items for delivery. During this operation a total of 278 sorties were flown to resupply units not accessible by road. Artillery Ammunition for the RAA Battery was delivered by CV-2 (Caribou) Low Level Extraction (LOLEX) while the Infantry Task Forces were resupplied exclusively by HU-1 helicopters and TF 3/319 by road convoy. A water point was operational in the TF 3/319 area throughout the operation.

b. Medical: The medical chain for Operation "HUMP" consisted of the following links:

(1). Unit aid men accompanied all units, platoon size and larger.

(2). Each Battalion Surgeon operated an aid station in the vicinity of the Battalion Command Post throughout the Operation.

(3). Medical evacuation was accomplished by helicopter in all cases.

(4). Wounded personnel were evacuated either to the 3rd Mobile Army Surgical Hospital (MASH) or to Brigade Clearing Station depending on the severity of the wound.

(5). Personnel treated who could not return to duty were kept in the 3rd MASH or Brigade Holding.

(6). All personnel and units in the medical chain are to be commended on the outstanding job done during this operation. Their prompt and correct actions undoubtedly saved the lives of numerous Bde personnel.

c. Transportation: Task Force 1/503d and 1/RAR moved to and from the operational area by helicopter while TF 3/319 moved by motor convoy. No administrative problems were encountered.

d. Communications: All communications during Operation "HUMP" were established using organic equipment. By using RC-292 antennaes [sic] in the Brigade CP and PRC-25 radios in the operational area, radio communications were maintained with all Task Force Headquarters and between ground units. Wire communications were used within TF 3/319 at all times and to a limited extent within the Infantry Task Forces at night. An Airborne radio relay was available at all times in case of radio communications problems.

7. COMMANDERS ANALYSIS: The 173d Airborne Brigade (Sep) Operation 28–65 (HUMP) conducted in Tan Uyen and Dong Thanh Districts of Bien Hoa Province from 5 to 9 November 1965 was by far the Brigade's most successful operation. On 8 November the Brigade's 1st Battalion (Airborne) 503d Infantry met and destroyed a Viet Cong main line regiment and sent its remnants fleeing into the jungle leaving their dead behind. The enemy kill, by body count, came to 403. This was the largest kill, by the smallest unit, in the shortest time in the war in Vietnam to date. The Brigade continued to simultaneously and effectively exercise its three most important capabilities of Intelligence Gathering, Tactical Operations and Civic Actions.

a. Intelligence Gathering: In all cases intelligence information received was analyzed and reacted upon immediately. Three examples are as follows:

(1). On D–Day a report was received which indicated that a large VC force was waiting in ambush around one of the Brigade's primary landing zones. Since it was possible that the report was correct and time was of essence, the decision was made to use the Alternative LZ and the suspected VC locations were hit by Air and Artillery.

(2). A Viet Cong that was killed by 1/RAR was carrying a plan for an attack on an outpost in the Bien Hoa Air Base area. Appropriate action was immediately taken to insure [sic] that any attacking force would be ambushed and destroyed. The same VC carried a diary which indicated the presence of a VC regiment somewhere in the Bde TAOR.

(3). A SPAR Report received on 7 November indicated that a large VC installation was located in the vicinity of TF 1/503d. Patrols from 1/503 made contact with the force late on 7 November and set the stage for the battle of 8 November 1965. It is believed that this force is the same as the one referred to in the VC diary in 7, (a), (2) above.

b. Tactical Operations: The tactical elements of the Brigade did an outstanding job during this operation. As the search of the TAOR was accomplished, ground and air forces were used very effectively to keep the VC off balance. Until the battle of 8 November the enemy had engaged in only limited harassing actions over widely scattered areas. Once the enemy was pinpointed, he was out maneuvered, out-fought, and severely beaten. The results of Operation "HUMP" are as follows:

(1). U.S. Forces   KHA—Forty-nine (49)
                                       WHA—Eighty-three (83)
                                       MIA—None
                                       CAPTURED—None
                                       WEAPONS LOST—None
                                       EQUIPMENT LOST—None

(2). Australian Forces   KHA—One (1)
                                       WHA—Six (6)
                                       MIA—One (1) (Presumed dead)
                                       CAPTURED—None
                                       WEAPONS LOST—None
                                       EQUIPMENT LOST—None

(3). New Zealand Forces: KHA—None
                                       WHA—None
                                       MIA—None
                                       CAPTURED—None
                                       WEAPONS LOST—None
                                       EQUIPMENT LOST—None

(4). Viet Cong Loses: KIA—403 (body count) 200 (Possible Additional)
                                       CAPTURED—Five (5)
                                       WEAPONS LOST—One (1) East German 7.9 LMG
                                                           One (1) French 7.5 LMG
                                                           One (1) MAT 49 (9mm)
                                                           One (1) U.S. Browning Automatic Rifle
                                       EQUIPMENT LOST—1000 rounds of assorted small arms ammunition, forty (40) magazines from ChiCom 7.62 LMG, misc. field gear.

c. Civic Actions: It is characteristic of this war that while the battle raged a few miles away, the supporting artillery was engaged in civic action operations in an attempt to win the people of the area for the Government of Vietnam. The civic action teams worked in the villages around position

"ACE," giving medical or dental aid to 258 civilian patients and distributing 250 pds of food to needy families.

    d. Conclusions and Lessons Learned:

        (1). Conclusions:

            (a). On 8 November the 173d Abn Bde (Sep) encountered and destroyed a Viet Cong main line regiment in War Zone "D," just North of Bien Hoa, RVN.

            (b). The flexibility of this Brigade and its supporting forces was demonstrated on several occasions during this operation. Examples include the following:

                i. Last minute decision to use the Alternate Landing Zone on D–Day and the simultaneous expenditure and immediate replacement of TAC Air on hand for LZ Preparation.

                ii. Tactical maneuvers accomplished by 1/503 and 1/RAR during the Operation and Medical Evacuation Operations on 8 and 9 November.

                iii. Extraction of the Brigade on 9 November rather than 10 November as originally planned from four (4) separate extraction zones (One of which was constructed by the ground forces). To further complicate matters, one helicopter broke down on the extraction zone of 1/503. The extraction operation was immediately shifted to the RAA Battery until the helicopter could be repaired.

            (c). The portion of the "Ho Chi Minh" Trail just northwest of the confluence of the Song Be and Dong Nai Rivers, long reputed to be a heavily used Viet Cong supply route, revealed no indications of recent traffic.

            (d). All intelligence information derived before and during an operation must be fully exploited, recorded, analyzed and acted on immediately. Proper reaction to intelligence information on this operation enabled the Brigade to fix and destroy a VC regiment.

            (e). The open area (just North of LZ KING) was found to be surrounded by recently prepared fortified positions, that could be used by the VC to ambush any heliborne force landing in that area.

            (f). This operation was the Brigade's first battle where it appeared that the majority of enemy casualties were caused by rifle and machine gun fire, rather than by mortar, artillery and air. Interviews with Bde individual riflemen indicated that they fired from 150–300 rounds from their M-16 rifles during the battle of 8 November and often saw the enemy fall after being hit by their fire. Machine gunners were also quite active. Both of these facts are dramatic reversals over World War II post battle analyses.

(g). The M-16 rifle performed well during the battle with relatively few stoppages experienced. The trouble that was experienced can be attributed to an accumulation of carbon in the chamber. This has resulted from a lack of chamber brushes and ruptured cartridge extractors which are urgently needed for M16 rifles.

(h). In several instances flame throwers could have been used by 1/503 however, the problem of getting the weapon into the area in time was prohibitive. Flame Thrower Teams are available with the Support Battalion and are being trained in repelling [*sic*] from helicopters into operational area.

(i). A recurring problem is for the man on the ground to identify his location. Marking rounds to be fired from the M-79 are urgently needed.

(j). The concept of attaching a FAC team to each infantry battalion to assist the Airborne FAC in the control and direction of strike aircraft and to advise the ground commandeer in the planning and execution of tactical air support is mandatory and has proven exceptionally effective.

(k). The air preparation of LZ KING for the assault of TF 1/503d consisted of napalm. Bombs could not be used because 1/RAR was located directly across the river.

(l). The two way Intelligence/Admin/Logistics Net employed during this operation functioned well.

(m). Long Range Patrols were used in conjunction with this operation. This was their first use within the Bde in combat a great distance from the main force. They made several sightings and gained valuable intelligence and experience by testing operational procedures.

(2). Lessons Learned:

(a). During any extraction it is imperative to know how many troops remain in the objective area and where they are located. During the conduct of extraction at night, this becomes even more important to preclude leaving personnel in the pick-up area and to insure [*sic*] that supporting Artillery and Air can be pulled in close to the perimeter. To mark LZ's at night, lights should be used which are directional in nature, allowing easy visibility by helicopter pilots and negating observation by VC in surrounding areas.

(b). In the dense jungle terrain of RVN most enemy contacts are made at distances of 15 to 30 meters. Once contact is made with an enemy having automatic weapons the contact force is relatively glued to its position and it is difficult to pull them back to allow heavy fire support to be brought to bear on enemy front line forces. It was proposed that on future approach marches approximately five fire teams of five men each precede the main body by 100 to 200 meters. In this manner the minimum of forces will be committed when contact is made, enabling the maximum freedom for maneuver of the main body.

(c). The difficult problem for the battalion commander after contact is to determine where all his forces are located before committing any more forces to movement or using his heavy fire support. The element in contact must also be given time to develop the situation before the decision is made to maneuver other elements or use the heavy fire support. Whenever the situation cannot be developed without excessive personnel losses the most effective approach is to break contact, strike the enemy with air and artillery, with an immediate follow-up by friendly maneuvering. If we can take an objective by fire power, we should do so.

(d). It is an advantage to set up a battalion base and operate from that base rather than constantly move the battalion as a whole. This procedure expedites logistical support and command and control. Heavier weapons such as 4.2 inch mortars can also be delivered into the base if needed. This procedure has been found to be an excellent way to search an area.

(e). On occasion it may be necessary to stop everything in order to carefully adjust artillery and TAC Air to place it exactly where it is needed. The fire often must be walked to the desired location. Use bullets and bombs, not bodies, to win battles.

(f). Preparation of landing zones in jungle terrain continues to be a problem. During this operation it was discovered that personnel with experience as a lumberjack produce five times the results of inexperienced personnel. Therefore a special team for LZ preparations is being organized and trained within this Brigade. This team will have necessary equipment and will be on call during operations to rappel from helicopters into the proposed LZ.

(g). The Air Force H-43 helicopters with its 200 foot lowering cable can be used effectively, but slowly, to evacuate personnel from jungle areas where no LZ is available. A cable hoist for the UH-1 helicopter is urgently needed.

(h). Experience has been that in requesting a Tactical Area of Responsibility (TAOR) for a specific operation it must be larger than the area of maneuver to include areas from which action may be generated. Fires must not be restricted to the maneuver area.

e. Summary: On 8 November 1965, when heavily engaged by overwhelming numbers, the leadership and will to fight demonstrated by the officers and men of this Brigade proved the superiority of the American

Paratrooper beyond any question of doubt. They decisively defeated a determined and numerically superior enemy force.

FOR THE COMMANDER:

LEO J. MERCIER
2d Lt, AGC
Asst Adj Gen

2 Incl
as
Distribution:
    2—MAC J3
    1—MAC J2
    1—MAC T
    1—CG, USARV
    1—CG, 1st Inf Div

Appendix 5

PRESIDENTIAL UNIT CITATION

(The "Distinguished Unit Citation" was redesignated the "Presidential Unit Citation" by Executive Order 10694, 10 January 1957. Why we were awarded the DUC, even though it was not an official award, is beyond me.)

GENERAL ORDERS

HEADQUARTERS
DEPARTMENT OF THE ARMY
No. 40   Washington, D.C., *31 October 1966*[1]

	Section
DISTINGUISHED UNIT CITATION—Award	I
PRESIDENTIAL UNIT CITATION—Award	II
VALOROUS UNIT CITATION—Award	III
MERITORIOUS UNIT COMMENDATION—Awards	IV

I__*DISTINGUISHED UNIT CITATION.* Award of the Distinguished Unit Citation by the President of the United States of America to the following units of the Armed Forces of the United States is confirmed as accordance with paragraph 194, AR 672-5-1. The text of the citation as announced by President Lyndon B. Johnson on 20 June 1966 reads as follows:

"By virtue of the authority vested in me as President of the United States and as Commander-in-Chief of the Armed Forces of the United States I have today (20 June 1966) awarded the Distinguished Unit Citation (First Oak Leaf Cluster) for extraordinary heroism to:

THE 1ST BATTALION (AIRBORNE), 503D INFANTRY, 173D
AIRBORNE BRIGADE (SEPARATE) UNITED STATES ARMY
and the
Attached Units___
HEADQUARTERS AND HEADQUARTERS COMPANY
COMPANY A, COMPANY B, COMPANY C
of the
1ST BATTALION (AIRBORNE), 503D INFANTRY, 173D

AIRBORNE BRIGADE (SEPARATE)
THE 1ST TEAM OF THE 3D RADIO RELAY UNIT
THE COMPOSITE SQUAD OF THE 173D ENGINEER COMPANY

The foregoing companies of and units attached to THE 1ST BATTAL-ION (AIRBORNE), 503D INFANTRY, 173D AIRBORNE BRIGADE (SEP-ARATE) distinguished themselves by extraordinary heroism in action against hostile forces in the vicinity of Bien Hoa, Republic of Vietnam, on 8 November 1965. The morning after the Battalion had conducted a search operation and learned from patrols that a strong hostile element was in the general area, COMPANY C, the lead Company, encountered a well-entrenched and camouflaged Viet Cong force. When the insurgents opened fire with a volume of automatic weapons fire, the United States forces retaliated. As the battle grew in intensity and it became evident that COMPANY C had engaged a battalion-size Viet Cong element which attempted to surround the flanks of the American unit, COMPANY B was committed to secure the right flank of COMPANY C. Simultaneously, elements of COMPANY A attacked the left flank of the insurgent force. Although COMPANY B met strong resistance and fought at close range in a dense jungle area, it succeeded in penetrating the hostile circle around COMPANY C. Then, as COMPANY B's open flank was being enveloped, the brave men of this Company broke a hostile encirclement for the second time. Despite the constant Viet Cong assaults, their continual attacks in human waves, and the many casualties sustained by the American units, the gallant and determined troops of the 1ST BATTALION (AIRBORNE), 503D INFANTRY repulsed the Viet Cong and inflicted severe losses upon them. After a battle which raged throughout the afternoon, elements of THE 1ST BATTALION (AIR-BORNE), 503D INFANTRY defeated a numerically superior hostile force and, on the following morning, counted four hundred and three Viet Cong dead in the immediate area. The devotion to duty, perseverance, and extraordinary heroism displayed by these members of THE 1ST BATTAL-ION (AIRBORNE), 503D INFANTRY and the attached units are in the highest traditions of the United States Army and reflect great credit upon themselves and the armed forces of their country."

Appendix 6

GLOSSARY

1/503	1st Battalion (Airborne), 503rd Infantry.
1LT	First Lieutenant.
1/RAR	1st Battalion, Royal Australian Regiment.
1SG	First Sergeant. An E-8.
24 hour	The first 12 hours are exactly the same. After 12 noon, add 100 for every hour. Thus, 2:00 p.m. becomes 1400, 6:00 p.m. becomes 1800, 11:00 p.m. becomes 2300.
2/503	2nd Battalion (Airborne), 503rd Infantry.
2LT	Second Lieutenant.
A	Alpha
AB	Air Base.
AK-47	Standard rifle used by the Viet Cong and NVA.
Alpha	Company A. Or first letter of the phonetic alphabet.
ARA	Aerial rocket artillery.
ARLNO	Artillery Liaison Officer
ARVN	Army of the Republic of Vietnam (South Vietnamese).
B	Bravo
Base camp	Usually a battalion, brigade or division sized headquarters.
Bde	Brigade.
BG	Brigadier General.
Bird	Any aircraft, but usually a helicopter.
Bn	Battalion.
Bravo	Company B. Second letter of the phonetic alphabet.
C and C	Command and Control helicopter. Used by battalion commanders, brigade commanders and division commanders.
Cav	1st Cavalry Division (Airmobile). Can also be used with a regiment designation.
CG	Commanding General.

CH-47	Chinook helicopter.
Charlie	Company C or could refer to the Viet Cong. Also, the third letter of the phonetic alphabet.
Chinook	CH-47 helicopter, used to carry cargo or troops.
CIB	Combat Infantryman's Badge.
CINCPAC	Commander-in-Chief, Pacific.
Claymore	Antipersonnel mine.
CMB	Combat Medic's Badge.
CO	Commanding Officer.
COL	Colonel.
Company	Included four rifle platoons, plus a headquarters unit. Total complement depended on type of infantry unit: airborne, airmobile, or conventional.
CONARC	Continental Army Command.
COSVN	Central Office for South Vietnam. Hanoi's forward element for its operations in the South.
Cover my 6	Along with "my 6 was covered" it meant covering one's back.
CP	Command Post.
CPT	Captain.
CSM	Command Sergeant Major. An E-9.
D Day	Day of assault.
D+1	Day of assault plus one day.
Delta	Company D. Fourth letter of the phonetic alphabet.
DO	Duty Officer.
Dust-off	Helicopter medevac.
E-1	Recruit.
E-2	Private.
E-3	Private First Class.
E-4	Specialist or Corporal.
E-5	Specialist or (Buck) Sergeant.
E-6	Specialist or Staff Sergeant.
E-7	Sergeant First Class or Platoon Sergeant.
E-8	Master Sergeant or 1ST Sergeant.
E-9	Sergeant Major or Command Sergeant Major.
FAC	Forward Aircraft Controller.
FNG	Fucking New Guy.

FO	Artillery Forward Observer.
FSCC	Fire Support Control Center.
G-1	General Staff Officer, Personnel.
G-2	General Staff Officer, Intelligence.
G-3	General Staff Officer, Operations.
G-4	General Staff Officer, Logistics.
G-5	General Staff Officer, Civil Affairs.
GEN	Four-Star General.
Grunt	Infantry soldier.
H&I	Harassing and Interdiction fires by field artillery.
H Hour	The hour of the attack.
Huey	UH-1B or UH-1D helicopters. B model was usually a gunship, D model was a troop carrier.
Ia	In Vietnamese means river.
KHA	Killed, hostile action.
KIA	Killed in action.
Leg	Any soldier, sailor, airman or marine who is not airborne qualified.
LP	Listening post.
LT	Lieutenant.
LTC	Lieutenant Colonel.
LZ	Landing Zone.
M-16	Standard rifle used by U.S. and ARVN forces.
MACV	Military Assistance Command Vietnam.
MAJ	Major.
Medevac	Medical evacuation by helicopter.
MG	Major General.
MSG	Master Sergeant. An E-8.
Mustang	A former enlisted man who earns an officer's commission.
NCO	Noncommissioned Officer. A sergeant, E-5 or above.
NVA	North Vietnamese Army. Same as PAVN.
OCS	Officer Candidate School.
OD	Olive drab.
OP	Observation post.
PAVN	People's Army of [North] Vietnam. Same as NVA.
PFC	Private First Class.
PJs	Para Jumpers. USAF parachute qualified survival medics.

Platoon	Four squads plus a platoon leader, platoon sergeant and an RTO.
PSG	Platoon Sergeant. An E-7.
RAR	Royal Australian Regiment.
ROTC	Reserve Officers Training Corps.
RTO	Radiotelephone operator.
S-1	Battalion or Brigade Staff Officer, Personnel.
S-2	Battalion or Brigade Staff Officer, Intelligence.
S-3	Battalion or Brigade Staff Officer, Operations.
S-4	Battalion or Brigade Staff Officer, Logistics.
S-5	Battalion or Brigade Staff Officer, Civil Affairs.
SFC	Sergeant First Class. Usually a platoon sergeant. An E-7.
SGM	Sergeant Major. An E-9.
SGT	Sergeant. An E-5, or used generically for all sergeants.
Snuffies	An affectionate term used by LTC Wilbur Jenkins, 1/8th Cavalry, 1st Air Cav Div, to describe all enlisted infantrymen.
Song	In Vietnamese it also means river.
SOP	Standard Operating Procedure.
SP4	Specialist Fourth Class. An E-4.
SP5	Specialist Fifth Class. An E-5.
SP6	Specialist Sixth Class. An E-6.
Squad	Ten men plus a squad leader.
SSG	Staff Sergeant. Usually a squad leader. An E-6.
TAOR	Tactical area of responsibility.
TO&E	Tables of Organization and Equipment. Specified the number of men in a unit, their equipment and what equipment each would be authorized.
TOC	Tactical operations center.
VC	Viet Cong or Victor Charlie.
WHA	Wounded, hostile action.
WIA	Wounded in action.
WO	Warrant Officer.
WP	White phosphorus round fired by artillery.
XO	Executive Officer.

CHAPTER NOTES

Preface

1. Dale Andrade, "Why Westmoreland Was Right," *Vietnam*, April 2009, 30.
2. Warren Wilkins, *Grab Their Belts to Fight Them* (Annapolis, MD: Naval Institute Press, 2011), 7.
3. George C. Herring, *America's Longest War: The United States and Vietnam, 1950–1975*, 4th ed. (New York: McGraw-Hill, 2002), 271.

Chapter 1

1. Larry H. Addington, *The Patterns of War Since the Eighteenth Century* (Bloomington: Indiana University Press, 1984), 258.
2. Mark Moyar, *Triumph Forsaken* (New York: Cambridge University Press, 2006), 6.
3. Fredrik Logevall, *Embers of War* (New York: Random House, 2012), xi–xii.
4. *Ibid.*, xiii–xiv.
5. Edward Doyle, Samuel Lipsman, and Stephen Weiss, *Passing the Torch (The Vietnam Experience)*, ed. Robert Manning (Boston: Boston Publishing, 1981–1988), 50.
6. Logevall, *Embers of War*, 270.
7. *Ibid.*, 339.
8. *Ibid.*, 341.
9. *Ibid.*, 354–355.
10. *Ibid.*, 358.
11. Martin Windrow, *The Last Valley* (New York: DaCapo, 2006), 233.
12. Stanley Karnow, *Vietnam: A History* (New York: Viking, 1983), 191.
13. Logevall, *Embers*, 394.
14. Bernard Fall, *Hell in a Very Small Place* (New York: DaCapo, 2002), 31–37.
15. Logevall, *Embers*, 384.
16. *Ibid.*, 392.
17. Moyar, *Triumph Forsaken*, 26.
18. Logevall, 394.
19. Karnow, *Vietnam*, 191–193.
20. Logevall, 405.
21. *Ibid.*, 409.
22. Karnow, Vietnam, 211–212.
23. Logevall, 412.
24. Fall, *Hell in a Very Small Place*, 133.
25. *Ibid.*, 134–154.
26. Windrow, *The Last Valley*, 412.
27. Moyar, *Triumph Forsaken*, 311.
28. Doyle, *Passing the Torch*, 72–73.
29. *Ibid.*
30. Fall, *Hell in a Very Small Place*, 483–484.
31. Windrow, 623–624.
32. Logevall, 534.
33. Moyar, 30.
34. Herring, *America's Longest War*, 49.
35. Logevall, 592–593.
36. *Ibid.*, 628–629.
37. Moss, *An American Ordeal*, 72–73.
38. Moyar, 34.
39. *Ibid.*, 55.
40. Herring, 66.
41. Doyle, 101–102.
42. Graham Greene, *The Quiet American* (London: William Heinemann, 1955), 31–32
43. Moyar, 67.
44. *Ibid.*, 73.
45. Karnow, 1983, 237.
46. David Halberstam, *The Best and*

the Brightest (New York: Random House, 1972), 12.

47. *Ibid.*, 11.

48. Doyle, 151–152.

49. Trinh Nhu et al., *Lich Su Bien Nien Xu Uy Nam Bo Va Trung Uong Cuc Mien Nam, 1954–1975* [Historical chronicle of the Cochin China Party Committee and the Central Office for South Vietnam, 1954–1975] (Hanoi: Ho Chi Minh National Political Studies Institute, Party History Institute, 2002), 180. Quoted in Wilkins, 7.

50. Wilkins, 8.

51. Moyar, 83.

52. Wilkins, 8.

53. *Ibid.*

54. *Ibid.*, 10.

55. Edward Lewis and Richard Rhodes, eds., *John F. Kennedy: Words to Remember* (n.p.: Hallmark Cards, 1967), 18–19.

56. Neil Sheehan, Hendrick Smith, E.W. Kenwoody, and Fox Butterfield, *The Pentagon Papers* (New York: Bantam, 1971), 99.

57. Halberstam, *The Best*, 169–173.

58. Robert Dalleck, *An Unfinished Life* (New York: Little, Brown & Co., 2003), 444–455.

59. Maitland and Weiss, *Raising*, 50–51.

60. Sheehan, *Shining Lie*, 262–263.

61. *Ibid.*, 259.

62. Moyar, 194–195.

63. Karnow, 1991, 309.

64. Halberstam, 290–291.

65. Moss, *Vietnam*, 387.

66. Lynn Montross, *Cavalry of the Sky* (New York: Harper & Brothers, 1954), 6.

67. *Ibid.*, 10.

68. Frederic A. Bergerson, *The Army Gets an Air Force* (Baltimore: Johns Hopkins University Press, 1980), 71.

69. James M. Gavin, "Cavalry, and I Don't Mean Horses," *Harper's*, April 1954, 54.

70. Shelby Stanton, *Anatomy of a Division* (New York: Warner Books, 1987), 14.

71. *Ibid.*, 15–17.

72. *Ibid.*, 20.

73. Carl Shuster, "Case Closed: The Gulf of Tonkin Incident," *Vietnam*, June 2008, 28–33.

74. Edwin E. Moise, *Tonkin Gulf and the Escalation of the Vietnam War* (Chapel Hill: University of North Carolina Press, 1996), 75–78.

75. Maitland, *Raising the States*, 154.

76. Moise, *Tonkin Gulf*, 79–80.

77. Shuster, *Vietnam*, 28–33.

78. Moise, 105–108.

79. *Ibid.*, 143.

80. Shuster, "Case Closed," 28–33.

81. Maclear, *The Ten Thousand*, 138.

82. Moss, *Vietnam*, 140–143.

83. *Ibid.*, 139.

84. Moyar, *Triumph*, 353.

85. Carland, *Stemming the Tide*, 16.

86. Moss, *Vietnam*, 160–161.

87. *Ibid.*, 377.

Chapter 2

1. Department of the Army, 24 Military History Detachment, *173d Airborne Brigade History* (APO San Francisco 96250: 30 April 1968).

2. Edward F. Murphy, *Dak To* (New York: Pocket Books, 1995), 17.

3. Shelby L. Stanton, *The Rise and Fall of an American Army* (Novato, CA: Presidio Press, 1985), 45.

4. Murphy, 19.

5. *Ibid.*, 18.

6. *Ibid.*, 10.

7. *Ibid.*, 10–11.

8. *Ibid.*, 12–13.

9. *Ibid.*, 10–16.

10. COL Richard H. Boland, interview by author, 24 December 2003.

11. *Ibid.*

12. Boland.

13. Richard White to Al Conetto, 27 October 1993 (Conetto letters).

14. GEN Wayne Downing to Al Conetto, 1 August 2006 (Conetto letters).

15. Stanton, *Rise and Fall*, 46.

16. Joe Diaz, "Memoirs of an Old Soldier," 6 January 1998.

17. Richard White to Al Conetto, 27 October 1993.

18. Harry Allen to Al Conetto, undated (Conetto Letters).

19. MG Ellis Williamson interview by John Carland, January 1993, 1.

20. Stanton, *Rise and Fall*, 46.

21. Walter B. Daniel to Al Conetto, 22 April 1996.

22. Department of the Army, *173d Airborne Brigade History*.

23. Bob Breen, *First to Fight* (Nashville: Battery Press, 1988), 103.

24. War Zones C and D descriptions contained in Military Encyclopedia Center of the Ministry of Defense, *Tu Dien Bach Khoa Quan Su Viet Nam*, 148: quoted in Wilkins, 100.

25. LTC Lowell D. Bittrich, "Vietnam, the 173d Abn Bde & the 9th VC Division," 1972–1973, 8–9.

26. Department of the Army, Headquarters, 173d Airborne Brigade (Separate), *Combat Operations After Action Report*, by 2LT Leo J. Mercier (APO U.S. Forces 96250, 19 December 1965), 2.

27. Michael Lee Lanning and Dan Cragg, *Inside the VC and the NVA* (New York: Ivy Books, 1992), 95.

Chapter 3

1. Department of the Army, Headquarters 173d Airborne Brigade (Separate), *Daily Staff Journal or Duty Officer's Log* (Bien Hoa, Republic of Vietnam, 1–15 November 1965), 0001–2400 5 Nov 1965, 1.

2. *Ibid.*, 2.

3. *Ibid.*, 3.

4. *Ibid.*, 4–5.

5. Department of the Army, Headquarters, 173d Airborne Brigade (Separate), *Critique of Operation Hump*, by BG Ellis W. Williamson (APO U.S. Forces 96250, 19 November 1965), 2.

6. Juan Jaime to Al Conetto, January 30, 1998, 1 (Conetto Letters).

7. COL Walter B. Daniel to Al Conetto, March 18, 1993 (Conetto Letters).

8. James Hutchens, *Beyond Combat* (Chicago: Moody Press, 1968), 99–101.

9. Department of the Army, *Daily Staff Journal*, 7.

10. Department of the Army, *Critique of Operation Hump*, 3.

11. Department of the Army, *Staff Journal*, 0001–2400 6 Nov 1965, 1–5.

12. John Holland, "My Recall of Operation Hump," September 3, 1996, 1.

13. COL John E. Tyler, "Operation Hump, The Battle on Hill 65," November 18, 1996, 1.

14. Department of the Army, *After Action*, 5.

15. Department of the Army, *Staff Journal*, 7 Nov 1965, 1–4.

16. Walter B. Daniel to Al Conetto, 31 May 1993 (Conetto Letters).

17. COL Walter B. Daniel to Al Conetto, March 18, 1993 (Conetto Letters); COL Walter B. Daniel to Al Conetto, May 31, 1993 (Conetto Letters).

18. LTC Lowell Bittrich, "Battle on Hill 65," 3.

19. Department of the Army, *Staff Journal*, 5.

20. COL Walter B. Daniel to Al Conetto, March 18, 1993 (Conetto Letters).

21. Juan Jaime to Al Conetto, January 30, 1998, 1 (Conetto Letters).

Chapter 4

1. Viet Cong newspaper article, *Quan Giai Phong* No. 69, 30 November 1965, "Head-on Battle Destroyed One Battalion of the U.S. Expeditionary Force-Three Comrades Repulsed 15 American Assaults, Killing Over 50 Enemy," quoted in Bob Breen, *First to Fight* (Nashville: Battery Press, 1988), 114.

2. Tom Marrinan, 173d Reunion notes, July 2–6 1997, 17.

3. Robert Blango, interviewed by author, June 7, 2003.

4. Dick North to Al Conetto, April 14 1993. Personal interview notes of 1/503rd officers and NCOs, January 1966, 9–10 (Conetto Letters).

5. Dick North to Al Conetto, date unknown, 6.

6. *Ibid.*

7. Headquarters, United States Army Vietnam, *Award of the Silver Star*. General Orders 954, APO San Francisco 96307. 10 February 1966.

8. *Ibid.*, 7.

9. Hutchens, *Beyond Combat*, 101.

10. Department of the Army, *Staff Journal*, 8 Nov 1965, 1.

11. Hutchens, *Beyond Combat*, 102.

12. Wilkins, 106–108.

13. Marc Oswald, John Rich, and Kenny Alphin, *The 8th of November*, directed by Gary Chapman (Nashville: Warmer Bros., 2005).

14. Hutchens, *Beyond Combat*, 102.

15. *Ibid.*, 103.

16. Blango, 2003.

17. Viet Cong newspaper article, *Quan Giai Phong* No. 69, in *First to Fight*, 115.

18. Rick Salas, phone interview by author, January 5, 1998 (Conetto Letters).

19. Wilkins, 108.

20. COL John E. Tyler, "Operation Hump," 2.

21. Henry Tucker, interview by Ed Noel, *Commercial Dispatch*, 1966.

22. Dick North to Al Conetto, *Hill 65*, October 25, 1985, 7.

23. Juan Jaime to Al Conetto, January 30, 1998, 1–2 (*Conetto Letters*).

24. Jaime, January 30, 1998, 2.

25. Jaime, 1998.

26. *Ibid.*

27. Blango, 2003.

28. LTC Lowell Bittrich, "Battle on Hill 65," May 1966, 5.

29. Department of the Army, *Staff Journal*, 8 November 1965, 2.

30. Bittrich, "Battle on Hill 65," 5.

31. Department of the Army, *Staff Journal*, 8 November 1965, 2.

32. Sam Scrimanger to Al Conetto, December 27, 1996, 2 (Conetto Letters).

33. Mike DeFrancesco to John Holland, email January 6, 1998, 2 (Conetto Letters).

34. CSM Bill Acebes to Al Conetto, November 29, 1997 (Conetto Letters).

35. Joe Diaz, "Memoirs of an Old Soldier," to Al Conetto, January 31, 2014, 2 (Conetto Letters).

36. Joe Diaz to Al Conetto, January 6, 1998, 2 (Conetto Letters).

37. Diaz, January 31, 2014, 2–3.

38. Dick North to Al Conetto, April 14, 1993. Personal interview notes of 1/503rd officers and NCOs, January 1966, 1–3.

39. Acebes to Al Conetto, November 29, 1997 (Conetto Letters).

40. Department of the Army, *Staff Journal*, 2.

41. John Holland, "My Recall of Operation Hump," September 3, 1996, 1.

42. *Ibid.*, 2.

43. *Ibid.*

44. *Ibid.*

45. Michael Casey, et al., eds., *The Army at War (The Vietnam Experience)*, ed. Robert Manning (Boston: Boston Publishing, 1981–88), 28.

46. Holland, 2.

47. Bittrich, 6–7.

48. Bittrich, 7.

49. Headquarters, United States Army Vietnam, *Award of the Silver Star*. General Orders 802, APO San Francisco 96307. 5 February 1966.

50. Bill Delia to Al Conetto, date unknown, 2 (Conetto Letters).

51. Joe Diaz to Al Conetto, 2.

52. Bill Delia to Al Conetto, 2.

53. Bittrich, 7–8.

54. Department of the Army, *Combat After Action Report*, 19 December 1965, 5.

55. Interviews by author, 173d Reunion, July 4–6, 1997, Tucson, 1.

56. *Ibid.*, 8–9.

57. Bittrich, 9.

58. Jamie, 3.

59. Hutchens, *Beyond Combat*, 107.

60. *Ibid.*, 108.

61. *Ibid.*, 109.

62. *Ibid.*

63. *Ibid.*, 107–111.

64. VC newspaper article, *Quan Giai Phong* No. 69.

65. Wilkins, 38.

66. Bittrich, 9.

67. Hutchens, 104.

68. Blango, 2003.

69. Dick North to Al Conetto, April 14, 1993, Personal interview notes, 6–7 (Conetto Letters).

70. COL John Tyler to Al Conetto, August 5, 1998, 1 (Conetto Letters).

71. Department of the Army, *Staff Journal*, 2.

Chapter 5

1. Walter B. Daniel to Al Conetto, 18 March 1993, 3.
2. COL Walter B. Daniel, "Operation Hump," November 30, 1996, 3.
3. *Ibid.*
4. Department of the Army, *Staff Journal*, 8 Nov 1965, 3.
5. Walt Daniel, 18 March 1993.
6. COL John E. Tyler to Al Conetto, 3 June 1993 (Conetto Letters).
7. Jack Fleming to Al Conetto, "Reflections on Operation Hump," 15 February 1998, 1–2.
8. Bittrich, "Battle on Hill 65," 11.
9. Rick Lyons email to Al Conetto, February 13, 2001, 1–2 (Conetto Letters).
10. COL Walter B. Daniel to Al Conetto, March 18, 1993 (Conetto Letters).
11. *Ibid.*
12. Dick North to Al Conetto, 14 April 1993, Rough notes, 3 (Conetto Letters).
13. Dick North, "Hill 65," 25 October 1985, 7 (Conetto Letters).
14. Dick North to Al Conetto, 14 April 1993.
15. COL John Tyler, "Operation Hump," 18 November 1996, 4.
16. Rick Lyons, 2001.
17. COL Walter B. Daniel to Al Conetto, 31 March 1993 (Conetto Letters).
18. Department of the Army, *Staff Journal*, 0001–2400 8 November 1965, 3.
19. Daniel, 1993.
20. Interviews by author, 173rd Reunion, 4–6 July 1997, Tucson, 11–13.
21. Mike DeFrancesco email to John Holland, 6 January 1998, 3 (Conetto Letters).
22. SMSgt. (Ret.) Robert L. Lapointe, *PJs in Vietnam: The Story of Air Rescue in Vietnam* (Anchorage, AK: Northern PJ Press, 1990), 158–160.
23. Department of the Army, *Staff Journal*, 4.
24. Bittrich, 10–11.
25. Dick North to Al Conetto, 14 April 1993, personal interview notes, 3 (Conetto Letters).

26. Department of the Army, *Ibid.*
27. Blango, 7 June 2003.
28. Joe Diaz to Al Conetto, 6 January 1998, 3 (Conetto Letters).
29. MG Ellis Williamson, *Operation Hump*, November 1996, 2.
30. MG Ellis W. Williamson interview with John Carland, 11–12.
31. Department of the Army, *Staff Journal*, 5.
32. *Ibid.*
33. Bittrich, "Battle on Hill 65," 11–12.
34. LTC Henry "Sonny" Tucker email to Al Conetto, June 21, 2006 (Conetto Letters).
35. Hutchens, *Beyond Combat*, 113–114.
36. Bittrich, "Battle for Hill 65," 11–12.
37. Blango, interview by author, 7 June 2003.
38. Diaz, 31 January 2014, 4.
39. Juan Jaime to Al Conetto, 30 January 1998, 3–4 (Conetto Letters).
40. Blango, interview by author, 7 June 2003.
41. Department of the Army, *Staff Journal*, 7.
42. Bittrich, "The Battle for Hill 65," 13.
43. Tyler, *Operation Hump*, 4.
44. Department of the Army, *Staff Journal*, 7.

Chapter 6

1. Department of the Army, *Staff Journal*, 0001–2400 9 November 1965, 2.
2. LaPointe, *PJs in Vietnam*, 160.
3. MG Williamson interview by John Carland, January 1993, 12.
4. Hutchens, *Beyond Combat*, 115.
5. Diaz, 31 January 2014. 4.
6. Breen, *First to Fight*, 10.
7. Mike DeFrancesco to John Holland, email 6 January 1998, 3 (Conetto Letters).
8. Interviews by author, 173d Reunion, 4–7 July 1997, 7.
9. Interview notes from 173d Reunion, 2–6 July 1997.
10. Juan Jaime to Al Conetto, 30 January 1998, 4 (Conetto Letters).
11. Hutchens, *Beyond Combat*, 116.

12. Department of the Army, *Staff Journal*, 2–4.

13. Tyler, *Operation Hump*, 7.

14. Department of the Army, *Staff Journal*, 5–7.

15. Bittrich, "Battle on Hill 65," 15.

16. 173rd Reunion notes, 4–6 July 1997, 17.

17. *Ibid.*, 13–14.

18. Department of the Army, *Staff Journal*, 7–8.

19. COL Walter B. Daniel to Al Conetto, 18 March 1993 (Conetto Letters).

20. Department of the Army, *Critique of Operation Hump*, 14.

21. Department of the Army, *Staff Journal*, 9.

22. Department of the Army, *Critique of Operation Hump*, 7.

23. *Ibid*, 8.

24. Headquarters, 173d Airborne Brigade (Separate), *Critique of Operation Hump* (APO San Francisco 96250, 15 November 1965), 7.

25. Dick North to Al Conetto, 14 April 1993, personal interview notes, 16 (Conetto Letters).

26. COL Walter B. Daniel to Al Conetto, 18 March 1993 (Conetto Letters).

27. Dick North to Al Conetto, *Ibid.*, 16.

28. Walter B. Daniel, "Operation Hump," 30 November 1996, 5.

29. Don Bliss email to Al Conetto, August 21, 2006 (Conetto Letters).

30. Department of the Army, *Staff Journal*, 10–11.

31. Bittrich, "The Battle for Hill 65," 16–17.

32. Sam Scrimanger, 3.

33. Interviews by author, 173rd Reunion, 4–6 July 1997, 10.

34. Bittrich, "The Battle for Hill 65," 18.

35. COL John Tyler in a letter to LTC Lowell Bittrich, 14 November 1996, 4 (Conetto Letters).

36. Lowell Bittrich, *The 173d Airborne Brigade and The 9th VC Division*, 1972–1973, 20.

37. Bittrich, *The 173d Airborne Brigade*, 20.

38. Neil Sheehan, "Vietcong Lose 391 in All-Day Battle," *New York Times*, 9 November 1965, sec. 1, 1.

39. Jack Foisie, "391 Viet Cong Killed in Head-On Battle With GIs," *Los Angeles Times*, 10 November 1965, sec. A, p. 1 and 16.

40. John Maffre, "GIs Break 2 Traps, Kill 391 Vietcong," *Washington Post*, 10 November 1965, A1, A16.

41. Times-Post Service, "U.S. Wins First 'Toe-to-Toe' Battle," *San Francisco Chronicle*, 10 November 1965, 1, 13.

42. Joe Schneider, "Paratroopers Crush VC Camp, Kill 391," *Pacific Stars and Stripes*, 11 November 1965, 1, 6.

43. COL John Tyler to Al Conetto, 3 June 1993 (Conetto Letters).

44. Hutchens, *Beyond Combat*, 124.

45. Karen Asher and Tim Duffie, "The Virtual Wall," The Virtual Wall/www.virtualwall.org (accessed December 24, 2014).

46. Vietnam Veterans Memorial Fund, Inc., *Vietnam Veterans Memorial Directory of Names* (Washington, D.C.: Vietnam Veterans, Memorial Fund, Inc., sixth printing, 1986.

47. Department of the Army, *Combat Operations After Action Report*, 6.

48. Department of the Army, *Combat Operations*, 7.

49. Headquarters, Department of the Army, *Distinguished Unit Citation*, General Orders Number 40 (Washington, D.C.: 31 October 1966), 1.

50. Department of the Army, Headquarters, 173rd Airborne Brigade (Separate), *Combat Commander's Note Number 85* (APO U.S. Forces 96250, 14 November 1965), 4.

51. MG Williamson interview by John Carland, January 1993, 13.

52. *Pacific Stars & Stripes*, November 12, 1965, 6.

53. COL Walter B. Daniel to Al Conetto, May 31, 1993 (Conetto Letters).

54. Hutchens, *Beyond Combat*, 117.

55. Carland, *Stemming the Tide*, 74.

56. MG Ellis Williamson to Al Conetto, March 30, 1993 (Conetto Letters).

57. *Ibid.*

58. Blango.

59. Wilkins, 109.

60. Interview notes from 173d reunion, 2–6 July 1997.

Chapter 7

1. LTG Hal Moore and Joseph Galloway, *We Were Soldiers Once ... and Young* (New York: HarperPerennial, 1993), 13–14.

2. *Ibid.*, 33.

3. Moore and Galloway, *We Were Soldiers*, 13–17.

4. *Ibid.*, 53.

5. *Ibid.*, 56.

6. *Ibid.*, 50.

7. *Ibid.*, 57–58.

8. *Ibid.*, 58–59.

9. *Ibid.*, 74.

10. *Ibid.*, 127–139.

11. *Ibid.*, 158–159.

12. *Ibid.*, 175.

13. *Ibid.*, 199–209.

14. Larry Gwin, *Baptism: A Vietnam Memoir* (New York, Ivy, 1999), 128–130.

15. Gwin, *Baptism*, 132–134.

16. Moore and Galloway, *We Were Soldiers*, 269–270.

17. *Ibid.*, 269.

18. *Ibid.*, 291.

19. Gwin, 145–146.

20. Moore, 303.

21. *Ibid.*, 309–311.

22. Gwin, 149–151.

23. *Ibid.*, 156.

24. Moore, 363.

25. *Ibid.*, 369.

26. *Ibid.*, 366.

27. Moss, *Vietnam*, 377.

28. Wilkins, 124.

Chapter 8

1. Walter B. Daniel, *Operation Hump (The Fighting on 8 and 9 November 1965)*, 30 November 1996, 1–2.

2. *Ibid.*, 5–6.

3. Moore and Galloway, *We Were Soldiers*, 1992, 341–342.

Chapter 9

1. LTG John J. Tolson, *Airmobility 1961–1971* (Washington, D.C.: Government Printing Office, 1973; reprint, Washington, D.C.: Government Printing Office, 1982), 22.

2. *Ibid.*, 51.

3. John D. Pomfret, "Johnson Orders 50,000 More Men to Vietnam and Doubles Draft; Again Urges U.N. to Seek Peace," *New York Times*, 29 July 1965, 1,11, and 12.

4. Bernard Fall, *Street Without Joy*, 4th ed. (Harrisburg: Stackpole, 1961), 207.

Chapter 11

1. Department of the Army, Headquarters, 173d Airborne Brigade (Separate), *Critique of Operation Hump* (APO U.S. Forces 96250), November 15, 1965.

Chapter 12

1. Pythia Press, "Pham Xuan An: Vietnam's Top Spy," Zalin Grant's War Tales, http://www.pythiapress.com (accessed August 8, 2014).

Chapter 13

1. Beth McHugh, "Post Traumatic Stress Disorder: What Causes It?" Your Online Counselor. http://youronlinecounselor.com/Articles/PTSD-causes.htm (accessed December 10, 2014).

2. Jonathan Shay, *Achilles in Vietnam* (New York: Touchstone, 1994), xx.

3. "The Winter of Your Discontent?" *Consumers Reports on Health*, February 1993, 15–16.

4. William Broyles, "Why Men Love War," *Esquire*, November 1984, 1–2.

5. *Ibid.*, 4.

Appendix 1

1. Hutchens, *Beyond Combat*, 112.
2. Marc Oswald, *8th of November: A True American Story of Honor* (Nashville: Warner Bros., 2005).

Appendix 4

1. Department of the Army, Headquarters 173d Airborne Brigade (Separate), *Combat Operations After Action Report*, (APO U.S. Forces 96250), 19 December 1965.

Appendix 5

1. Headquarters, Department of the Army, *Award of Distinguished Unit Citation*. General Orders 40, Washington, D.C. 31 October 1966, pg. 1.

Bibliography

Books

Addington, Larry H. *The Patterns of War Since the Eighteenth Century.* Bloomington: Indiana University Press, 1984.

Alphin, Big Kenny, John Rich, and Allen Rucker. *Big & Rich: All Access.* New York: Center Street, 2007.

Baker, Mark. *Nam.* New York: Berkley, 1983.

Bergerson, Frederic A. *The Army Gets an Air Force.* Baltimore: Johns Hopkins University Press, 1980.

Breen, Bob. *First to Fight.* Nashville: The Battery Press, 1988.

Broyles, William. *Brothers in Arms: A Journey From War to Peace.* New York: Alfred A. Knopf, 1986; Avon, 1987.

Buell, Thomas B., Clifton R. Franks, John A. Hixson, David R. Mets, Bruce R. Pirnie, James F. Ransome, Jr., and Thomas R. Stone. *The Second World War: Europe and the Mediterranean,* ed. Thomas E. Griess. Wayne, NJ: Avery, 1984.

Carland, John M. *Combat Operations: Stemming the Tide, May 1965 to October 1966.* Washington, D.C.: Government Printing Office, 2000.

Casey, Michael, Clark Dougan, Denis Kennedy, and Shelby Stanton, eds. *The Army at War (The Vietnam Experience),* ed. Robert Manning. Boston: Boston Publishing, 1981–1988.

Casey, Michael, Clark Dougan, Samuel Lipsman, Jack Sweetman, and Stephen Weiss. *Flags Into Battle (The Vietnam Experience),* ed. Robert Manning. Boston: Boston Publishing, 1987.

Coleman, J.D. *Pleiku: The Dawn of Helicopter Warfare in Vietnam.* New York: St. Martin's Press, 1988.

Dalleck, Robert. *An Unfinished Life.* New York: Little, Brown and Company, 2003.

Dean, Chuck. *Nam Vet: Making Peace With Your Past.* Portland: Multnomah, 1988.

Downs, Frederick. *No Longer Enemies, Not Yet Friends.* New York: W.W. Norton, 1991.

Doyle, Edward, and Samuel Lipsman. *Setting the Stage (The Vietnam Experience),* ed. Robert Manning. Boston: Boston Publishing, 1981–1988.

Doyle, Edward, Samuel Lipsman, and Stephen Weiss. *Passing the Torch (The Vietnam Experience),* ed. Robert Manning. Boston: Boston Publishing, 1981–1988.

Eaton, Edgar W. *Mekong Mud Dogs.* Great Britain: amazon.co.uk, 2014.

Ebert, James R. *A Life in a Year.* New York: Ballantine, 2004.

Fall, Bernard B. *Hell in a Very Small Place.* New York: Da Capo, 2002.

_____. *Last Reflections on a War.* New York: Schocken, 1972.

_____. *Street Without Joy,* 4th ed. Harrisburg, PA: Stackpole, 1961.

Greene, Graham. *The Quiet American.* London: William Heinemann, 1955.

Grossman, LTC Dave. *On Killing.* New York: Little, Brown and Company, 1995.

Gwin, Larry. *Baptism*. New York: Ivy Books, 1999.

Hackworth, COL David H. *About Face*. New York: Touchstone, 1990.

_____. *Steel My Soldiers' Hearts*. Touchstone, 2003.

Halberstam, David. *The Best and the Brightest*. New York: Random House, 1972.

Herr, Michael. *Dispatches*. New York: Avon, 1978.

Herring, George C. *America's Longest War: The United States and Vietnam, 1950–1975*, 3rd ed. New York: McGraw-Hill, 1996.

_____. *America's Longest War: The United States and Vietnam, 1950–1975*, 4th ed. New York: McGraw Hill, 2002.

Herrington, Stuart A. *Silence Was a Weapon*. New York: Ivy Books, 1987.

Hung, Nguyen Tien, and Jerrold L. Schecter. *The Palace File*. Perennial Library, 1989.

Hutchens, James M. *Beyond Combat*. Chicago: Moody Press, 1968; Shepherd's Press, 1986.

Just, Ward. *To What End*. New York: Public Affairs, 1968.

Karnow, Stanley. *Vietnam: A History*. New York: Viking, 1983.

_____. *Vietnam: A History*. New York: Penguin, 1991.

Lang, George, Raymond L. Collins, and Gerard F. White. *Medal of Honor Recipients 1863–1994*. New York: Facts On File, 1995.

Langguth, A.J. *Our Vietnam: The War, 1954–1975*. New York: Simon & Schuster, 2000.

Lanning, Michael Lee, and Dan Cragg. *Inside the VC and the NVA*. New York: Ivy, 1994.

LaPointe, Robert L. *PJs In Vietnam: The Story of Air Rescue in Vietnam*. Anchorage, AK: Northern PJ Press. 1990.

Lewis, Edward, and Richard Rhodes. *John F. Kennedy: Words to Remember*. n.p.: Hallmark Cards, 1967.

Logevall, Fredrik. *Embers of War*. New York: Random House, 2012.

Macdonald, Peter. *Giap: The Victor in Vietnam*. New York: W.W. Norton, 1993.

Maclear, Michael. *The Ten Thousand Day War*. New York: St. Martin's Press, 1981.

MacMillan, Margaret. *Nixon and Mao*. New York: Random House, 2008.

Mahedy, William P. *Out of the Night: The Spiritual Journey of Vietnam Vets*. New York: Ballantine, 1986.

Maitland, Terrence, and Stephen Weiss. *Raising the Stakes (The Vietnam Experience)*, ed. Robert Manning. Boston: Boston Publishing, 1981–1988.

Martin, Robert J., ed. *The 173rd Airborne Brigade (SEP)*. Paducah, KY: Turner, 1993.

Mason, Patience H.C. *Recovering from the War*. New York: Penguin, 1990.

Mason, Robert. *Chickenhawk: Back in the World: Life After Vietnam*. New York: Penguin, 1984.

McDonough, James. *Platoon Leader*. Novato, CA: Presidio, 1985.

McMaster, H.R. *Dereliction of Duty*. New York: HarperPerennial, 1998.

McNamara, Robert S. *In Retrospect*. New York: Times Books, 1995.

Moise, Edwin E. *Tonkin Gulf and the Escalation of the Vietnam War*. Chapel Hill: University of North Carolina Press, 1996.

Montross, Lynn. *Cavalry of the Sky*. New York: Harper & Brothers, 1954.

Moore, LTG Harold G., and Joseph L. Galloway. *We Are Soldiers Still*. New York: HarperCollins, 2008.

_____. *We Were Soldiers Once ... And Young*. New York: Random House, 1992.

Moss, George Donelson. *Vietnam, An American Ordeal*. Edgewood Cliffs, NJ: Prentice-Hall, 1990.

Moyar, Mark. *Triumph Forsaken*. New York: Cambridge University Press, 2006.

Murphy, Edward F. *Dak To*. New York: Pocket Books, 1995.

O'Brien, Tim. *The Things They Carried*. New York: Penguin, 1990.

Palmer, LTG Dave R. *Summons of the Trumpet*. Novato, CA: Presidio, 1978.

Pike, Douglas. *PAVN: People's Army of Vietnam*. Novato, CA: Presidio, 1986.

Ricks, Thomas E. *The Generals*. New York: Penguin, 2012.

Saunders, Stephen D. *Breaking Squelch*. Marsh Lake Productions, 2005.

Schmitz, David. *The Tet Offensive: Politics, War, and Public Opinion*. Landham, MD: Rowman & Littlefield, 2005.

Shay, Jonathan. *Achilles in Vietnam*. New York: Simon & Schuster, 1995.

Sheehan, Neil. *A Bright Shining Lie*. New York: Random House, 1988; Vintage, 1989.

Sheehan, Neil, Hendrick Smith, E.W. Foxwoody, and Fox Butterfield. *The Pentagon Papers*. New York: Bantam, 1971.

Snyder, Don J. *Soldier's Disgrace*. Dublin, NH: Yankee, 1987.

Sorley, Lewis. *Westmoreland: The General Who Lost Vietnam*. New York: Houghton Mifflin Harcourt, 2011.

Stanton, Shelby L. *Anatomy of a Division*. Novato, CA: Presidio, 1987; Warner, 1989.

_____. *The Rise and Fall of an American Army*. Novato: Presidio, 1985.

_____. *Vietnam Order of Battle*. Washington, D.C.: U.S. News Books, 1981.

Summers, COL Harry G. *On Strategy*. Novato, CA: Presidio, 1982.

Tolson, LTG John J. *Airmobility 1961–1971*. Washington, D.C.: Government Printing Office, 1973; reprint, Washington, D.C.: Government Printing Office, 1982.

Webb, James. *Fields of Fire*. New York: Bantam, 1979.

Westmoreland, GEN William C. *A Soldier Reports*. New York: Da Capo, 1989.

Wilkins, Warren. *Grab Their Belts to Fight Them*. Annapolis, MD: Naval Institute Press, 2011.

Windrow, Martin. *The Last Valley*. New York: Da Capo, 2006.

Magazine Articles

Andrade, Dale. "Why Westmoreland Was Right." *Vietnam*, April 2009, 30.

Broyles, William. "Why Men Love War." *Esquire*, November 1984. (Downloaded from the Internet on November 26, 2006.)

Gavin, James M. "Cavalry, and I Don't Mean Horses." *Harper's*, April 1954, 54–60.

Shuster, Carl. "Case Closed: The Gulf of Tonkin Incident." *Vietnam*, June 2008, 28–33.

Vanderpool, Jay D. "We Armed the Helicopter." *U.S. Army Aviation Digest*, June 1971, 3–6, 24–29.

Newspaper Articles

Foisie, Jack. "391 Viet Cong Killed in Head-On Battle With GIs." *Los Angeles Times*, 10 November 1965, sec. A, 1 and 16.

Noel, Ed. Interview with CPT Henry Tucker. *Commercial Dispatch*, 1966.

North, Dick. "This is the North." *Yukon Daily News*, 1 September 1966, 16.

Pomfret, John D. "Johnson Orders 50,000 More Men to Vietnam and Doubles Draft; Again Urges U.N. to Seek Peace." *New York Times*, 29 July 1965, 1 and 11.

Schneider, Joe. "Paratroops Crush VC Camp, Kill 391." *Pacific Stars and Stripes*, 11 November 1965, 1 and 6.

Sheehan, Neil. "Vietcong Lose 391 In All-Day Battle." *New York Times*, 9 November 1965, 1.

Times-Post Service, "U.S. Wins First 'Toe-to-Toe' Battle." *San Francisco Chronicle*, 10 November 1965, 1 and 13.

Websites

McHugh, Beth. "Post Traumatic Stress Disorder: What Causes It?" Your Online Counselor, http://youronline counselor.com/Articles/PTSD-Causes. htm (accessed December 10, 2014).

Pythia Press. "Pham Xuan An: Vietnam's Top Spy." Zalin Grant's War Tales. http://www.pythiapress.com (accessed August 8, 2014).

Videos

Oswald, Marc, John Rich, and Kenny Alphin. *The 8th of November: A True American Story of Honor*. Directed by Gary Chapman. 51 min. September 2005. Digital Video Disc.

_____. *8th of November: Vietnam Interviews*. Directed by Gary Chapman. (Translated by Pham Van Son.) 49 Min. September 2005. Digital Video Disc.

Sound Recordings

Rich, John, and Big Kenny Alphin. *8th of November, Comin' To Your City*. Warner Bros. CD. 2005.

Unpublished Materials

(All of the following are transcripts in the hand of Al Conetto, Walla Walla, WA.)

Acebes, William, to Al Conetto, 29 November 1997.

Allen, Harry, to Al Conetto, undated.

Bittrich, LTC Lowell D. "Battle of Hill 65 (Operation HUMP 5 to 9 November 1965)."

_____. "Vietnam: The 173rd Abn Bde & The 9th VC Division," 1972–1973.

Blango, Robert, 173rd Reunion interview by author, 7 June 2003.

Bliss, Don, to Al Conetto, 21 August 2006.

Boland, COL Richard H. Interview by author, 24 December 2003.

_____. Interview by author, 19–20 February 2005.

Conetto, 1LT Al, to Mr. and Mrs. Joseph Conetto, 12 August 1965.

_____, to Mr. and Mrs. James Mace, 19 September 1965.

_____, to Mr. and Mrs. James Mace, 17 October 1965.

Daniel, COL Walter B., to Al Conetto, 18 March 1993.

_____, to Al Conetto, 31 March 1993.

_____, to Al Conetto, 31 May 1993.

DeFrancisco, Mike, to Al Conetto, 6 January 1998.

Delia, Bill, to Al Conetto, date unknown.

Diaz, Joe, to Al Conetto. 6 January 1998. "Memoirs of an Old Soldier."

Downing, GEN Wayne, to Al Conetto, 1 August 2006.

Fleming, Jack, to Al Conetto, 15 February 1998.

Gaudet, Ken, to Al Conetto, 7 May 1993.

Hemphill, Thomas, to Al Conetto, May 6, 2001.

_____, to Al Conetto, April 13, 2001.

Henry, Bill to Al Conetto, September 18, 2014.

Holland, John. "My Recall of Operation Hump," 3 September 1996.

Jaime, Juan, to Al Conetto, 30 January 1998.

Lyons, Rick, to Al Conetto, 13 February 2001.

Moore, John R., William Workman, John Holland, Ron Kerns, Russ Roever, Harold Dale, and Tom Marrinan. 173rd Reunion interviews by author, 2–6 July 1997.

North, Dick. "Hill 65," 25 October 1985.

_____, to Al Conetto, 14 April 1993. Personal interview notes of 1/503rd officers and NCOs, January 1966.

_____, to Al Conetto, 14 April 1993. Rough notes.

Salas, Rick, to Al Conetto. 5 January 1998.

Scrimanger, Sam, to Al Conetto. 27 December 1996.

Sheathelm, Glenn, to Al Conetto, 7 July 2007. Rough notes.

Shelfer, Robert, to Al Conetto, 20 December 1993.

Tucker, LTC Henry "Sonny," email to Al Conetto, 21 June 2006.

Tyler, COL John E., to Al Conetto, 3 June 1993.

_____. "Operation Hump, The Battle on Hill 65, War Zone D Republic of Vietnam, November 5 Through 9, 1965," 18 November 1996.

White, Richard, to Al Conetto, 27 October 1993.

Williamson, MG Ellis, to Al Conetto, 30 March 1993.

_____. Interview by John Carland, January 1993.

_____. "Operation Hump, 5–9 November 1965, Statement of MG Ellis Williamson, November 1996.

Public Documents

Department of the Army. 24 Military History Detachment. *173rd Airborne Brigade History*. APO San Francisco 96250: 30 April 1968.

Department of the Army. Headquarters, 173d Airborne Brigade (Separate). *Combat Operations After Action Report*, by 2LT Leo J. Mercier. APO U.S. Forces 96250: 19 December 1965.

Department of the Army. Headquarters, 173d Airborne Brigade (Separate). *Combat Commander's Note Number 85*. APO U.S. Forces 96250: 14 November 1965.

Department of the Army. Headquarters, 173d Airborne Brigade (Separate). *Critique of Operation Hump*, by BG Ellis W. Williamson. APO U.S. Forces 96250: 15 November 1965.

Department of the Army. Headquarters, 173rd Airborne Brigade (Separate). *Daily Staff Journal or Duty Officer's Log*. Bien Hoa, Republic of Vietnam: 1–15 November 1965.

Headquarters, Department of the Army. *Distinguished Unit Citation*. General Orders Number 30. Washington, D.C.: 31 October 1966.

Headquarters, United States Army Vietnam. *Award of the Silver Star*. General Orders Number 802. APO San Francisco 96307: 5 February 1966.

Headquarters, United States Army Vietnam. *Award of the Silver Star*. General Orders Number 954. APO San Francisco 96307: 10 February 1966.

Author's Service
Record

I was commissioned as an Army 2LT on January 24, 1964 upon graduation from San Jose State University. I served as a communications platoon leader, mortar platoon leader, and rifle platoon leader with the 11th Air Assault Division (TEST) at Fort Benning, GA. The 11th was then re-designated the 1st Cavalry Division (Airmobile). I was promoted to 1LT in July 1965 and then went with the Cav to Vietnam in August.

I was transferred to the 173rd Airborne Brigade and again was a rifle platoon leader with A Company, 1st Battalion (Airborne), 503rd Infantry. The Hump was the most significant battle I was involved in during my 17 months in Vietnam.

I was promoted to Captain in November 1966 and returned to Vietnam in July 1967. I was initially assigned to the 1st Battalion, 8th Cavalry, 1st Cavalry Division as a logistics officer. In October I was given command of D Company. Afterwards I was transferred to Division Headquarters as the G2 Briefing Officer to the Commanding General.

I left the Army in January 1970.

I earned the following:

> Combat Infantryman's Badge
> Paratrooper's Badge
> Bronze Star for Meritorious Service
> Army Commendation Medal with Oak Leaf Cluster
> Air Medal
> Vietnam Service Medal
> Vietnam Campaign Medal
> National Defense Medal
> Presidential Unit Citation

INDEX

Numbers in **bold italics** indicate pages with illustrations.